ROBERT E. FORMAN

is Professor of Sociology at the University of Toledo. He is the author of "Neighborhood Interaction in a Homogeneous Community" (with Theodore Caplow), "Delinquency Rates and Opportunities for Subculture Transmission," and other articles on sociological problems of minority groups.

BLACK GHETTOS
WHITE GHETTOS
and
SLUMS

ROBERT E. FORMAN

A SPECTRUM BOOK

PRENTICE-HALL, INC.   ENGLEWOOD CLIFFS, NEW JERSEY

Acknowledgment is gratefully made to the following:

To Harcourt Brace Jovanovich, Inc., for permission to quote from *Black Metropolis*, by St. Clair Drake and Horace Cayton (New York, 1962).

To Arno Press, Inc., for permission to quote from *The Negro in Chicago*, Chicago Commission on Race Relations (New York, Arno Press edition, 1968).

To Harper & Row, Publishers, Inc., for permission to quote from *Forbidden Neighbors*, by Charles Abrams (New York, 1955).

To University of Minnesota Press for permission to quote from *Racial Policies and Practices of Real Estate Brokers*, by Rose Helper (Minneapolis, 1969) © 1969 University of Minnesota.

To Karl E. and Alma F. Taeuber and to Aldine Publishing Company for permission to quote from *Negroes in Cities*, by Karl E. and Alma F. Taeuber (Chicago, 1965) © 1965 Karl E. and Alma F. Taeuber.

To Harcourt Brace Jovanovich, Inc., for permission to quote from *The Negro Ghetto*, by Robert C. Weaver (New York, 1948).

To The Regents of the University of California for permission to quote from *Residence and Race*, by Davis McEntire (Berkeley & Los Angeles, University of California Press, 1960).

To The Macmillan Company and to Jonathan Cape Ltd. for permission to quote from *Manchild in the Promised Land*, by Claude Brown (New York and London, 1965) © 1965 The Macmillan Company.

To Harper & Row, Publishers, Inc., for permission to quote from *Shook-up Generation*, by Harrison E. Salisbury (New York, 1958).

PRENTICE-HALL INTERNATIONAL, INC. (*London*)
PRENTICE-HALL OF AUSTRALIA, PTY. LTD. (*Sydney*)
PRENTICE-HALL OF CANADA, LTD. (*Toronto*)
PRENTICE-HALL OF INDIA PRIVATE LIMITED (*New Delhi*)
PRENTICE-HALL OF JAPAN, INC. (*Tokyo*)

Contents

Preface

This book is about one of the major issues in American black-white relationships—housing and residential segregation in cities. The theoretical orientation stems from classical urban human ecology, which views the city as made up of a number of "natural areas," including those that are focused upon here—slums and ghettos.

This approach leads to asking about characteristics of each individual area and how it relates to other areas in the city. It encourages viewing an area within the perspective of time as one looks for both change and stability. Comparisons between types of area also suggest themselves, raising questions in this case about similarities and differences between the slums and ghettos of blacks, of immigrants, and of southern white "hillbillies." The literature on immigrants is fascinating in its own right, but I have used it here only insofar as it assists in present-day understanding of black ghettos and slums.

An explanation about word usage might be appropriate. Within just a few years, *black* has become a term preferred by many to *Negro*. The reader will find that I have employed both words in this book, usage being guided by these considerations: Where the writing clearly is expressing my ideas and is referring to current times, I have ordinarily used *black*. Where I have discussed or paraphrased a work that uses *Negro*, I have generally used that term, primarily for smoother reading and to avoid the impression that I am trying to influence the reader's perception of the work (apart from my discussion of it). Additionally, as used by the U.S. Census Bureau *Negro* is a technical term, as is *nonwhite* (which includes Negroes, Orientals, American Indians, and so forth), so that clarity in the description of census material, particularly in chapter 2, necessitates the use of census terms.

The author of any book owes a debt of gratitude to innumerable people who helped to shape his ideas during his lifetime. More immediately, specific acknowledgment is made of the contribution of colleagues Barry Beckham and Rose Helper for substantive assistance in the areas of population and the real-estate broker, respectively, and for critical readings of portions of the manuscript. Appreciation is expressed to department chairman Sidney Kaplan and former chairman Neil Palmer for encouragement and for facilitating my work in various ways. I am grateful to attorney Frank S. Merritt of Toledo's Advocates for Basic Legal Equality for assistance in and a critical reading of portions of the manuscript touching on legal matters. Recognition should be given graduate students David Brubaker, Herbert Douglas, Leo Lackamp, and Shirley Swora for suggestions and helpful discussions. Mr. Douglas also gave a substantial part of the manuscript the benefit of a reading from a black perspective.

I am thankful that editor Michael Hunter saw promise in an earlier version of this work and offered an ideal combination of encouragement, criticism, and freedom as I continued. Readers will not observe the specific contributions of production editor Marjorie Streeter, but let them be assured that her thorough conscientious work is responsible for many improvements in the manuscript.

I wish to dedicate this book to all my former teachers.

Toledo, Ohio   ROBERT E. FORMAN

1 | *The Black Ghetto*

The main theme of this work is the black ghetto. But the black ghetto exists within a social context and can best be understood by relating it to that context. Consequently three subsidiary themes will be considered. Because the black ghetto is a concentration of minority-group people it should be helpful to compare it with other types of minority-group concentration, both past and present. One of our concerns will then be a comparison of the black ghetto to other ghettos. Second, because a ghetto population implies a nonghetto population that may cause or contribute to the perpetuation of the ghetto, we will try to discover what the ghetto can tell us about the nonghetto population—in this case, the native white American. Third, because ghettos exist in cities and are influenced by the ways in which cities operate, our understanding of the black ghetto should be increased by viewing it as part of a larger urban complex. In short, we will attempt to understand the black ghetto by relating it to other ghettos, to areas and people outside the ghettos, and to the working of the city as a whole.

Robert C. Weaver, whose career has combined scholarly activities with social and public service, has warned about the "tendency to treat current problems as though they were unique and devoid of historical precedents. "Actually," he says, "this is not only untrue but dangerously misleading." [1] Weaver's warning seems especially well-taken and we will try to heed it.

In attempting to isolate the intertwined factors of racial characteristics, economic status, minority subculture, majority culture, and the dynamics of the urban setting itself, we will draw on evidence about the immigrant experience. Both blacks and immigrants have in common that they came to America's Northern cities poorly prepared educationally and economically; both differed culturally and to at least some extent physically from the native white Americans; both lived in slums and ghettos and slum-ghettos. As far back as 1899 W. E. B. DuBois noted that the "sociological effect" of Negroes was the same as "illiterate foreigners." [2]

GHETTOS

Considering the amount of controversy over issues pertaining to blacks in cities it is not surprising that there is not even agreement over the use of the word *ghetto*. Banfield claims that using that term to refer to all Negro neighborhoods "misrepresents the situation seriously and even dangerously," because it "tends to condition Negroes to the idea—which is usually a half-truth at most—that white prejudice 'forces' them to live in poor housing and among other Negroes." [3] On the other side, Kenneth Clark titled his book *Dark Ghetto* and wrote: "The dark ghetto's invisible walls have been erected by the white society, by those who have power, both to confine those who have no power and to perpetuate their powerlessness." [4] Drake and Cayton considered *ghetto* to be a "harsh term," and reported its use by black leaders in Chicago "when they want to shock complacency into action." [5] Despite their differences of opinion these writers do agree that a ghetto is an undesirable place in which people are *forced* to live.

A major concern of this book is with the extent to which blacks are forced to live with each other shut in by invisible walls. The connotations of harshness and forced segregation come from the original use of the term *ghetto* in medieval Europe to refer to the section of the city where Jews lived. Although Jews originally settled near each other for personal and community convenience, by the 15th century they were required to live within a legally prescribed ghetto area, generally deteriorated and overcrowded and walled off from the rest of the city. Ghetto gates were closed at night and severe punishments were inflicted upon Jews who had not managed to get back inside the walls in time.[6] Emancipation from the legal restrictions came only gradually during the nineteenth century and as late as 1917 in Russia. Even after it was no longer legally required, the European ghetto remained a distinct cultural area inhabited by Jews who lived there voluntarily.

The fact of a distinct group living together voluntarily has led to another established usage of the term *ghetto,* as pointed out by Robert Park. " 'Ghetto,' as it is here conceived, is no longer a term that is limited in its application to the Jewish people. It has come into use in recent times as a common noun—a term which applies to any segregated racial or cultural group." [7] Because segregation was not forced upon all such groups, Park's statement implies that ghetto segregation may be voluntary with the group. Other sociologists specifically recognize that ghetto segregation may be either "self-imposed" or involuntary.[8]

It is this broader meaning that will be intended here by use of the word *ghetto:* any area in a city which is inhabited primarily by a racially or culturally distinct group as a result of either voluntary or involuntary segregation.

GHETTOS AND SLUMS

Although the terms *slum* and *ghetto* are frequently used interchangeably, they refer to different phenomena and should not be confused. A slum area is one of overcrowded poor-quality housing containing "a subculture with a set of norms and values, which is reflected in poor sanitation and health practices, deviant behavior, and characteristic attributes of apathy and social isolation." [9] Whereas residence in a ghetto is the result of racial or cultural characteristics, residence in a slum is determined primarily by economic factors. The typical slum resident lives in poor housing because he cannot afford to live in anything better. While *slum* implies poverty, this is not necessarily true of the ghetto. The expression *gilded ghetto* recognizes that even well-to-do members of a minority group may live in relative isolation from larger society, whether this is the result of voluntary or of involuntary segregation. A slum-ghetto would be an area inhabited by economically poor segregated minority-group members.

The diagrams below are intended to illustrate some of the various relationships possible between slum and ghetto. Theoretically, slum and

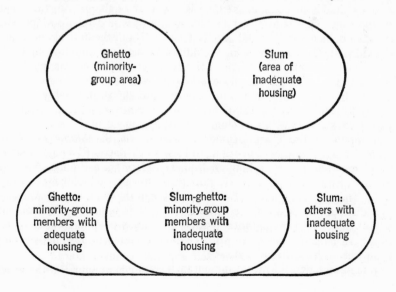

ghetto could be completely separate from each other, as in the first diagram, so that all those in the ghetto would be able to afford at least minimally adequate housing and none of the residents of the slums would be members of a ghetto minority group. The possibility seems to be mainly a theoretical one. A more realistic situation is illustrated in the second diagram. This model recognizes that some residents of the slums may simply be poor people who are not members of the ghetto minority group. It also takes into account that some residents in the ghetto may have housing that is adequate and hence not slum housing. There would, of course, be various degrees of overlap of slum and ghetto in different specific situations. The extreme possibility would be that of complete overlap—in which case every ghetto minority-group member would live in a slum but no one else would.

PRACTICAL IMPLICATIONS

The distinction between slum and ghetto is of much more than academic interest. There are practical implications that are relevant to dealing with the many problems of the ghetto effectively and intelligently. The National Advisory Commission on Civil Disorders charged that black unrest was due primarily to "white racism." [10] Banfield believes that the cause is basically one of income and social class and that if all poor blacks could be magically transformed racially into whites they would still have the same problems and difficulties.[11] Is it a matter of racial attitudes or economics? One is a matter of the ghetto, the other of the slum. One is a matter of human attitudes and relationships, the other of dollars and material goods. There are both theoretical and practical advantages in emphasizing the difference between slum and ghetto.[12]

Helping to contribute to the confusion between slum and ghetto is the fact that they have usually overlapped each other to a considerable degree. In earlier days immigrant ghettos were almost invariably in slum areas. In Chicago in the 1890s the "greater ghetto area . . . was practically coextensive with the 'slum district' as defined in the seventh special report of the Commissioner of Labor, on the *Slums of Great Cities*." [13] At about the same time, in New York, Jacob Riis commented: "One may find for the asking an Italian, a German, a French, African, Spanish, Bohemian, Russian, Scandinavian, Jewish, and Chinese Colony. . . . The one thing you shall vainly ask for in the chief city of America is a distinctively American community. There is none . . . among the tenements." [14] An Immigration Commission study of slum areas in seven Northern cities in the early 20th century found very few native-born family heads living in those areas.[15]

Slum and tenement meant immigrant ghetto just as they later came to mean black ghetto. It seems likely, though, that the immigrant slum-ghettos established a tradition of the native white American looking down upon their residents. With so many unlettered and unskilled immigrants it was almost impossible for a native white American to be so unsuccessful as to have to live in the slums. He could freely look with disdain upon slum dwellers because they did not include people he considered to be like himself.

BLACK GHETTOS AND WHITE GHETTOS

Areas of concentration of Negroes in Northern cities are discernible at least as far back as 1820, when the Five Points area of New York City was inhabited by "freed Negro slaves and low-class Irish." [16] By the middle of the 19th century Negro ghetto areas existed also in Boston and Philadelphia.[17] In clustering together in ghetto areas the Negroes were little different from other minority groups. The Irish, fleeing the potato famine of the 1840s, were the first mass immigration group to settle in American cities. Like later groups, their members settled near each other.

One definite difference is evident between blacks and other groups, however, for the latter tended much more to settle in colonies of former neighbors. Thus, not only were there Irish colonies, but within them each family "tried to live near friends and relatives from the same village." [18] Similarly, Thomas and Znaniecki found that Polish immigrants who had come from the same communities in Poland "always associate with each other more willingly" than with other Poles.[19] Zorbaugh noted the same characteristic for the Sicilians in Chicago. "Larrabee Street is a little Altavilla; the people along Cambridge have come from Alimena and Chiusa Sclafana; the people on Townsend from Bagheria; and the people on Milton from Sambuca-Zabut." [20] Even the "hillbillies" moving to Chicago in the 1960s showed the same tendency. "Entire blocks in Uptown are inhabited by the former residents of a single Alabama or West Virginia county. Apartment buildings are filled with members of a single mountain clan." [21]

For so many different groups to have followed this practice for over a century suggests that there are positive values to be derived from such concentration. For the immigrants such voluntary segregation meant that they could reduce the rate of transition from their native culture to the urban American way of life and thus minimize "culture shock." Immigrants established their own churches with services in their own languages, developed their own native-language newspapers, and established their own clubs and mutual-aid societies. If the immigrant faced difficulties, it was with the support of the centuries-old culture and traditions that he and his neighbors had carried to the new American urban environment.

So great was the sense of insulation from larger society that some immigrants hardly seemed to think of themselves as having left the Old Country. Thus women in Boston who ventured a few blocks outside the Italian colony would say, "I have been down to America today," [22] and a Croatian in Chicago could mention that men might live in his neighborhood for years and only go out into the "real America" once or twice.[23] Culturally then, the immigrant could continue to live in Italy or Croatia or Poland as transplanted to the New World and become "Americanized" more nearly at his own pace and on his own terms.

Although Negroes were also concentrated in their ghettos they did not cluster together in family or back-home locality groupings to the same extent. Regarding this lack of a strong tendency to cluster, Glazer and Moynihan commented: "There was little clubbing together of the South Carolinians versus the North Carolinians versus the Virginians—life in these places was either not different enough, or the basis of the differences was not attractive enough, to create strong local groups with strong local attachments . . . without the historical experiences that create an élan and a morale, what is there to lead them to build their own life, to patronize their own?" [24]

One might conclude that ghetto clustering is not functional for American natives except for the fact that it also is practiced by hillbilly migrants, suggesting it is of value to them. Both Negro and hillbilly subcultures represent versions of a Southern rural way of life. If clustering is common in one, then why not in the other? It could be due to either a lack of advantage in grouping together or an inadequate social base for doing so. The latter reason seems more likely. Both immigrant and hillbilly cultures have placed strong emphasis on family and kinship, and both were intact, even if economically poor, ways of life. For Negroes, however, the slave system destroyed strong traditional family and kinship patterns, and Negro communities in the South were kept subordinate to the dominant white communities and were not independent and complete communities in their own right. There was little for blacks to build upon and little from the old environment they were anxious to preserve in the new. Spear concluded: "Negroes were tied together less by a common cultural heritage than by a common set of grievances." [25]

Blacks were thus denied one of the advantages resulting from ghetto segregation, the support given the individual in a strange new urban setting by a familiar community maintaining a way of life with which he identified. There was at least one aspect of the ghetto which the Negro was able to benefit from as well as the immigrant, though—insulation from the attitudes of the native whites. Even by the middle of the nineteenth century there was definite prejudice felt by white natives against both "foreigners" and Negroes.[26] Near the turn of the century Steiner observed that foreigners "prefer to be among their own . . . because among their own, they are safe from that ridicule which borders on cruelty, and with which the average American treats nearly every stranger not of his complexion or speech." [27] Some sixty years later Spear attributed the existence of the black ghetto to "an almost impervious wall of hostility and discrimination." [28]

FORMATION OF THE BLACK GHETTO

In the Southern cities before the Civil War there was little residential segregation of Negro slaves. Both the desires of most slave owners and the needs of the Southern slave system led to having slaves living on their owners' premises where they could be supervised. Although they may have lived in separate buildings their comings and going were closely controlled by their owners with the support of the local police. A slave going on an errand for his master would be given a note explaining his mission and apparent freedom. Although a few slaves had enough independence to have their own housing and jobs, reporting back periodically and turning over part of their earnings to their owners, they were not common. The usual arrangement was for the slave to live on his master's property, a situation which was hardly conducive to ghetto segregation.[29]

In the North we can note some variations in the Negro experience which might be classified into three periods: (1) before the Civil War; (2) from the Civil War to World War I; (3) from World War I to the present. While there are some elements common to all three periods, there seem to be enough differences to justfy the classification.

BEFORE THE CIVIL WAR

Not too much need be said about this period. The fact of ghetto concentration during this time has already been noted. Before the Civil War the Negro in the North had a disadvantage encountered by no other group in this country in that his brothers to the south were legally held as slaves. A federal government that tolerated slavery in the South could hardly vigorously press for equality in the North. About the only thing the Negro could do was accept whatever rights the Northerner saw fit to "give" him.

FROM THE CIVIL WAR TO THE GREAT MIGRATION

The period following the Civil War was one of general improvement in the status of the Negro in Northern cities, although not to the extent that racial discrimination or segregation became unimportant. The stigma of currently existing slavery had been removed and Negroes had acquired a number of elementary civil rights. Undoubtedly of considerable importance is that not only was the Negro population a quite small proportion of the total population (2 percent or less) of these cities but that a number of these Negroes were native Northerners who were urbanized in their attitudes and behavior and familiar with the ways of the city. As such they were in a position to advance themselves and many of them did. Drake and Cayton refer to such people as the "Old Settlers." "The successful Negroes of the era, many of them former slaves, interpreted their own careers as proof that some day black men would be accepted as individuals and Americans." [30]

The Old-Settler Negroes compared very favorably with foreign immigrants of the time. Jacob Riis said that there was "no more clean and orderly community in New York" than theirs, adding that in the matter of cleanliness the Negro was "immensely the superior of the lowest of the whites, the Italians and Polish Jews. . . ." [31] Riis' observation was confirmed by a New York *World* article a few years later which commented that "the average Negro is . . . law-abiding and proves a good-paying tenant." [32] He was still charged a higher rent than whites, however.

Osofsky wrote about this period that "it was generally recognized that significant progress was made in the area of race relations subject to law since the end of the Civil War" and refers to the "easing of racial tensions." Respectable Negroes found courteous treatment and acceptance in New York's best hotels, restaurants, and churches. [33] Similarly, in Chicago the Old Settlers told of Negro clerks working in leading downtown stores, Negro doctors having white patients, courteous service given Negroes in downtown restaurants, and a minimum of racial prejudice generally. [34] DuBois reported in 1899 that although there was resistance among Philadelphia whites to living near Negroes, the "sentiment has greatly lessened in intensity during the last two decades." [35] During this same period Negroes in Columbus, Ohio, had been elected to the City Council and the Board of Education, and had been appointed to important positions in city government, although they made up only a small percentage of that city's total population. They also held some of the better jobs within the working class. [36] It seems possible that, had conditions not changed greatly, Negroes could have continued merging into the life of the cities in a fashion similar to that of the immigrants.

THE GREAT MIGRATION

Regardless of what might have been, what did happen was that the early 20th century saw a great increase in the migration of poorly educated, unsophisticated Negroes from the South. World War I brought about the start of the "Great Migration." Numerically, the Old Settlers were overwhelmed, and it quickly developed that the *typical* black person in the Northern city had become the new migrant from the South. In other words, "black" came to equal "ignorant Southerner." The Old Settlers complained about the uncouth manners of the newcomers and argued that distinctions should be made within the Negro group, but to little avail. The Great Migration resulted in greater prejudice and discrimination being directed against *all* Negroes, new and old alike. Understandably, some of the bitterest hostility toward the migrants came from the black Old Settlers, whose status declined as a result of being identified with them and who thought of the migrants as being "lazy," "dirty," "undesirable," "riff-raff." [37] Their "low standard of living and careless appearance [made] them unwelcome to the better class of blacks" in Philadelphia.[38]

A similar phenomenon may be observed in the case of the Jews. The German Jews, who came in the earlier part of the 19th century, had become quite Americanized and were well integrated into the life of the community when suddenly large numbers of Eastern Jews—both backward and highly distinctive culturally—flooded into American cities. Regarding Chicago, Wirth notes that the established Jews, comparable to the Negro Old Settlers, "sensed that all the progress they had made in breaking down barriers, in preventing the development of a ghetto, and in gaining recognition for themselves, as persons rather than as Jews . . . might now, with the new connotation that was attached to the word *Jew,* come to a sudden halt." [39] For both Negroes and Jews, the status of *all* members of the group fell because *most* of them were of low status.

In Chicago, Drake and Cayton believed that the Great Migration and the resulting riot of 1919 "profoundly altered relationships between Negroes and the white residents of Chicago." [40] "The early 20th century in New York City and in the North generally was a period of intensified racial alienation. Racial antagonism was rekindled in a variety of ways." [41] White churches, for example, that had accepted Negro members when there were only a few, sought segregation in one form or another when the Negro population started rapidly increasing. Negro communicants were encouraged to set up congregations of their own, join existing Negro congregations, or attend services separately held for

Negroes by their own church. The end result of such practices was to lead Dr. Martin Luther King, Jr., to observe many years later that 11:00 Sunday morning was the most segregated hour in the week.

Discrimination also increased in hotels and restaurants, and in employment and the labor unions. The New York state legislature even tried to reestablish the state law prohibiting black-white intermarriage.[42] The same phenomenon was also evident in Toledo, in which a Negro weekly newspaper observed in 1923: "As the number of Negroes in Toledo increases the relationship between the races changes. The most obvious and fundamental change is the constantly widening gap between the races in social life and especially in public life." [43] The position of Negroes in the cities was too tenuous at the start to resist successfully the effects of the Great Migration, and so it is from the time of World War I that the modern period of the Negro ghetto may be dated.

Although able to point to many changes in the Chicago black ghetto between 1920 and 1966, Spear still concluded: "Nevertheless, in many significant ways, remarkably little had changed since 1920. Increased numbers had vastly expanded the ghetto, but had not changed its basic structure. Negroes were still unable to obtain housing beyond the confines of the ghetto. . . . The same restrictions that had limited Negro opportunities in the early twentieth century still operated in 1966. . . . No other ethnic enclave in Chicago had changed so little over the past fifty years." [44] A great deal of the material to be covered here seems to support Spear's conclusion.

———

1. Robert C. Weaver, "Class, Race, and Urban Renewal," *Land Economics,* 36, No. 3 (August 1960), 245.

2. W. E. B. DuBois, *The Philadelphia Negro* (1899; reprint ed. New York: Benjamin Blom, Inc., 1967), p. 82.

3. Edward C. Banfield, *The Unheavenly City: The Nature and Future of Our Urban Crisis* (Boston: Little, Brown and Company, 1970), pp. 79–80.

4. Kenneth B. Clark, *Dark Ghetto* (New York: Harper & Row, Publishers, 1965), p. 11.

5. St. Clair Drake and Horace R. Cayton, *Black Metropolis* (New York: Harper Torchbook, Harper & Row, Publishers, 1962), p. 383.

6. Louis Wirth, *The Ghetto* (Chicago: University of Chicago Press, 1928, 1956), chapters 1–3.

7. Robert Park, "Foreword," in Wirth, *The Ghetto,* pp. v–vi.

8. *See* Charles S. Johnson, *Patterns of Negro Segregation* (New York: Harper & Row, Publishers, 1943), pp. 3–4; Noel P. Gist and Sylvia Fleis Fava, *Urban Society* (New York: Thomas Y. Crowell Company, 1964), pp.

106–7; Ralph Thomlinson, *Urban Structure* (New York: Random House, Inc., 1969), p. 171.

9. Marshall B. Clinard, *Slums and Community Development* (New York: The Free Press, 1966), p. 3.

10. *Report of the National Advisory Commission on Civil Disorders* (Washington, D.C.: Government Printing Office, 1968), p. 5.

11. Banfield, *The Unheavenly City*, p. 72 ff.

12. The distinction is consistently made in an action-oriented report, *One Year Later,* published by Urban America, Inc., and The Urban Coalition (New York: Praeger Publishers, Inc., 1969); *also cf.* Charles Abrams, *Forbidden Neighbors* (New York: Harper & Row, Publishers, 1955), pp. 76 ff.

13. Wirth, *The Ghetto*, pp. 198–99.

14. Francesco Cordasco, ed., *Jacob Riis Revisited* (Garden City, N.Y.: Doubleday & Company, Inc., 1968), p. 18.

15. Henry Pratt Fairchild, *Immigration* (New York: The Macmillan Company, 1913), pp. 235–36.

16. Roi Ottley and William J. Weatherby, eds., *The Negro in New York* (New York: The New York Public Library; Dobbs Ferry, N.Y.: Oceana Publications, Inc., 1967), p. 75.

17. Oscar Handlin, *Boston's Immigrants* (Cambridge, Mass.: Harvard University Press, 1959), pp. 96–97; DuBois, *The Philadelphia Negro,* Chaps. iii, iv; Leon F. Litwack, *North of Slavery* (Chicago: University of Chicago Press, 1961), p. 168.

18. William V. Shannon, *The American Irish* (New York: The Macmillan Company, 1963), p. 34.

19. William I. Thomas and Florian Znaniecki, *The Polish Peasant in Europe and America* (Boston: Gorham Press, 1920), V, 32–33.

20. Harvey W. Zorbaugh, *The Gold Coast and the Slum* (Chicago: University of Chicago Press, 1929), p. 164.

21. Chicago *Tribune* Magazine, September 22, 1968, p. 26.

22. Quoted in Walter Firey, *Land Use in Central Boston* (Cambridge, Mass.: Harvard University Press, 1947), p. 211.

23. Edith Abbott, *The Tenements of Chicago, 1908–1935* (Chicago: University of Chicago Press, 1936), p. 115.

24. Nathan Glazer and Daniel Patrick Moynihan, *Beyond the Melting Pot* (Cambridge, Mass.: The M.I.T. Press and Harvard University Press, 1963), p. 33.

25. Allan H. Spear, *Black Chicago* (Chicago: University of Chicago Press, 1967), p. 228.

26. Robert Ernst, *Immigrant Life in New York City, 1825–1863* (Port Washington, N.Y.: Ira J. Friedman, Inc., 1965; copyright © 1949), p. 40.

27. Edward A. Steiner, *On the Trail of the Immigrant* (New York: Fleming H. Revell Company, 1906), p. 263.

28. Spear, *Black Chicago*, p. 229.

29. Richard C. Wade, *Slavery in the Cities* (New York: Oxford University Press, Inc., 1964).

30. Drake and Cayton, *Black Metropolis*, p. 51.

31. Cordasco, ed., *Jacob Riis Revisited*, p. 52.

32. Quoted in Ottley and Weatherby, *The Negro in New York*, p. 184.

33. Gilbert Osofsky, *Harlem: The Making of a Ghetto* (New York: Harper Torchbooks, 1968; copyright © Harper & Row, Publishers, 1963), pp. 36–37.

34. Drake and Cayton, *Black Metropolis*, p. 74.

35. DuBois, *The Philadelphia Negro*, p. 295n.

36. Abrams, *Forbidden Neighbors*, pp. 20–21.

37. Osofsky, *Harlem*, p. 43.

38. DuBois, *The Philadelphia Negro*, p. 81.

39. Wirth, *The Ghetto*, p. 183.

40. Drake and Cayton, *Black Metropolis*, pp. 74–75.

41. Osofsky, *Harlem*, p. 41.

42. *Ibid.*, pp. 41–42.

43. Toledo *Observer*, November 10, 1923.

44. Spear, *Black Chicago*, p. 224.

2 | Black Ghetto Growth

The modern black ghetto began with the Great Migration. In 1860, just before the beginning of the Civil War, 92 percent of all U.S. Negroes lived in the South. Fifty years later, in 1910, the figure was still over 89 percent. Despite the vast changes that took place in the North during that half century—the growth of cities, formation of large corporations, technological and industrial development—the early 20th century found the American racial population distribution little different from what it had been in the middle of the 19th century. A major reason why changes in the North could affect the South so little was that the North could draw for its human raw materials upon the nations of Europe. Immigrants supplied the population needs of the burgeoning Northern cities.

By the early part of the 20th century, however, the coming of large numbers of immigrants was not considered by everyone to be an unmixed blessing. The closing of the frontier by the late 19th century and the establishment of Arizona as the last state within the American continental boundaries in 1912 provided evidence to all that the era of wide open land in the West was over. There was not the same need for people that there had been earlier.

Helping to decrease the desire of the natives for continued immigration was the fact that by the turn of the century the character of immigration had changed. Before the 1880s most European newcomers were of the "old immigration"; by the end of that decade most were of the "new immigration." Those of the old immigration came from northern and western Europe, which means that they tended to resemble the Yankees physically and culturally and that they were usually Protestant. They came at a time when rural areas were still being developed and they were able to spread out on farms and in small towns across the countryside. The new immigration, on the other hand, came from southern and eastern Europe; the people tended to be shorter and darker and to differ more culturally, and were usually of the Roman Catholic, Eastern Orthodox, or Jewish religions. The people of the new immigration also tended to pack into ghetto areas in the northern cities where their distinctive language, dress, and customs made them very noticeable to native Americans. In addition, they came in much larger numbers—at two and three times the rate of the old immigration.

A special case is that of the Irish. Large numbers fled from Ireland in the 1840s because of a blight which destroyed the potato crop, producing famine that resulted in more than two million deaths.[1] Arriving in the New World poor in both money and physical condition, they clustered together in cities on the Eastern Coast. Although they resembled the Yankees physically, they had sharp political and social differences with Anglo culture (differences of the type still causing trouble in Northern Ireland), and of course they were Roman Catholics. In some ways, then, the Irish resembled the new immigration which would come later. Their settlements were the prototypes of the northern racial ghettos which are our concern.

BLACKS AND IMMIGRANTS IN THE "EAST-NORTH"

Just what do we mean when we speak of the North? Data according to census "regions" are apt to be somewhat misleading for our purposes. Of all Negroes in the two northern census regions in 1970—the Northeast and North Central—88 percent were concentrated in the eight states of the East North Central and Middle Atlantic census "divisions." Furthermore, throughout the 20th century these same eight states have contained about 40 percent of the total United States population and from two-thirds to three-fourths of all Negroes outside the South. For purposes of discussion these two divisions will be considered collectively as the *East-North*. The states of the East-North are shown on the map below; they include most of the area commonly called the *North* when the term is used in the context of the race issue.

It is interesting to compare the East-North area with what Roberts in 1912 called the "zone of the new immigration." This zone, north of the angle shown on the map, included only 18 percent of the land area of the United States but more than 80 percent of the new-immigration foreign-born in the country.[2] Despite some differences between immigrants and Negroes, the area in which most new-immigration newcomers settled was the one into which Negroes leaving the South migrated. The evidence concerning this migration seems to support the conclusion that from the standpoint of the economic or manpower needs of the Northern cities, the immigrants and the Negroes fulfilled a similar function.

As of 1910 more than 40 percent of the total U.S. population lived in the East-North, and eight million, or better than 20 percent, were foreign-born. By way of contrast, the 719,000 Negroes made up less than 2 percent of the East-North population. While the foreign-born population had increased by practically two million people in the 1900–1910 decade the Negro population went up by only 135,000. This is a ratio of increase of nearly 15 foreign-born for every Negro in the decade just preceding World War I.

Comparison of the "East-North" (shown in heavy outline) to the "zone of new immigration" (included within angle on map), according to Roberts in 1912. The immigration zone included only 18 percent of the land area of the United States but more than 80 percent of the new immigrants. In 1970 the East-North contained almost 75 percent of all U.S. Negroes who lived outside the South.

Although there were great differences in relative numbers of Negroes and immigrants they were quite similar in some demographic respects. For example, 78 percent of the East-North foreign-born and 79 percent of the Negroes were urban, in contrast to the native white population, which was only 57 percent urban.

The category of *urban* as used here is that of the U.S. Census Bureau, which classifies a person as urban if he lives in an incorporated center of 2,500 or more. Another indicator of urbanization that places the emphasis upon larger cities is the number of people living in cities of 100,000 or more—i.e., in what the Census Bureau calls *principal cities*. When we look at the proportions of the urban population of the East-North area we see that not only were both Negroes and the foreign-born heavily urban, but that they tended to be concentrated in the principal cities. Of the East-North urban foreign-born in 1910, 70 percent lived in principal cities; the corresponding figure for Negroes was 61 percent. Both figures were considerably higher than the 46 percent for the native whites.

THE EFFECTS OF WORLD WAR I

World War I had two consequences that encouraged internal migration. The war effectively curtailed migration from Europe at the same time that it greatly stimulated industrial production. The situation was intensified by the entry of America into the war in 1917. Mobilizing an armed force of millions of men cut further into the labor force, while production of military goods created further demand for workers. If additional workers were to be found it would have to be within the country. The North looked southward.

The magnitude of the population changes affecting the North is revealed by a comparison of the World War I decade of 1910–1920 with the one which preceded it. We have already shown that the East-North gained approximately 15 foreign-born for every Negro between 1900 and 1910. In the following decade, however, this tremendous imbalance actually reversed, so that in the East-North the gain of almost 400,000 Negroes was larger than that of foreign-born by a ratio of better than three to two. A long-established pattern was overthrown as the South replaced Europe as the major source of migrant population for the North. The immigration restrictions imposed by the legislation of the 1920s would continue the new pattern.

Demographic data provide evidence of the extent of the Great Migration. Between 1910 and 1920 the state of Mississippi actually declined in population. "The principal factor in bringing about the decline . . . was the migration northward of large numbers of Negroes during the war." [3]

Although the census figures are according to decade, it should be emphasized that most of the change took place in the last five years of the decade under the influence of World War I. To get more workers, northern interests sent recruiters into the South to seek both black and white labor. "Special trains ran between points in Mississippi and northern industrial centers, taking on the appearance of holiday excursions." [4]

Drake and Cayton note:

> Prior to 1915, however, there had been little to encourage plantation laborers to risk life in the city streets. Now there were jobs to attract them. Recruiting agents traveled south, begging Negroes to come north.

They sometimes carried free tickets in their pockets, and always glowing promises on their tongues. For the first time, southern Negroes were actually being invited, even urged to come to Chicago. They came in droves. . . . And as each wave arrived, the migrants wrote the folks back home about the wonderful North. A flood of relatives and friends followed in their wake.[5]

Northern industries advertised in Negro papers for Southern Negro workers and utilized the Federal Department of Labor to recruit and transport workers from the South.[6] In some cases, southern workers walked off their jobs in the middle of the day to take advantage of the recruiter's offer, going north to take over the better paying but "heavy work done by Italians, Montenegrins, Roumanians, Greeks and other foreigners before the European war broke out." [7]

Some local governments in the South retaliated by requiring labor recruiters to purchase licenses, the extreme case probably being Macon, Georgia, which set a fee of $25,000 for the license and in addition required that the recruiter be recommended by 10 local ministers, 10 manufacturers, and 25 businessmen. Montgomery, Alabama, imposed fines and jail sentences on any person or organization "enticing, persuading, or influencing" labor to leave Montgomery.[8] Agents were harassed and intimidated in various ways.

The fact that Negroes seemed so ready to leave the South even prompted some Southern whites to question the desirability of the South as a place for Negroes to live. In 1916 the *Atlanta Constitution* called attention to local variations in the rates at which Negroes were leaving, noting that Negroes in Georgia counties in which lynchings had taken place were "most eager to believe what the emigration agents told them," and that few Negroes had left one county which had never had a lynching. The article commented: "Mob law as we have known it in Georgia has furnished emigration agents with all the leverage they want." [9] Other newspapers referred to other aspects of racial discrimination, such as the insecurity of Negroes that resulted from a lack of legal protection, police harassment of Negroes, educational disadvantages, and rises in the cost of living—many of these factors being the same ones that Negroes gave as reasons for moving North. There is little evidence, however, that appreciable change took place in the Southern race relations pattern or that the South was effective in its attempt to halt the black flow northward.

The magnitude of the World War I phase of the Great Migration may be realized by a comparison of some simple data. In the 1910–1920 decade alone the percentage of U.S. Negroes who lived in the South decreased by 3.9 points, a greater reduction than that for the preceding 50 years. Had the change continued at the earlier rate the percentage of Negroes living in the South that was actually reached in 1920 would not have been attained until after 1970. The 1910–1920 period compressed five decades into one and set a pattern which would affect race relations for perhaps the remainder of the century.

The 1920 census showed not only that Negroes had moved north in unprecedented numbers, but that their targets had been the cities in general and the large cities in particular. The percentage of East-North Negroes who were urban had increased from 79 to 87 percent, surpassing the 83 percent figure for the foreign-born, and both being considerably higher than the 64 percent for the native whites; of the Negroes who were urban, 70 percent lived in the principal cities. The similarity of the Negroes to the foreign-born and the difference of both of them from the native whites were still quite evident.

MIGRATION SINCE WORLD WAR I

The decade of the 20s was one of economic prosperity and revolutionary change in everyday living as mass distribution was achieved of such basic consumer items as automobiles, radios, and household appliances. Construction of roads and highways as well as home building and modernization were additional elements that stimulated the demand for products of the urban North. The resulting job opportunities, plus the ravages of the boll weavil in the South, encouraged a continuation of the Great Migration, and Negroes responded by moving northward in record numbers. The 1930 census found that the Negro population in the East-North had increased by 673,000, an increase more than half again as large as that of the World War I decade and almost double the increase of the foreign-born. The foreign-born had already started to become an element of decreasing importance in the population just as the Negro was becoming progressively more important.

If the Northern city had little to offer Negroes in the depression 30s, the rural South had even less. "With the collapse of cotton tenancy in the South, and because of discrimination in the dispensing of relief and emergency employment, thousands of Negroes set out for Chicago." [10] Although there were generally no jobs for the newcomers, Negro leaders pointed out the similarity of Negro migrants to the white "Okies" and "Arkies" who moved to California during the same period, also without possibility of regular employment. Despite the depression, the East-North saw a gain in the Negro population almost as large as during the World War I decade.

By 1940 more than one Negro in six (18.2 percent) was living in the East-North area—almost 80 percent of all Negroes outside the South. World War II and the succeeding twenty-five years may be considered as simply an expanded version of World War I and the 20s. The same dynamics operated, but on a much larger scale, as more men were called into uniform and more equipment per man was needed, much of it being produced by the cities of the North. The decade of prosperity following World War I has been more than matched by the continued economic well-being of the United States as a whole up into the 70s.

Beginning after World War II another major force—the mechanization of Southern agriculture—contributed substantially to the northward population movement. Agricultural products differ as to the ease with which they may be handled by machines. Wheat was one of the easiest crops to work by machine, and effective harvesters were developed during the 19th century that enabled relatively few people to work a large area. Cotton, on the other hand, proved to be very resistant to cultivating and picking machines. The necessity for hand picking meant that each share-cropping family could ordinarily tend only 10 to 20 acres.

When successful mechanical cotton cultivators and pickers were developed and adopted following World War II, the dislocation of share-croppers on cotton plantations was tremendous. One family, or a small number of day laborers, could now accomplish the work that formerly required a dozen or more families.[11] The unbelievable rapidity of mechanization of cotton culture is indicated by the fact that in 1950 just 8 percent of the cotton crop was harvested mechanically. Within only 14 years machine picking of cotton had increased to 80 percent.[12] Share-cropper families, both white and black, were pushed off the land in vast numbers. Many of them went North.

When we survey the entire period from 1910 to 1970 we see that a profound population redistribution has taken place. For every decade, the South experienced a net loss through migration of the nonwhite population while the North experienced a comparable gain.[13] By 1970 more than one-third of all Negroes in the country lived in the East-North, where they made up one-tenth of its population. The extent of urbanization of the Northern Negro seems almost incredible, with more than 95 percent living in cities and 80 percent of these in cities of 100,000 or more. Thus the data surveyed here record the transformation of a people from predominantly rural Southerners to highly urbanized Northerners.

The almost explosive expansion of black ghettos beginning with World War I and their subsequent growth had an immense impact upon the patterns of race and residence in Northern cities.[14] In the 1910–1920 decade the black population more than doubled in Chicago, quadrupled in Cleveland, and increased sevenfold in Detroit. Because the Negro was distinctive physically every increase was clearly evident. It is possible that the cities might even have been able to handle this influx had the pressure eased afterward, but the flow northward during the 20s again doubled the enlarged Negro populations of the East-North principal cities.

Native whites dealt with the immigrants by shutting off the supply at its source; not able to do this with Negroes, they bottled them up in the ghetto and fought its enlargement. One consequence of this is that the white has become extremely conscious of ghetto growth and expansion—into white areas. The problem of the black ghetto is not one of static areas—a white neighborhood here and a black one there; overhanging the entire modern period of the black ghetto have been the dynamic facts of its increase in population, white resistance to enlargement of its area, building up of back-pressure, and breaking through of its boundaries.

CHANGES IN MIGRATION PATTERNS

The role of migration has been stressed so far as the major determinant of ghetto growth. The other way in which a population may be enlarged is natural increase—an excess of births over deaths. For most of the modern period there seems little question but that migration has been the primary factor in the black ghetto. It is estimated that 94 percent of the increase in Negro population for Chicago between 1910 and 1920 was the result of migration. Both the 1910 and 1920 censuses found that more than three-fourths of Chicago's Negroes were born in other states.[15] In the North as a whole in both the 1920s and 1930s the fertility of urban Negroes was even below the level needed to maintain the population.[16] Substantial ghetto growth could only have been the result of migration.

Studies made during the late 1960s seemed to indicate that the rate of migration to the North was slowing down, so that ghetto growth was becoming mainly a function of natural increase.[17] These studies were not supported, however, by the 1970 census, which showed that during the 1960s the South had a net loss of almost 1.4 million blacks—a loss roughly the same as that of the 1940s and 1950s. Although not all those who left the South went North, "the destination of Southern Negroes did not change drastically during 1960–70." [18] The East-North showed a net gain in Negro population of .9 million through migration, almost as large as each of the preceding two decades.[19] Migration and natural increase together gave the East-North a gain of nearly 2.2 million in the Negro population, a larger increase than in any preceding decade. (See Table 1 on page 21). By 1970 there were more than three times as many Negroes in the East-North as in 1940, and 11 times as many as in 1910.

TABLE 1. NEGRO POPULATION DATA, 1910–1970 *

	1910	1920	1930	1940	1950	1960	1970
# Negroes in U.S.	9,828	10,463	11,891	12,866	15,042	18,860	22,673
% Negroes in South	89.1	85.2	78.7	77.0	68.0	60.0	53.2
% Negroes in East-North	7.3	10.7	16.7	18.5	24.4	30.0	34.5
# Negroes in East-North	719	1,115	1,983	2,338	3,679	5,670	7,827
Net loss fr. nonwhite migration fr. South in prec. decade	197	522	872	407	1,599	1,436	1,380
Increase in # East-North Negroes in prec. decade	135	396	868	355	1,341	1,991	2,157
% East-North pop. Negro	1.9	2.5	3.8	4.4	6.1	8.1	9.9
% East-North Negroes urban	79.0	86.7	90.1	90.9	94.6	96.2	97.4
% East-North Negroes in principal cities	48.0	59.6	69.0	6.76	74.8	77.5	77.7
# East-North Negroes in principal cities	345	678	1,368	1,610	2,773 †	4,390 †	6,081

* Population figures in thousands.   † Taken as 98 percent of "nonwhites."

Source: United States Census. Net migration data for 1910–1940 from Karl E. and Alma F. Taeuber, "The Negro Population in the United States," in *American Negro Reference Book* (Englewood Cliffs, New Jersey: Prentice-Hall, Inc., 1966).

NEGRO FERTILITY

In considering Negro fertility it is helpful to keep in mind some basic population principles which are characteristic of populations around the world. Nonurban populations, whether in primitive or contemporary societies or rural populations in westernized societies, generally have high rates of fertility. High fertility rates have been functional in such societies because of high death rates and the fact that children could do some of the work of the society and thus be economic assets instead of liabilities.

Urbanization, education, and increased wealth, on the other hand, ordinarily tend to reduce fertility rates. Consequently, the more urbanized countries in the world have a lower average fertility rate than the less urbanized ones, and the urban population within each country generally has a lower fertility rate than the rural population. In the city the child is economically more of a liability than an asset as parents face various demands on their time and money. Even within the city those with more education and income tend to have fewer children than those who are lower socioeconomically.[20] The almost universal pattern, interrelating fertility and migration, has been for the excess population produced by high rural fertility to migrate to the city, thus contributing to its growth. This has been characteristic of the United States and was clearly documented in England as early as the 17th century.[21]

American Negro population data reflect these general characteristics. In the 1920s and 1930s Negro rural farm fertility was high, leading to migration cityward, and urban fertility was low, even below the replacement level. Whites showed a similar pattern.[22] Beginning with World War II both white and nonwhite urban fertility increased to well above the replacement level, but with the nonwhite rate higher than that of the whites. The Taeubers point out, though, that a distorted view can result from simply comparing crude birth rates of whites and Negroes for central cities, because the composition of the respective populations is different. Most Negroes live in the central cities and many of them are recent migrants. Migrants tend to be young and consequently to be in the high fertility ages, whereas whites in the central cities tend to be older and, therefore, to have fewer births.[23]

In view of the rural background of so many migrants to the city it would not be surprising if they initially at least had high rates of fertility simply because that had been their practice in the past. In a study in Cincinnati Beckham found that Negro mothers native to the city had fewer children than Negro mothers born in rural areas.[24] Similar findings have also been reported by others.[25] This suggests that Negro urban fertility will tend to decline as does that of other native urbanites in response to the realities of life in the city.

For the country as a whole, white and nonwhite fertility trends have followed the same pattern in recent decades. Peak fertility for both groups was reached in 1957 and both declined regularly during the next 10 years.[26] Fertility may be measured by the *fertility ratio,* or *child-woman ratio,* based on census enumeration. The ratio for Northern Negroes in 1970 was 468, compared to 399 for Northern whites. The corresponding figures for 1960 were 627 and 549. While the Negro ratios for both years were from 14 to 17 percent higher than those for the white, they had both declined by about one-fourth during the decade. The 1970 Negro ratio was thus smaller than the 1960 white ratio.[27]

The generally found relationship of education and socioeconomic level to fertility is characteristic of urban Negroes in that increased educational level is associated with lower fertility.[28] While both white and nonwhite mothers with high school educations have the same number of children, nonwhite mothers with at least four years of college have fewer children than comparable white mothers. It is only at an educational level of less than four years of high school that nonwhite mothers have more children.[29] These data suggest that rising educational and social levels of Negroes would lead to decreased fertility as families have fewer children and seek to do more for each one.

---

1. Cecil Woodham-Smith, *The Great Hunger* (New York: Harper & Row, Publishers, 1962), p. 411.

2. Peter Roberts, *The New Immigration* (New York: The Macmillan Company, 1912), pp. 156–57.

3. William S. Rossiter, *Increase of Population in the United States,* Census Monographs I, U.S. Census Bureau (Washington, D.C.: Government Printing Office, 1922), p. 56.

4. *Ibid.*

5. St. Clair Drake and Horace R. Cayton, *Black Metropolis* (New York: (Harper Torchbook, Harper & Row, Publishers, 1962), p. 58.

6. Chicago Commission on Race Relations, *The Negro in Chicago* (Chicago: University of Chicago Press, 1922; reprinted by Arno Press, New York, 1968), pp. 86–87.

7. Allon Schoener, ed., *Harlem on My Mind* (New York: Random House Inc., 1968), pp. 29–30.

8. Drake and Cayton, *Black Metropolis,* pp. 58–59.

9. Quoted in Chicago Commission, *The Negro in Chicago,* p. 84.

10. Drake and Cayton, *Black Metropolis,* p. 88.

11. Harry C. Dillingham and David F. Sly, "The Mechanical Cotton Picker, Negro Migration, and the Integration Movement," *Human Organization*, XXV, No. 4 (Winter, 1966), 344–51. The authors report that even a relatively small mechanical picker can harvest an acre of cotton in six man-hours, compared to seventy-four man-hours by hand—a ratio of better than twelve to one.

12. Calvin L. Beale, "The Negro in American Agriculture," in John P. Davis, ed., *American Negro Reference Book* (Englewood Cliffs, N.J.: Prentice-Hall, Inc., 1966), p. 111C.

13. Karl E. Taeuber and Alma F. Taeuber, "The Negro Population in the United States," in Davis, *American Negro Reference Book*, Table III, p. 112.

14. Charles E. Silberman, *Crisis in Black and White* (New York: Vintage Books, Random House, Inc., 1964), p. 34.

15. Otis Dudley Duncan and Beverly Duncan, *The Negro Population of Chicago* (Chicago: University of Chicago Press, 1957), p. 302; Allan H. Spear, *Black Chicago* (Chicago: University of Chicago Press, 1967), p. 142.

16. Gunnar Myrdal (with the assistance of Arnold Rose and Richard Sterner), *An American Dilemma* (New York: Harper & Row, Publishers, 1944), p. 160.

17. Reynolds Farley and Karl E. Taeuber, "Population Trends and Residential Segregation Since 1960," *Science*, March 1, 1968, pp. 953–56; Urban America, Inc., and The Urban Coalition, *One Year Later* (New York: Praeger Publishers, Inc., 1969), p. 111.

18. U.S. Department of Commerce Census News Release, Washington, D.C., March 3, 1971, p. 3.

19. *Ibid.*, Table 5.

20. See any standard text on population such as Ralph Thomlinson, *Population Dynamics* (New York: Random House, Inc., 1965), chapter 9.

21. John Graunt, *Natural and Political Observations Made Upon the Bills of Mortality* (London: Roycroft, 1662; reprinted by The Johns Hopkins Press, Baltimore, 1939).

22. Myrdal, *An American Dilemma*, p. 160.

23. Taeuber and Taeuber, "The Negro Population in the United States; p. 151.

24. Barry Beckham, "Factors Influencing Fertility Among Urban Negroes," *Social Science*, XLV, No. 3 (June 1970), 170–71.

25. Pascal K. Whelpton, Arthur A. Campbell, and John E. Patterson, *Fertility and Family Planning in the United States* (Princeton, N.J.: Princeton University Press, 1966).

26. *Vital Statistics of the United States, 1967*, Vol. I, Department of Health, Education and Welfare (Washington, D.C.: Government Printing Office, 1967), pp. 1–5.

27. Computed by Barry Beckham (1970 census data from Census Report PC (V2)-1). As breakdowns above age five were in ten-year intervals, the

formula used was: (number of children under 5) divided by (women aged 15–44) multiplied by (1,000). *See also* Wilmoth A. Carter, "New Life for the Cities," *Civil Rights Digest,* III, No. 3 (Summer 1970), 36–41.

28. Taeuber and Taeuber, "The Negro Population in the United States," p. 151.

29. *Report of the National Advisory Commission on Civil Disorders* (Washington, D.C.: Government Printing Office, 1968), p. 116.

3 | Ghetto Development

THE IMMIGRANT GHETTO PRECEDENT

There seem to be a number of similarities between the immigrant ghetto of the past and the present black ghetto. It is likely that this is not just coincidental, though, but rather that the immigrant ghetto set the pattern for the way in which the native white would view ghettos and their occupants. To clarify some of these issues let us briefly review some aspects of immigrant ghettos.

The early Irish were certainly not welcomed by native Americans, who saw "that the Irish, crowding into the cities, posed problems in housing, police, and schools; they meant higher tax rates and heavier burdens in the support of poorhouses and private charitable institutions. Moreover, the Irish did not seem to practice thrift, self-denial, and other virtues desirable in the 'worthy, laboring poor.' They seemed drunken, dissolute, permanently sunk in poverty." [1] There were still many slum-dwelling Irish in New York City by 1890, and Riis judged that they were seriously corrupted by tenement life.[2]

Neither were the new-immigration ghetto residents well regarded. Concerning the reaction toward them which native whites developed in the 1890s Higham wrote: "An initial distrust, compounded largely out of their culture and appearance, swelled into a pressing sense of menace, into hatred, and into violence." [3] Roberts referred to those "who say that we get the dregs of Europe in the new immigration." [4] Regarding the Italians and the Jews (one a nationality and the other a religious group) Riis claimed: "The two races, differing hopelessly in much, have this in common: they carry their slums with them wherever they go." [5] Riis, it should be remembered, was a reformer who was sympathetic toward the immigrants. Ten years later, while not denying the charge that the Italian immigrant was dirty, he argued that the cause was the inadequacy of slum-ghetto plumbing.[6] That he had to explain this could indicate that at least some people were unaware of the inadequacies of slum housing and viewed the lack of cleanliness as an inborn trait.

There is a great deal of agreement that immigrants were in fact dirty.

Citing various sources, Fairchild observed: "In the foregoing quotations, frequent reference is made to the filthy conditions in which the dwellings of the foreign-born are kept. It is the current idea among a large class of people that extreme uncleanliness characterizes the great majority of immigrant homes. Unfortunately there is all too large a basis of truth for this impression." [7] He did note, though, that "negligence on the part of city authorities" resulted in filthy-appearing streets. Roberts similarly conceded that "we all say the 'dirty foreigners,' " but pointed out: "Few of us think of the greedy landlord, the indifferent Board of Health, the indolent street cleaner, and the absence of the garbage man." [8] Thus although there seemed to be little opposition to the view that foreigners were dirty, those who championed their cause argued that it was due to the poor quality of housing and sanitation provided by the natives, who, of course, were the ones criticizing the foreigners. The low status of the immigrants, which ironically was determined in part by their filthiness, hampered their obtaining better services and facilities from city and landlord.

Nor were foreigners viewed highly by all those in the real-estate business. A 1923 textbook on real-estate practices referred to the "marked change" that took place when immigrants moved into an area, with it "sinking lower and lower until foreigners of the lowest and most undesirable type, begin to infest the section, living in overcrowded quarters and under unsanitary conditions." [9] A survival of this type of thinking may be found in a real-estate game, originally copyrighted in 1935 but still popular, in which the three cheapest and least desirable properties on the playing board are Mediterranean Avenue, Baltic Avenue, and Oriental Avenue.

Immigrant ghetto residents were frequent victims of a variety of types of exploitation, sometimes even before they left the ship.[10] Of the 19th-century Italian immigrants Firey found: "Nearly all were illiterate peasants who possessed no skills and were easy prey for employment agents, loan sharks, and other exploiters." [11] Writing of the new immigration in general Roberts observed: "When this helpless, inarticulate mass of foreigners invades a section of our cities, the birds of prey—both foreign and native-born—are there to feed upon their ignorance, weakness, and vanity." [12] Instead of adequate housing the immigrants found "avarice, that saw in the homeless crowds from over the sea only a chance for business, and exploited them to the uttermost." [13]

How highly was the foreigner valued? How much support was there in society for a ghetto resident having a feeling of "immigrant pride?" Let an observation of Riis suggest an answer: "The horse that pulls the dirt cart one of these laborers loads and unloads is of ever so much more account to the employer . . . than he and all that belongs to him.

Ask the owner; he will not attempt to deny it, if the horse is worth anything. The man, too, knows it." [14]

When we thus review the overall position of the immigrant ghetto residents it is difficult not to conclude that they were a lowly regarded lot living under miserable conditions. They seem to have been hardly the type of people the typical native, white, middle-class person would want marrying into his family or even living in his neighborhood. There is evidence on this point from work done by Bogardus in the 1920s. He administered his "social-distance scale" to 1,728 native-born Americans from all regions of the United States; his sample contained some Negroes, Jews, and Orientals, but there were very few with new-immigration ancestry. Bogardus judged that his sample was overrepresentative of the "more thoughtful and forward-looking members of American life rather than . . . narrow-minded, older, or conservative Americans." Yet the percentage of this young liberal sample willing to have a member of a new-immigration nationality marry into the family ranged from a high of only 16 percent (for Russians) down to less than 5 percent (for Syrians and Serbo-Croatians). Bogardus' respondents were no more willing to have a Serbo-Croatian as a neighbor than a Negro—both were acceptable to only 12 percent of the sample—while Russian Jews and Bulgarians were only slightly more popular, with figures of 16 percent. All were in sharp contrast to Swedes, Germans, and those from Great Britain, who were welcomed as neighbors by 75 percent or more of the sample.[15] The voluntary segregation of the immigrants in their own ghettos must have met with the wholehearted approval of native Americans.

Although there appears to be a basic similarity between the black and immigrant ghettos as they and their occupants have been viewed by the native white, there have been definite differences, however, in the native's response to the attempts of ghetto-dwellers to leave their respective ghettos and move out into larger society. This difference in response is largely the determiner of the difference between a voluntary and an involuntary ghetto.

MOVEMENT OF GHETTO RESIDENTS

There are two ways in which ghetto residents may move. The first is as part of the movement of a whole ghetto—i.e., when its boundaries change as a result of movement or expansion of the ghetto as a whole. This process is referred to as invasion, and will be discussed shortly. The person in an invaded area faces the prospect of another group moving in and surrounding him. The second way is as individuals moving out of the ghetto into the community at large. Such a move both reflects and causes a lessened interest in following the way of life prevalent within the ghetto. It was a move many immigrants eventually took, but one which has frequently been unavailable to the black for reasons that are a concern of a substantial portion of this book. In its briefest form, the thesis being presented here is that as a result of housing and real-estate patterns which have been developed during the period of the modern black ghetto, an attempted move of the second type by an individual has usually been viewed by others as the initial step in a move of the first type—invasion by the ghetto.

INVASION AND SEGREGATION

American cities have consistently been active, growing, dynamic places. Changes in land use and growth in population inevitably produce changes in the boundaries of the different parts, or natural areas, of cities. In the case of ghettos, the establishment of some by new groups and the expansion of others have meant that their boundary lines have usually been in a state of flux. The term *invasion* has long been used in urban human ecology to refer to the process of one group moving into the area of another and taking it over. The end-stage of invasion is referred to as *succession*. When the invading group is clearly different racially and/or culturally from the original group (which may have been an invading group itself earlier) the invasion process is quite easy to follow. It has taken place repeatedly in American cities for more than a century.

Riis provides an example of successive invasions in New York City over a period of several decades prior to 1890:

> There is a church on Mulberry Street that has stood for two generations as a sort of milestone of these migrations. Built originally for the worship of staid New Yorkers of the 'old stock,' it was engulfed by the colored tide [during the Civil War]. . . . Within the past decade the advance wave of the Italian onset reached it, and today the arms of United Italy adorn its front. The negroes have made a stand at several points . . . but their main body, still pursued by the Italian foe, is on the march yet.[16]

The same process was observed in Chicago in the early 20th century:

> The Negro has slowly but steadily pushed his way in among the Sicilians, who, in turn, have begun to move northward toward North Avenue, into the German slum.[17]

Whatever the locale or the specific invading group, the process of invasion in itself tends to produce considerable hostility between the new and old group.

"This is *our* neighborhood, a *Swedish* neighborhood," a minister of a Swedish church in Chicago argued in explaining why he opposed a new playground in the area. "The dark people have come in farther south in the ward. If a playground is put in our neighborhood we fear these people will come with their children to live in the neighborhood. . . ." The "dark people" were not Negroes, but Sicilians. The time was the early 20th century. Two Swedish girls tried to chase Sicilian girls out of a city park, shouting, "Get out! Dagoes! Dagoes! You can't play here!" Not only was the neighborhood Swedish, but one of the public parks of the City of Chicago had come to be considered as Swedish, too. By 1910 the area had become overwhelmingly Sicilian.[18]

The Sicilian area was in turn invaded by the Negro. "On the school and public playgrounds are reenacted the scenes of a generation ago when the Sicilian was forcing out the Swede. The Negro child is often mistreated and ostracized. There are gang fights on playground and street. . . . Sicilian fathers protest to the schools against admitting Negro children." [19] But the invasion proceeded successfully. Population invasion has a long tradition in American cities. Yet, material about the ghettos up to World War I indicates that the Negroes were simply one among many ethnic groups who competed with each other within the slums in the constant process of settling, expanding and invading, and relocating. Within the ghettos the Sicilians were undoubtedly no more welcome to the Swedes than the Negroes were later to the Sicilians. From outside the ghettos, the Negroes were apparently looked upon with not much less favor than a number of new immigration nationalities.

This material on immigrants and Negroes points up what is almost a paradoxical combination of long-established characteristics of the native white American urbanite in his relationship with ghetto residents. First, the native white from early in the 19th century has successfully sought isolation of himself from the residents of slum ghettos—whether such ghettos were Negro or immigrant.[20] Frequently all that was required was the greater economic power of the native whites who could pay enough to move into areas which the ghetto residents could not afford. In mid-19th-century Boston, as the Irish concentrated in the North End and South Cove, "the original inhabitants of every class abandoned their homes to move into the West End, which . . . became a stronghold of middle-class homes with luxurious fringes of monied elegance." [21]

The native whites responded to the new immigration in a similar fashion, fleeing from the invading foreigners:

> Many changes take place when foreigners come into a block. The English-speaking do their best to keep them out, but some one wants to sell and get more for his property from a foreigner than from a 'white man,' and the highest bidder gets it. In a section of Pittsburgh, the 'Ginnies' rent the houses in the alleys which are vacated by the English-speaking residents; not long after the 'white folks' in the houses facing the street imagine that strong odors crawl over the fence, strains of weird music, so very different from that they are accustomed to, are heard . . . they can't stand it and out they go.[22]

This quotation implies that the English-speaking "whites" considered themselves to be racially different from the new-immigration foreigners, as well as documenting the tendency of native whites to separate themselves from the immigrants. Economic differences between natives and immigrants, plus the tendency of immigrants to cluster together, could produce almost complete mutual isolation of the two groups.

GHETTO CHARACTERISTICS

The second trait of the native white is his willingness to accept as a neighbor those who no longer have *ghetto characteristics*—different language, mannerisms, and dress which in themselves would give the person a different appearance—and perhaps most important in a status-conscious society which tends to equate slum and ghetto—a person who has acquired the economic means to move into a native white neighborhood. Economic success would generally be correlated with loss of ghetto characteristics, in most cases probably as a direct cause. Thus, as a cocoon shelters the ugly caterpillar while it undergoes a metamorphosis to emerge as a beautiful butterfly, so the slum-ghetto sheltered the ugly immigrant until he or his children could emerge as beautiful Americanized "natives." To guarantee that the transformation process would take place before immigrants could inflict themselves upon normal native whites, one author of a textbook in real-estate fundamentals advocated as late as 1932 that "undesirable elements of Southern Europe" should be kept "segregated in sections by themselves for at least one generation." [23]

But what about the prejudice with which the native viewed those of the new immigration? It became very difficult to maintain and apply to those successful "Americans" with the well-behaved children who had just moved in next door. Of course, it was mainly those who were most successful and most Americanized who would seek to move out of the ghetto. If the new immigration gave us the "dregs of Europe," the new neighbors were "the exception that proves the rule."

What are here termed ghetto characteristics are what Abrams seemed to have in mind when he referred to the distinction that some real-estate agents have made between "a 'good' Jew to whom property may be sold, and . . . the long-nosed, bearded variety of the anti-Semitic caricature." [24] The caricature Jew would *look* Jewish, and not just in his physical appearance. His manner of dress would be different, he might use typically Jewish gestures, he would speak with an accent. He would reek of the ghetto; let him stay there where he "belongs." But an Americanized Jew would not be that different culturally from everyone else and so would be acceptable as a neighbor.

Even WASPs (White Anglo-Saxon Protestants) can have ghetto characteristics, as illustrated by the "hillbillies," whose ghettos have been a part of a number of Northern cities for the past few decades. Like many blacks they have been forced out of the rural South by economic conditions and have arrived in the city with the same lack of urban skills and education. Like the immigrants of the past they have clustered together according to their former community. In this most recent case of the continuing process of population invasion, "the first Southern white Anglo-Saxon Protestant to move in on a Chicago block has about the same impact as a Negro. Chicagoans panic and move out as fast as possible, although a few remain to fight a rear-guard action." [25] Yet, as a Chicago businessman who does volunteer work to assist them points out: "You've got to realize that the white southern migrant, unlike the Negro or Puerto Rican, faces what is basically just a one-generation problem. All he has to do is lose his southern accent and move out of the migrant community and nobody recognizes him anymore." [26] He would no longer have ghetto characteristics.

SEGREGATION AND GHETTO CHARACTERISTICS

What is the significance of involuntary ghetto segregation? On a theoretical level, it is a denial of the basic American right of any citizen to live anywhere he wishes and can afford and for whatever reasons are important to him. On a practical level, where a man lives can affect his earning power, social status, opportunities for his children, the suitability and convenience of his housing, chances for social mobility, goods and services available, and so forth. We will consider some of these factors in greater detail later.

Regardless of race, the housing of the very poor is going to be of poor quality simply because of economic factors, so that there is little additional disadvantage from having to live in a ghetto-slum as compared to a non-ghetto-slum. If the poverty is the result of racial discrimination in education or employment, then slum housing becomes in effect ghetto housing, and the ghetto characteristics of the residents may in themselves result in continued racial discrimination, thus perpetuating the slum-ghetto.

The problem of the poor, regardless of race, is a separate one of providing adequate low-income housing; it is not the central problem of the ghetto as a ghetto. Rather, the crucial issue seems to be whether those who are more successful can live outside the ghetto if they wish. The question is whether any ghetto will be voluntary or involuntary.

Weaver found that in Chicago before World War I, "the Negro was not the worst-housed ethnic group in the city. That dubious distinction fell upon the Italians who were the most recent migrant group. . . . As early as 1912, however, it was clear that poor housing among Italians could be a temporary situation. . . . There were no strong barriers to the movement of Italians out of the run-down areas where they were concentrated. . . . Pre-World War I Chicago, had however, already begun to adopt customs and attitudes to limit greatly the Negro's enjoyment of similar opportunities." [27] These customs and attitudes continued into subsequent decades. Abbott commented in the 1930s that although the Negro poor faced housing problems similar to those of the Poles, Jews, and Italians who also were poor, "prejudice among the white people" kept even well-to-do Negroes from moving out into areas offering good housing, a handicap not faced by the economically successful of other groups.[28]

It is this difference in ability to move out of the slums that led Harrington to distinguish between the "old slums" and the "new slums." The old, ethnic or immigrant, slums offered miserable housing conditions, but they also offered a goad to improvement and a "culture of aspiration." The new slums, which are overwhelmingly racial slums, present an "environment of pessimism and hopelessness" because of their residents' inability to escape them.[29]

We noted earlier that the native white American has generally refused to live near those who had ghetto characteristics—whether those of the immigrant or those of the black—but that he usually accepted people who came from ghetto groups, provided the individuals had lost their ghetto characteristics. Such ghetto characteristics suggested teeming slums inhabited by strange groups with all sorts of unusual beliefs and customs. The very fact that a person from an immigrant ghetto sought to move out into an "American" neighborhood could be taken as evidence that he was renouncing ghetto ways and hence could be accepted as a neighbor. Even the "dark people," who appeared to be so formidable a problem when huddled solidly together in Little Sicily, proved to be within the range of assimilation after a period of "Americanization." The Americanized immigrant no longer suggested to anyone who saw him the poverty (with its concomitant threat to social status to those who associated with him), congestion, filth, disease, gambling, addictions, crime, vice, and personal demoralization that have been the perennial lot of the slum-ghetto dweller.[30]

That Negroid physical characteristics may be considered ghetto characteristics is undoubtedly due to the fact that such a very high proportion of blacks in cities do live in black ghettos. Certainly though, black ghetto does not automatically mean black slum. The black ghetto includes stable, successful families at both the working-class and middle-class levels. But the native white's preoccupation with both color and social status may encourage him not to make distinctions within the ghetto population and thus to ascribe to *all* members of the ghetto the characteristics of those in the slum.

Clinard's observations seem relevant here: "A slum also has an image in the eyes of the larger community. There is a societal reaction to slum dwellers. The nonslum dweller often associates the physical appearance and difficult living conditions of the slum with belief in the 'natural inferiority' of those who live in the slums. As a slum is an inferior place, those who live there are also inferior." [31] This image, or mental blueprint, which the white has of the slum-ghetto, complete with all its undesirable characteristics, leads him to equate the "threat" of a Negro neighbor on his block with that of hauling the slum-ghetto in toto right onto his street. This leads him to resist the movement of *any* black person into his neighborhood.

As one resident of a white, middle-class neighborhood described the reaction when a middle-class black family moved onto his street: "There were wild yarns everywhere . . . Harlem was emigrating en masse to our neighborhood. Scenes of crime and passion were envisioned in Springfield Gardens, our quiet residential community in Queens, New York." [32] Helper made the same observation from a more objective position about whites' reactions to a black neighbor: "They fear that their neighborhood will deteriorate if Negroes come because of their manner of living in other areas: *they associate Negroes with the undesirable slum* (dirt, noise, squalor, stealing, vice), something to be avoided if possible." [33]

Naturally, whites resist. The ultimate irony is that in resisting, they continue the pattern of racial residential segregation which dams people up in the ghetto, increasing the congestion which both perpetuates and increases the *slum* conditions which support the slum-ghetto image that justifies the segregation. One can hardly find a better example of a vicious circle.

THE SELF-FULFILLING PROPHECY

Robert Merton has developed the concept of the "self-fulfilling prophecy." [34] Put briefly, there is a self-fulfilling prophecy situation when people believe that a certain thing will happen and when that belief causes them to act in a way that brings about the expected result. Had they believed something else, they would have acted differently and some other result would have ensued. One can see the self-fulfilling prophecy phenomenon at work on the residential segregation scene. The white identifies the social pathology of the slum ghetto with blacks and fears that if one black family moves into his area it will soon go all black and become a slum. Without denying that there is a high incidence of social pathology in any slum-ghetto, one may ask, how realistic are the white's fears that *his* neighborhood will become a slum? The answer is that the greater the belief that it will happen, the more people will act in a way that will make their expectations come true. The prophecy will fulfill itself, as the Commission on Civil Disorders has pointed out.[35]

Consider the opposite possibility. People do *not* believe that one black neighbor equals a black slum-ghetto. They would then not resist a black family moving into their neighborhood. Not being dammed up artificially as a result of segregation, black ghetto residents would then not be subject to the social pathology of the slum, resulting from congestion. With less social pathology, the image which whites have of blacks would change, which would facilitate accepting blacks as neighbors. With blacks more widely distributed around the city, black physical characteristics would lose significance as ghetto characteristics. Under these conditions it would be impossible for any area into which blacks moved to become a slum-ghetto because there would not be the pent-up housing demand forcing blacks to move almost solidly into any area they could get, overcrowding it.

The situation which Drake and Cayton described in *Black Metropolis* —their name for the Chicago Black Belt—in the 1940s is little different today: "The existence of these [social pathology] conditions has become a convenient rationalization for keeping Negroes segregated. . . . As it becomes increasingly crowded—and 'blighted'—Black Metropolis's reputation becomes ever more unsavory. The city assumes that *any* Negroes who move *anywhere* will become the focal point for another little Black Belt with a similar reputation." [36] Thus, restrictive segregation perpetuates conditions which cause whites to maintain segregation— a circular process to which Myrdal also called attention.[37]

As with the immigrants, many blacks might choose to remain in areas inhabited mostly by themselves. An important point needs to be made. If all locations in a metropolitan area were made readily available to blacks it would be impossible for solid slum-ghetto areas to develop everywhere. There simply are not enough blacks to go around. They are a minority of the population in all metropolitan areas, and in most central cities.

We need to raise another question. Is the resistance of whites to having black neighbors due just to ghetto characteristics; isn't there an additional factor of racial prejudice, so that the white would not want a black neighbor regardless of his social characteristics? A definitive answer to this question cannot be given under the present circumstances, although some aspects can be suggested. First, the question assumes that the presence of one black family does not mean that the neighborhood will ever go all black, as is likely to be the case under present segregation conditions. Second, it also assumes that the black neighbor is at least equal in economic and occupational level to the present residents of the area and also has similar behavioral standards. Third, because of the first two conditions there would be no reason to expect that the black family would have an adverse effect on property values, thus threatening the economic investment of the whites in their homes.

These conditions approach those under which the Americanized immigrant moved out into native white neighborhoods, keeping in mind that he also had been defined by many as racially inferior. Although some native whites undoubtedly resented the fact that "Dagoes" or "Bohunks" were moving into their neighborhoods and were not overly congenial to their new neighbors, they managed to get along and came to think of each other as individuals rather than just as members of groups. The same thing could probably happen with blacks if some of the social and economic supports for racial prejudice were removed or weakened.

RESTRICTIVE SEGREGATION

Involuntary ghetto segregation may be either *restrictive* or *nonrestrictive*. One might conceive of a situation in which, although the two races lived in separate areas in the city, the quality, availability, cost, and variety of housing would be equal for both groups. This would be nonrestrictive segregation. This possibility was implied by Myrdal in the 1940s when he stressed that "if white people insist on segregation," the society should provide sufficient housing to prevent "scandalous housing conditions for Negroes" and the social pathology resulting from "doubling up." [38]

There is no legal way in which involuntary segregation may be maintained, however. (See p. 53 and chapter 10.) While nonrestrictive segregation would at least meet the housing needs of blacks, it is neither a legal nor a practical possibility for American society. But considering nonrestrictive segregation does help to emphasize the importance of restrictive segregation in contributing to the problem of the black ghetto. It is not just a matter of racial segregation, but of a form of segregation that has produced crowding and congestion, increasing social pathology within the ghetto—thus perpetuating the negative image that encourages continued resistance to its expansion, the familiar pattern of a vicious circle.

---

1. William V. Shannon, *The American Irish* (New York: The Macmillan Company, 1963), p. 39.

2. Francesco Cordasco, ed., *Jacob Riis Revisited* (Garden City, N.Y.: Doubleday & Company, Inc., 1968), pp. 19–20; *see also* p. 91.

3. John Higham, *Strangers in the Land* (New Brunswick, N.J.: Rutgers University Press, 1955), p. 87.

4. Peter Roberts, *The New Immigration* (New York: The Macmillan Company, 1912), p. 128.

5. Cordasco, *Jacob Riis Revisited*, p. 23.

6. *Ibid.*, p. 362.

7. Henry Pratt Fairchild, *Immigration* (New York: The Macmillan Company, 1913), pp. 242–43.

8. Roberts, *The New Immigration*, p. 162.

9. Quoted in Charles Abrams, *Forbidden Neighbors* (New York: Harper & Row, Publishers, 1955), p. 159.

10. Robert Ernst, *Immigrant Life in New York City, 1825–1863* (Port Washington, N.Y.: Ira J. Friedman, Inc., 1965; copyright © 1949), p. 27.

11. Walter Firey, *Land Use in Central Boston* (Cambridge, Mass.: Harvard University Press, 1947), p. 183.

12. Roberts, *The New Immigration*, p. 163.

13. Cordasco, *Jacob Riis Revisited*, p. 304.

14. *Ibid.*, pp. 34–35.

15. Emory S. Bogardus, *Immigration and Race Attitudes* (Lexington, Mass.: D. C. Heath & Co., 1928), p. 25.

16. Cordasco, *Jacob Riis Revisited*, p. 22.

17. Harvey W. Zorbaugh, *The Gold Coast and the Slum* (Chicago: University of Chicago Press, 1929), p. 147.

18. *Ibid.*, pp. 160–61.

19. *Ibid.*, p. 148.

20. See Ernst, *Immigrant Life*, chapters 4 and 5; Leon Litwack, *North of Slavery* (Chicago: University of Chicago Press, 1961), pp. 168 ff.

21. Oscar Handlin, *Boston's Immigrants* (Cambridge, Mass.: Harvard University Press, 1959), p. 96.

22. Roberts, *The New Immigration*, p. 161.

23. Quoted in Abrams, *Forbidden Neighbors*, p. 160.

24. *Ibid.*, p. 235.

25. Hal Bruno, "Chicago's Hillbilly Ghetto," *The Reporter*, June 4, 1964, p. 29.

26. Chicago *Tribune* Magazine, September 22, 1968, p. 33.

27. Robert C. Weaver, *The Negro Ghetto* (New York: Harcourt Brace Jovanovich, Inc., 1948), pp. 17–18.

28. Edith Abbott, *The Tenements of Chicago, 1908–1935* (Chicago: University of Chicago Press, 1936), p. 125.

29. Michael Harrington, *The Other America* (New York: The Macmillan Company, 1962), chapter 8.

30. Cf. St. Clair Drake and Horace R. Cayton, *Black Metropolis* (New York: Harper Torchbook, Harper & Row, Publishers, 1962), p. 175.

31. Marshall B. Clinard, *Slums and Community Development* (New York: The Free Press, 1966), p. 14.

32. Ralph Bass, "Prejudice Won't Make Us Sell Our House," *Coronet*, July 1959, pp. 103–7.

33. Rose Helper, *Racial Policies and Practices of Real Estate Brokers* (Minneapolis: University of Minnesota Press, 1969), p. 79 (emphasis added).

34. Robert K. Merton, *Social Theory and Social Structure* (New York: The Free Press, 1957), pp. 421–36; 1968 edition, pp. 475–90.

35. *Report of the National Advisory Commission on Civil Disorders* (Washington, D.C.: Government Printing Office, 1968), p. 119.

36. Drake and Cayton, *Black Metropolis*, p. 211 (emphasis in original).

37. Gunnar Myrdal (with the assistance of Arnold Rose and Richard Sterner), *An American Dilemma* (New York: Harper & Row, Publishers, 1944), p. 623.

38. *Ibid.*, pp. 626–27.

4 | *Racial Segregation*

THE EXTENT OF SEGREGATION

The very existence of "black belts" and "white areas" is evidence of residential segregation, but we may still ask how pervasive it is and how much variation there is from place to place. Thorough work on this question has been done by Karl and Alma Taeuber and is reported on in their book, *Negroes in Cities*. The Taeubers developed a "segregation index" which expresses the amount of segregation on a scale with a theoretical range of from zero to 100. Assume a city in which 20 percent of the population is nonwhite. If race were completely irrelevant to housing location then each block in the city would contain, on the average, 20 percent of nonwhites. A city in which each block contained the same percentage of nonwhites as the city as a whole would have a segregation index of zero and would be considered completely unsegregated. For values greater than zero: "The higher the value, the greater the degree of residential segregation. . . . The value of the index may be interpreted as showing the minimum percentage of nonwhites who would have to change the block on which they live in order to produce an unsegregated distribution. . . ." [1]

The Taeubers computed segregation indexes for 207 American cities using data from the 1960 census. The index values obtained ranged from 60.4 (San Jose, California) to 98.1 (Fort Lauderdale, Florida). Most cities had values in the upper range of scores, with half of the cities above 87.8.[2] The Taeubers were also able to compute segregation-index values for a smaller number of cities for 1940 and 1950. Their data for large Northern cities are given in Table 2.

Of the 18 cities for which data are given, only four showed a decrease in segregation over both decades covered. For 10 cities a decrease in segregation in one decade was offset by an increase in the other. On the whole, however, the data indicate a small decrease in segregation between 1940 and 1960, more cities having decreased in the latter decade than in the earlier one. Even this conclusion must be advanced

TABLE 2. INDEXES OF RESIDENTIAL SEGREGATION FOR SELECTED NORTHERN CITIES, 1940, 1950,1960

City	1940	1950	1960	Change 1940–50	Change 1950–60
Akron, Ohio	82.2	87.6	88.1	5.4	0.5
Buffalo, N.Y.	87.9	89.5	86.5	1.6	−3.0
Chicago, Ill.	95.0	92.1	92.6	−2.9	0.5
Cincinnati, Ohio	90.6	91.2	89.0	0.6	−2.2
Cleveland, Ohio	92.0	91.5	91.3	−0.5	−0.2
Columbus, Ohio	87.1	88.9	85.3	1.8	−3.6
Dayton, Ohio	91.5	93.3	91.3	1.8	−2.0
Detroit, Mich.	89.9	88.8	84.5	−1.1	−4.3
Gary, Indiana	88.3	93.8	92.8	5.5	−1.0
Indianapolis, Ind.	90.4	91.4	91.6	1.0	0.2
Jersey City, N.J.	79.5	80.5	77.9	1.0	−2.6
Milwaukee, Wis.	92.9	91.6	88.1	−1.3	−3.5
Newark, N.J.	77.4	76.9	71.6	−0.5	−5.3
New York, N.Y.	86.8	87.3	79.3	0.5	−8.0
Philadelphia, Pa.	88.0	89.0	87.1	1.0	−1.9
Pittsburgh, Pa.	82.0	84.0	84.6	2.0	0.6
Rochester, N.Y.	85.5	86.9	82.4	1.4	−4.5
Toledo, Ohio	91.0	91.5	91.8	0.5	0.3

Source: Karl E. and Alma F. Taeuber, *Negroes in Cities* (Chicago: Aldine Publishing Company, 1965), pp. 39–40.

cautiously, though, because the segregation index may be affected by the way in which areas of Negro housing expand.

Because of the block-by-block pattern of expansion of black areas there will always be some blocks at any one time which are "changing" and which are occupied by both whites and blacks. Statistically, these blocks look "integrated" and thus tend to reduce the segregation index score although they will soon become almost solidly black. An indicator of "true" residential integration would be the existence of urban areas which remain racially mixed over a period of time. Using census-tract data for a limited number of cities the Taeubers sought to locate "Stable Interracial Areas"—areas in which the size of both the white and non-white populations had remained relatively unchanged throughout a decade. For the period of 1940–1960 for the three Northern cities studied—Detroit, Cleveland, and Philadelphia—they found only one census tract in one city for one decade (Philadelphia, 1940–1950) that they could consider a Stable Interracial Area.[3] Similar, although not directly comparable, data for Chicago indicated that it also lacked stable interracial neighborhoods.[4] Earlier data showed that Philadelphia had six Stable Interracial Areas in 1930–1940 and Cleveland had one in 1920–1930, but they obviously failed to survive as integrated areas.[5] Statistical evidence up to 1960 confirms the surface impression that the amount of segregation in Northern cities has been considerable indeed.

More recent data point to an increase in the extent of segregation during the 60s. A number of cities had special censuses conducted during the middle of the decade. A Census Bureau analysis of data for 12 of these cities indicates a clear tendency for census tracts almost solidly Negro—75 percent Negro or more—to have increased since 1960 at the expense of tracts with smaller proportions of Negroes. Thus, in Cleveland, while 72 percent of all Negroes lived in almost solidly Negro tracts in 1960, 80 percent of all Negroes were living in such tracts by 1965. By mid-decade the percentages for Buffalo, New York, and Evansville, Indiana, had increased respectively from 35 percent and 34 percent to 69 percent and 59 percent—amazing increases for a period of only about five years. The extent of segregation is also indicated by considering the opposite extreme: only 4 percent of Cleveland's Negroes and 8 percent of Buffalo's Negroes lived in census tracts that were less than 25 percent Negro.[6]

Using data from these same special censuses, Farley and Taeuber computed a "dissimilarity index" similar to that of the Taeubers' segregation index discussed above. Of the 13 cities studied, the index went down in only two: Fort Wayne, Indiana, and Sacramento, California. Fort Wayne was the only one of seven Northern cities studied that showed a decline in segregation, and that decline was only about a half point. Cautioning that the cities available for study did not constitute a random sample of all American cities, Farley and Taeuber saw no evidence in their data of a decline in the extent of segregation during the 1960s. They concluded: "Stability in segregation patterns has been maintained despite massive demographic transformation, marked advances in Negro economic welfare, urban renewal and other clearance and resettlement programs, considerable undoubling of living quarters and diminished room-crowding, high vacancy rates in many of the worst slums, and an array of federal, state, and local anti-discrimination laws and regulations." [7]

SOME EFFECTS OF RESIDENTIAL SEGREGATION

We may begin by noting Johnson's observation that "racial segregation in residential areas provides the basic structure for other forms of institutional segregation." [8] The implications of this statement alone are considerable, but it is beyond the scope of this work to survey many of them and to review all the negative consequences of segregation. Instead, only a few of what the writer believes are commonly regarded as basic rights of all American citizens—and that are frequently denied by residential segregation—will be examined.

Segregation keeps many blacks from living in the type of housing that best meets their needs. All but the most wealthy people face economic limitations to their housing choices, of course, and blacks cannot be immune to this, but a ghetto covers only a portion of a city and can offer only the kind of housing that was built there at some time in the past for people whose housing needs may have been quite different from contemporary blacks. The ghetto generally provides very little new housing and a relatively small proportion of single-family housing, a handicap particularly affecting middle-class families.[9] The ghetto resident may find it practically impossible to buy a new single-family house on a reasonably sized lot of the kind simply taken for granted by white suburbanites.

The Chicago Commission on Race Relations reported on the difficulties faced by Negroes in trying to obtain suitable housing during and shortly after World War I. The Commission found that the shortage of homes of a suitable size in the Black Belt forced many Negroes to take large old houses whose expenses could only be met by taking in lodgers, with the consequent loss of privacy and greater risk of sexual irregularities.[10] Similar conditions existed in New York.[11] Some 35 years later Duncan and Duncan found the same situation—doubling-up and taking in lodgers to meet the high costs of too large dwelling units.[12] In other cases, the only units available may be too small for the family. Thus, a disruption of family life caused by simply not being able to obtain housing which meets the needs of the family in size and room arrangement is one consequence of segregation.

A serious and growing economic problem for blacks is that ghetto residence in itself limits the ability to obtain jobs because of location and transportation factors. Such factors are in addition to other employment difficulties caused by racial discrimination in hiring and promoting and by inadequacies in training and education. With the expansion of urban areas, most of the new industrial and service jobs are located in outlying or suburban areas, with a consequent loss of such types of jobs in the inner parts of the city. The new jobs developing in the central business district are primarily in the business and professional category.

A study in Chicago found that between 1955 and 1965 there was a loss of 90,000 jobs within the west and south black-ghetto areas in that city.[13] The decline in jobs in inner-city areas has been particularly pronounced in the Northern and Western cities in which so many blacks are located. Between 1960 and 1964, although manufacturing employment increased in the nation as a whole, it decreased in most of the major Northern central cities.[14] Also, new public service institutions, such as hospitals, that provide employment for a wide range of skill levels, are tending to be located in suburban areas.[15] A city planner for Cleveland stated: "Most of the employment opportunities opening up are in the suburban communities, many of them . . . are quite some distance from where the Negro population lives." [16] Even the problem of learning about job openings and applying for employment is greatly increased in difficulty when the jobs are far from ghetto areas.

Although there has been a considerable increase in the total number of jobs in the greater Chicago area, many of them are practically inaccessible to Black Belt residents. The director of the Chicago Urban League explained: "More than 300 firms in the area send us job listings. Then, when we talk to guys who are qualified, they say, 'I can't drive thirty-two miles one way every day. I'm going to work in town.' Negroes must then seek work at less money somewhere near the inner city." [17]

A survey at Argonne National Laboratory, on the outskirts of Chicago, found that its Negro employees had a 50-mile daily round trip to and from work. Such a trip becomes a considerable expense in itself, leading the United States Commission on Civil Rights to point out: "Where Negroes are able to obtain employment in suburban communities, they incur extra costs because they often cannot live within a reasonable distance of their work and must commute." The Commission cited the case of the Cleveland, Ohio, suburb of Solon—"a city with one Negro resident"—which has 4,500 workers who commute daily from Cleveland to work in Solon industries.[18]

The total cost of operating an automobile—including depreciation, insurance, tires, repairs, and so forth—is likely to be not less than eight cents a mile. Using this figure, a daily round trip of 50 miles would cost $4 a day and between $80–$90 a month. This could be considered a "segregation tax" imposed on blacks but not on the white who can locate in a suburb near his job. The black may instead take a lower-paying job in the central city, but then he pays the "tax" in the form of lower income. As a ghetto resident generally pays more for his housing than a white pays for comparable accommodations, this might be considered another form of tax imposed by segregation.

Such a trip, for dependability, requires a relatively new and well-maintained auto. A car pool that depends on the car of only one person in the group, which is not uncommon, leaves the rest of the group stranded if the driver is sick or not working. Public transportation lines have been planned more to bring white suburban workers into the city than to transport inner-city workers to outlying industrial sites. Although there have been some federally supported programs subsidizing mass transportation, one writer comments: "This 'carry them out to work at dawn and bring them back at night' approach smacks of the old plantation system, however, especially when the worker can afford housing near his job and is denied it only because of his race. When a federal subsidy is involved, it amounts to subsidizing segregation." [19]

The location of jobs and transportation is not just a problem of the giant cities. A 1965 study in Toledo, whose population is near 400,000, found that 40 percent of the residents of a Model Neighborhood area— an inner-city black-ghetto area participating in the federal Model Cities program—relied either on public transportation or walking to get to work. About one in seven Model Neighborhood residents reported having to give up the chance to take a job because of inadequate public transportation. Those who did use public transportation to get to work reported an average trip time of approximately an hour each way, more than three time as long as the work trip for those with cars. In addition, there are a number of major employment sites in outlying parts of the Toledo metropolitan area that are practically inaccessible by public transportation.[20]

The Report of the National Advisory Commission on Civil Disorders also called attention to the fact that most new jobs were being created in suburbs and outlying areas and judged that "this trend is likely to continue indefinitely." [21] The location of industry in outlying areas is not for the purpose of avoiding the ghetto area as such, but because space for the most efficient plant-layout and transportation needs can be obtained most readily and cheaply on large tracts of open land away from the high land costs and congestion of the central city.[22] The present decentralization of industry is a continuation of a trend which was evident even in the 19th century.[23]

The Commission does not consider it likely that industry could be lured back to the city. The only other alternatives are to make housing available to black workers in suburbs near their jobs or to develop an elaborate mass-transportation system between ghetto and suburb. The Commission stated, however, that carrying out such a system "on a large scale will be very costly." It did note that many more existing central-city jobs could be made available to Negroes "if employers cease racial discrimination in their hiring and promotion practices." The Commission concluded: "Nevertheless, as the total number of Negro central city job-seekers continues to rise, the need to link them with emerging new employment in the suburbs will become increasingly urgent." [24] In view of the poor prognosis both for substantial numbers of new inner-city jobs and for mass transportation to jobs in outlying areas, the most feasible alternative seems to be making housing available to blacks in suburban areas—the very areas which have been most resistant to decreased residential segregation in the past. The National Committee Against Discrimination in Housing has charged that suburbs in the New York City area have been willing to relax land-zoning restrictions to attract business and industry from New York City and Newark, but have tightened residential controls to keep racial minority workers in the jobs thus created from living there near the jobs.[25]

The effect of segregation in handicapping the employment possibilities and resulting earning potential of blacks is readily demonstrable and easily comprehended in a country that emphasizes economic striving and material well-being. The additional money that a black spends in transportation costs to get to his job is not available to meet family needs, whether for medical care, education, or recreation. His children are similarly handicapped if he must take a lower-paying inner-city job; in either case his disadvantage is passed along to his children, who may also suffer additional economic loss as adults simply because the school they went to was in a ghetto area. The name or location of a school will identify it with the ghetto, and, particularly in the case of high schools, it is likely to have an unfavorable reputation in the community, so that its graduates have more difficulty in obtaining jobs simply because they attended it. The young people are aware of this, which tends to stifle their motivation while in school.

Aside from the economic consequences of segregation there are other effects. Approximately one person out of every nine in the United States is black, and segregation isolates this population of about 23 million people from the rest of the country—an unhealthy situation for an interdependent urban society. Lack of understanding, suspicion, and hostility develop easily in such circumstances. A young Negro in Cleveland testified before the United States Civil Rights Commission that he never knew a white person until he was 14 or 15 years old: "I just didn't know them. I didn't think they even existed because I looked at my arm and my face, it was brown and I thought that was natural because everyone else around me was brown." A teacher in a ghetto junior high school testified that students did not seem to realize that there were whites in Cleveland, and that they thought "that the white community is something that is way out, it is out of Cleveland." [26]

Some adults come to realize the isolation they had as children from other segments of society. One woman who grew up in St. Paul and years later met a Negro leader originally from that city also realized that he had "spent a good part of his childhood on a street and in a condition I had literally never seen. . . . We speak of St. Paul and we speak not only of different worlds but actually of different cities." [27] She noted that St. Paul then had a population of less than 300,000 and could be circumnavigated by car in less than an hour.

Even when blacks and whites become neighbors the ignorance resulting from earlier isolation can persist into the new situation. Damerell tells of a middle-class black family that moved into the middle-class suburb of Teaneck, New Jersey. When a white neighbor came to the house soliciting for a charity drive she thoroughly looked over the house and commented: " 'Oh, you live beautifully!' 'What do you mean?' asked [the black lady of the house]. 'How did you *expect* me to live?' 'I had no idea,' said the woman, who lived in the same sort of split-level herself." [28]

SEGREGATION, INTEGRATION, AND NONSEGREGATION

In considering alternatives to the present almost complete residential segregation of the races it seems helpful to follow Weissbourd and Channick in distinguishing between desegregation and integration. They explain: "If some Negroes choose to live in separate communities as white ethnic groups have done, as long as the decision is theirs we have a condition of desegregation. Desegregation is, therefore, different from integration, for it includes separate Negro and white neighborhoods as well as mixed ones." [29] Nonsegregation seems preferable to their term, desegregation, which tends to emphasize the process of change. Nonsegregation implies both the right of people to remain indefinitely where they are, even if in ghetto areas, and the elimination of restrictions on moving into other areas. Nonsegregation would provide for voluntary ghetto residence, while integration could result in involuntary nonghetto residence. Only white ethnocentrism could lead to the belief that all blacks would want to live in predominantly white areas.

A number of writers have commented on the attraction of a ghetto for its residents. In the late 19th century DuBois observed: "The Negro who ventures away from the mass of his people and their organized life, finds himself alone, shunned and taunted, stared at and made uncomfortable. . . . Thus he remains far from friends and the concentrated social life of the church, and feels in all its bitterness what it means to be a social outcast." [30] Wirth similarly contrasted the "cold, artificial life" outside the Jewish ghetto with the "warmth and familiarity" within.[31]

Weaver pointed out in the 1940s that blacks who moved outside of established ghettos were likely to be "suspect by other Negroes." [32] He also noted that Negro businessmen or professionals who did so were likely to suffer reduced income, a motive for remaining in the ghetto that was characteristic of 19th-century Irish businessmen and professionals as well.[33] Black leaders have emphasized political and other advantages that come from the concentration of black population. It would also be no small satisfaction simply to know one was living in an area where one's racial characteristics were accepted by its residents. Given the possible advantages and attractions of a ghetto area for many of its residents and the recognition that cultural pluralism is a valid philosophy within the American system of values, a system of eliminating segregation through a program of "ghetto elimination" does not seem justifiable.

Discussing voluntary segregation, the Advisory Commission on Civil Disorders states: "The experience of other ethnic groups indicates that some Negro households would be scattered in largely white residential areas. Others—probably a large number—would voluntarily cluster together in largely Negro neighborhoods." [34] Let us consider how feasible such a system of nonsegregation would be.

We will start with a consequence of the present system of restrictive segregation. Because housing for blacks has been yielded only slowly and grudgingly by the white community there has been a continuous "backpressure" within the black ghetto for more housing. Realizing this, most whites believe that an area opened to blacks will undergo "massive racial transition" and become all black.[35] This means that a white seeing a black move into his all-white area responds not to the individual black neighbor himself, but to what the newcomer symbolizes for the future of the neighborhood. The prophecy then becomes likely to fulfill itself. With nonsegregation, the pent-up housing demand would be met and whites would not need to fear that their neighborhood would go all black if one or a few blacks moved in.

But would whites accept even a few blacks into a white neighborhood? Numerous writers, both white and black, going back at least as far as the late 19th century, have made statements that would answer this question affirmatively, their common theme being that whites do not mind having some Negro *neighbors* but that most of them do not want to live in a solidly or predominantly black *neighborhood*. In 1899 DuBois commented that "one Negro family would be tolerated where six would be objected to." [36] During World War II Myrdal concluded that whites move out of an area because they "feel that their neighborhood is doomed to be predominantly Negro. . . ." [37] At about the same time Drake and Cayton found in Chicago that: "Most of the white people did not object to the presence of a few Negroes, but they were afraid that they, as individual white families, would become completely isolated in a Negro area." [38]

In the 1950s Abrams, citing various examples of interracial housing, stated: "It is not the presence of the minority per se that arouses fears but fear of an impending minority homogeneity. In a stabilized area where there is no fear that a neighborhood will be overwhelmed by one group, there is no danger to investment or social prestige." [39] McEntire in 1960 cited studies of white neighborhoods that successfully absorbed small numbers of nonwhites and pointed out that whites respond to the expected "future racial composition of the neighborhood" and are likely to leave an area which is due to "go Negro." [40] Weaver has also said: "Most white middle-class families will not long remain in a neighborhood where they are a racial minority." [41]

A study reported on in 1960 by Eleanor P. Wolf found that neighborhoods could successfully absorb small numbers of nonwhite families when these were not regarded as the beginning of a mass invasion.[42] Helper found that even Chicago realtors "had the impression that white people would not move if they could be sure that they would not be surrounded by Negroes. . . ." [43] Community leaders from suburban areas near Oakland, California, testified before the Commission on Civil Rights in 1967 that what whites feared was "an avalanche . . . of minority groups moving into the community" and "the concentration" of minority-group members.[44]

This presents a paradox: A number of workers over a considerable span of years in a variety of settings have observed that whites do not appear to mind having *some Negro neighbors* but would not want to live in a *predominantly Negro neighborhood*. Negroes are actually a minority of the population in each of the metropolitan areas and a substantial number would want to remain voluntarily in black communities, leaving only a portion of the total who would both be able to and desire to move out into white neighborhoods. With nonsegregation they could be scattered about the metropolitan area so they would in fact be only a minority in any particular neighborhood—the very situation whites say would not disturb them. Yet our cities have evolved a pattern of restrictive segregation that produces a block-by-block expansion of a solid black ghetto.

Published evidence points to a similarity between black and white views regarding racial proportions in mixed neighborhoods. In the 1950s, Saul Alinsky asked a group of white Chicago race rioters if they would mind living in a neighborhood which had only 5 percent blacks. The leader answered: "Mister, if we could have 5 percent or even a little bit more, but we knew for sure, and I mean for sure, that that was all there was going to be—you have no idea how we would jump at it." [45] Only a few years later a study of Chicago Negroes showed that only five percent of them would prefer to live in a mostly white neighborhood, a percentage not greatly different from that found in other northern metropolitan areas.[46] With Negroes a minority of the population of Chicago in 1970, it is evident that if five percent of them lived in predominantly white neighborhoods, they would make up less than five percent of such a neighborhood's population, a situation even white race rioters conceded would be acceptable to them.

SEGREGATION, CULTURE, AND
GHETTO CHARACTERISTICS

The black may point out that the white objects to being in a neighborhood in which he is heavily outnumbered by blacks, but that he expects the black to be content in a neighborhood in which he is heavily outnumbered by whites. One might conclude that the whites' reaction is simply a matter of racial prejudice based on physical traits; this writer would suggest that the cultural component cannot be neglected and may be of primary importance, for in addition to the physical differences many blacks will also differ culturally to some extent from most native whites, just as immigrants differed culturally in earlier times. A recent study, for instance, has found extensive differences according to race in young people's popular music interests.[47]

Both ghetto residence and black pride would tend to accentuate such cultural differences. This is little different from the situation for immigrants, however, whose national pride and ghetto clustering tended to keep them distinct from American culture. It was noted earlier, though, that those who moved out from the immigrant ghettos to native white areas were the ones who had given up most of their Old World culture and become "Americanized." The native whites would accept people who were culturally similar to themselves and reject those who were culturally distinct, even among whites. Thus in rejecting a predominantly black neighborhood the white is probably rejecting living in a neighborhood which is culturally and not just racially different.

Adopting native, white, American culture has different meaning for blacks and immigrants. The immigrant's child could renounce Old-Country ways because they provided a foundation from which he could continue the process his parents began by migrating. He could minimize the importance of the illustrious accomplishments of Polish heroes in history because they would not aid him in America, except that their very existence gave him the confidence to reject them. The immigrant, or more likely his child, could afford psychologically to become Americanized.*

Americanization for the black, on the other hand, began in slave days and resulted in his coming to accept the white's rationalization that he was inferior to them. Although there have been black-pride move-

---

* This does not overlook the culture conflict faced by the immigrant's child as a "marginal man," who partook of both cultures but was firmly established in neither. He did, after all, have the option of continuing to follow his parents' culture and even to outdo them in it through the psychological process of compensation. He nevertheless generally chose Americanization and could feel he was better off by so doing.

ments earlier, it is only in recent years that they have become a mass phenomenon. Just as with the immigrants, group pride can best be supported in the ghetto. There is considerable psychological risk to the black in rejecting black culture before it is firmly established either in himself or in his group, which is what the white suburbanite would have him do by moving out into a predominantly white neighborhood and living a "white" way of life as a small minority of the local population.

Ghetto residence may thus offer social and psychological advantages to at least some blacks and at the same time be responsible for some economic and social drawbacks. Are the disadvantages of the ghetto so great that it should be eliminated and blacks distributed around the city in a manner that would produce a value of zero on the Taeubers' segregation index? To phrase the question this way is to continue the traditional race-relations pattern in which whites do the deciding and then do things "for" or "to" the blacks. It seem evident that the "mix" of favorable and unfavorable aspects of ghetto vs. nonghetto residence would be different for different individuals and families. The question cannot be decided in the abstract but must be answered by each person or family. The conclusion these considerations suggest, then, is that some degree of segregation may be desired by at least some blacks for whom the advantages of the ghetto outweigh the disadvantages. The obvious solution to this issue is that ghetto residence be voluntary. The next two chapters will survey evidence that indicates that it is not.

───────────

1. Karl E. Taeuber and Alma F. Taeuber, *Negroes in Cities* (Chicago: Aldine Publishing Company, 1965), p. 30.

2. *Ibid.,* p. 34.

3. *Ibid.,* pp. 102–8, 246–47.

4. *Ibid.,* p. 104.

5. *Ibid.,* p. 110.

6. *Report of the National Advisory Commission on Civil Disorders* (Washington, D.C.: Government Printing Office, 1968), pp. 120–21.

7. Reynolds Farley and Karl E. Taeuber, "Population Trends and Residential Segregation Since 1960," *Science,* March 1, 1968, p. 955.

8. Charles S. Johnson, *Patterns of Negro Segregation* (New York: Harper & Row, Publishers, 1943), p. 8.

9. E. Franklin Frazier, *The Negro in the United States* (New York: The Macmillan Company, 1949), p. 301.

10. Chicago Commission on Race Relations, *The Negro in Chicago* (Chicago: University of Chicago Press, 1922; reprinted by Arno Press, Inc., New York, 1968), p. 158.

11. Gilbert Osofsky, *Harlem: The Making of a Ghetto* (New York: Harper Torchbooks, 1968; copyright © Harper & Row, Publishers, 1963), pp. 137–38.

12. Otis Dudley Duncan and Beverly Duncan, *The Negro Population of Chicago* (Chicago: University of Chicago Press, 1957), p. 19.

13. Pierre de Vise, *Chicago's Widening Color Gap*, Chicago, Interuniversity Social Research Committee–Report Number 2 (December 1967), p. 74.

14. Daniel P. Moynihan, "Employment, Income, and the Ordeal of the Negro Family," *Daedalus*, Fall 1965.

15. Dorothy Newman, "The Decentralization of Jobs," *Monthly Labor Review*, May 1967.

16. U.S. Civil Rights Commission, *A Time to Listen . . . A Time to Act* (Washington, D.C.: Government Printing Office, 1967), p. 59.

17. Jerry De Muth, "No Housing Where the Jobs Are," *Progressive*, June, 1968, p. 39.

18. U.S. Civil Rights Commission, *A Time to Listen*, pp. 70–71.

19. De Muth, "No Housing" p. 40.

20. "Model Cities Program: Draft for Discussion," (mimeographed report, Toledo, Ohio, 1968), pp. 247–54.

21. *Report of the National Advisory Commission on Civil Disorders*, p. 217.

22. U.S. Civil Rights Commission, *A Time to Listen*, pp. 58–59.

23. Adna F. Weber, *The Growth of Cities in the Nineteenth Century* (New York: The Macmillan Company, 1899); Miles L. Colean, *Renewing Our Cities* (New York: The Twentieth Century Fund, 1953), p. 66.

24. *Report of the National Advisory Commission on Civil Disorders*, p. 217.

25. *City*, June–July 1970, p. 5.

26. U.S. Civil Rights Commission, *A Time to Listen*, p. 9.

27. Midge Decter, "St. Paul and the American Tradition," *Harpers Magazine*, CCXXXVIII, No. 1429 (June, 1969), 57.

28. Reginald G. Damerell, *Triumph in a White Suburb* (New York: William Morrow & Co., Inc., 1968), pp. 125–26 (emphasis in original).

29. Bernard Weissbourd and Herbert Channick, "An Urban Strategy," *The Center Magazine*, I, No. 6 (September 1968), 4–5.

30. W. E. B. DuBois, *The Philadelphia Negro* (1899; reprinted, New York: Benjamin Blom, Inc., 1967), p. 297.

31. Louis Wirth, *The Ghetto* (Chicago: University of Chicago Press, 1928, 1956), pp. 122–23.

32. Robert C. Weaver, *The Negro Ghetto* (New York: Harcourt Brace Jovanovich, Inc., 1948), p. 240.

33. William V. Shannon, *The American Irish* (New York: The Macmillan Company, 1963), p. 36.

34. *Report of the National Advisory Commission on Civil Disorders,* p. 219.

35. *Ibid.,* p. 119.

36. DuBois, *The Philadelphia Negro,* p. 297.

37. Gunnar Myrdal (with the assistance of Arnold Rose and Richard Sterner), *An American Dilemma* (New York: Harper & Row, Publishers, 1944), p. 623.

38. St. Clair Drake and Horace R. Cayton, *Black Metropolis* (New York: Harper Torchbook, Harper & Row, Publishers, 1962), p. 189.

39. Charles Abrams, *Forbidden Neighbors* (New York: Harper & Row, Publishers, 1955), p. 319.

40. Davis McEntire, *Residence and Race* (Berkeley & Los Angeles: University of California Press, 1960), p. 83.

41. Robert C. Weaver, "Class, Race, and Urban Renewal," *Land Economics,* 36, No. 3 (August 1960), pp. 245–51.

42. Eleanor P. Wolf, "Some Factors Affecting Residential Decisions in a Racially Changing Neighborhood," *Journal of Intergroup Relations,* I, No. 3 (Summer 1960).

43. Rose Helper, *Racial Policies and Practices of Real Estate Brokers* (Minneapolis: University of Minnesota Press, 1969), p. 131.

44. U.S. Civil Rights Comm., *A Time to Listen,* p. 73.

45. *Report of U.S. Civil Rights Commission* (Washington, D.C.: Government Printing Office, 1959), p. 444.

46. Gary T. Marx, *Protest and Prejudice* (New York: Harper & Row, Publishers, 1967), p. 176.

47. John P. Robinson and Paul Hirsch, "It's the Sound that Does It," *Psychology Today,* III (October 1969), 42–45.

5 | Maintaining Segregation, I

The means used to maintain restrictive residential segregation are so varied and are interrelated in such a complex fashion that a mutually exclusive systematic classification seems impractical, if not impossible. Instead, four major types will be suggested:

Establishment of racial areas by local ordinance
Institutional means
Quasi-institutional means
Informal means

The first two types will be covered in this chapter; the others in the following one.

LOCAL ORDINANCES

Some cities in the South and on the West Coast actually passed ordinances stating that nonwhites could only live in certain specified areas of the city. San Francisco was the first, in 1890, with a law that Chinese could live only in a certain part of the city and requiring those who lived elsewhere to move to the area designated for Chinese. Legislation in Southern cities attempted to establish either all-Negro or all-white blocks or to establish segregated districts in which it was illegal for members of the prohibited race to live (this could force whites to move if they lived in an area designated for blacks). Despite the fact that such legislation was declared unconstitutional by the U.S. Supreme Court by 1917, attempts were still made to establish segregated areas by law as late as 1935 in Oklahoma City and 1940 in North Carolina.[1]

INSTITUTIONAL MEANS

RESTRICTIVE COVENANTS

The device that came closest to establishing racial districts in the North by legal means was the restrictive covenant. In establishing a covenant, a group of property owners would make a legally binding agreement among themselves not to convey or lease their properties to certain classes of people, such as Negroes. The same effect could be obtained by writing provisions into the property deed prohibiting sale to or use of the property by certain classes of people. Such prohibitions were legally enforceable, so that if the owner of a restricted property sold it to a prohibited person, other parties to the agreement could take the matter to court and have the sale voided against the wishes of both buyer and seller.

The restrictive covenant, then, was placed on property owned by whites to keep it from being sold to "undesirables." As with so many other phenomena covered in this work there are parallels between other groups and the blacks, because the latter were not always the only ones considered to be undesirable. Covenants were also aimed at a variety of other minority groups—Mexicans, Orientals, American Indians, and "persons whose blood is not entirely of the white race," as well as such white groups as Armenians, Syrians, Jews, "Balkan races," Hindus, "Spanish Americans," "former residents of the Turkish Empire," and "South Europeans." [2] Abrams commented that it became fashionable to prohibit as many groups as possible to emphasize the "exclusiveness" of a residential development and that it became considered unethical for developers *not* to have covenants keeping out minorities.[3]

Weaver called restrictive covenants "the most dangerous" of all the means used to effect residential segregation, pointing out that they gave "legal sanction . . . and the appearance of respectability to residential segregation." [4] They did just that. In 1948 the U.S. Supreme Court ruled that restrictive covenants could not be legally enforced in the courts— thus eliminating the major sanction which made them effective—but for 30 years they held sway in American cities and had a profound effect upon the racial residential patterns which might have developed in quite a different fashion had there not been restrictive covenants.*

---

* The issue of covenants came before the Supreme Court in 1926, but the Court ruled that they were merely agreements between private parties and hence could not constitutionally be prohibited. The 1948 decision accepted that the Court could not prevent such agreements but held that when the parties to an agreement brought

Chicago made early and extensive use of restrictive covenants, which may be why it is one of the most completely segregated cities in the country. (See Table 1, Chapter 4.) Covenants were employed most fully in areas of the city adjacent to the existing Black Belt and thus impeded the normal expansion of black areas.[5] A member of the Chicago Real Estate Board described in a speech in 1928 how a "fine network of contracts that like a marvelous delicately woven chain of armor is being raised from the northern gates of Hyde Park . . . to . . . all the far-flung white communities of the South Side." [6]

Under such circumstances how could the Black Belt ever expand? The very success of the restrictions against expansion produced the conditions that could force it. Damming up the black population in restricted ghettos led to greater overcrowding and consequently greater pressures for additional housing. Under the "law of supply and demand," black buyers were eventually ready to pay such inflated values for houses in white areas that it was disadvantageous for the owners to continue to resist. At that point, they generally either renounced their covenants or failed to seek redress against those who did, and the area turned black. It hardly needs emphasis that the whole process of determining land usage was controlled by the whites—they "protected" their property against the blacks but reserved the right to change if it became advantageous.

It is impossible to estimate the extent to which covenants have contributed to even the present-day image of the black ghetto as a congested, dammed-up part of the city, fairly bursting at the seams and threatening to engulf the adjacent white community. Had the Black Belt not been so consistently resisted, which in turn made it so overcrowded and increased social pathology within it, the whole pattern of urban race relations might have been considerably different.

The restrictive covenant was placed on property owned by whites to keep it from being sold to "undesirables." Note that in order to do this the whites had to restrict their own freedom; they could sell their own property only in accordance with the terms of the covenants. This situation worked to the advantage of the large property owners at the expense of the smaller owners. Large, white, real-estate companies could break covenants with relative ease, selling or renting property to blacks at the most financially advantageous terms. The small property owners faced a dilemma: "If they sold to Negroes and broke the covenants, the property owners' associations would challenge the transactions; whereas, if they did not sell to Negroes, either they would find themselves stranded in all-Negro communities, unable because of the covenants to rent any

---

the matter to the courts for enforcement, it then became a public issue and that the powers of government could not be used to enforce racial discrimination.

portion of their property to Negroes, or they would have to sell at a loss to the larger real-estate companies." [7] It would not be surprising if a good deal of the frustration and anger which this situation would tend to produce resulted in hostility being directed toward the Negroes, who could be defined as the "cause" of the problem, rather than toward the exploitation by wealthy whites of the whole system of racial residential segregation. By making neighborhoods the battlegrounds in a war of residential segregation in which the stakes were the lifetime investments of everyday people, segregation in general and restrictive covenants in particular contributed immensely to increasing the tensions and hatreds in both races.

In 1944 Myrdal gave his opinion that if the U.S. Supreme Court were to rule against restrictive covenants, "segregation in the North would be nearly doomed." [8] Four years later the Court did so rule and in the more than two decades following that ruling the pattern of restrictive segregation remained practically unchanged. How could Myrdal, whose study was so thorough and perceptive, have so misjudged the situation of residential segregation? The only conclusion is that he underestimated the number of ways in which segregation can be maintained either without the support of law or in violation of it. We shall explore this after a brief digression to consider a topic which underlies many beliefs and practices concerning race and real estate.

PROPERTY VALUES—A DIGRESSION

Whenever the matter of white-black housing arrangements arises, either lurking in the background or openly expressed will be the question of effects upon property values. "As early as 1793, the attempt to locate 'a Negro hut' in Salem, Massachusetts, prompted a white minister to protest that such buildings depreciated property, drove out decent residents, and generally injured the welfare of the neighborhood." [9] More than 160 years later another white minister defended opposition to a housing development that would have taken in 10 or 12 middle-class Negro families in Deerfield, Illinois, by stating: "I can say that almost without exception the large number of worried people who have sought me out in the last week are concerned primarily with economic loss, not with depriving the Negro of his just due. This is the critical issue as I see it. . . . " [10]

Concerning Northern cities in the 19th century, before the Civil War, Litwack wrote: "The vigorous exclusion of Negroes from white residential neighborhoods made escape from the ghetto virtually impossible. The fear of depreciated property values overrode virtually every other consideration." [11] The Great Migration renewed concern with property values. The Chicago Commission on Race Relations reported: "No single factor has complicated the relations of Negroes and whites in Chicago more than the widespread feeling of white people that the presence of Negroes in a neighborhood is a cause of serious depreciation of property values. To the extent that people feel that their financial interests are affected, antagonisms are accentuated." [12] Neighborhood property-owners' associations emphasized property values in their publicity materials.[13]

Before World War II, real-estate brokers in Chicago were stimulating sales by telling property owners that " 'the neighborhood was going colored and the values of their investments would fall anyhow.' " [14] The same tactics were still being used in the 1960s.[15] Helper found that most brokers mentioned the likelihood of price decline as a reason for not selling a house in a white neighborhood to a black.[16] Fears of effect on property values have frequently been mentioned in connection with opposition to public-housing projects. Certainly the belief that lowered property values result from Negro occupancy seems to be an important underpinning of the entire system of racial residential segregation.

There are two factors that on a logical basis would indicate *higher* property values in black areas. One is the greater demand for housing for blacks that results from the back-pressure in the ghetto because of the reluctance of whites to provide for black population growth. Another factor is the considerable economic return produced by a building in a black area as a result of relatively high rents, greater crowding, and lessened maintenance. These characteristics will be documented in Chapter 7. For both Chicago and New York there are instances reported in which landlords evicted white tenants in order to take in blacks for rents as much as two or three times as high as those whites were charged.[17] A building producing twice the income it did earlier can hardly, by the normal operation of principles of economics, be less valuable. The rush of blacks to New York at the beginning of the Great Migration "ballooned Harlem real estate to fantastic prices, a swell that almost made the community's people dizzy." [18] Similarly, in Chicago after World War II, real-estate men found that it was more profitable to rent to Negroes than whites, so that whether renting or buying, blacks felt the effects of "inflated prices for property." [19] These do not sound like the conditions that would produce economic loss.

Yet whites have frequently lost substantial amounts of money as a result of the transition of their properties to Negro occupancy. Wherever whites have had losses as a result of racial change the reason has generally been the same at any time over the past half-century and regardless of the particular city.

As Osofsky explains: "The very setting in which whites were confronted with Negro neighbors for the first time led to less than level-headed reasoning. The first impulse of many 'in a rather panicky state of mind' was to sell at whatever their property would bring and move elsewhere." [20] The

Chicago Commission on Race Relations likewise concluded: "The principal influence of Negroes upon property values is psychological, due to the deep-seated and general prejudice of whites against Negroes, which begets and sustains the belief that Negroes destroy property values wherever they go." [21] The Chicago Commission found that: "When values fall extremely due to a selling panic among white owners, it is often followed by a decided recovery as the Negro demand grows." Real-estate dealers told the Commission that "if the white owners were not overanxious to sell when the Negro 'invasion' begins, they might later on obtain as much or more for their property than they could have obtained before the advent of the Negroes." [22] The explanation offered half a century ago by the Chicago Commission can hardly be improved upon, except to put it in the theoretical context of the self-fulfilling prophecy. Whites believe that blacks lower property values, and because of this belief they panic and sell at too-low prices; having experienced a loss, they find their belief confirmed that blacks lower property values. They have made their belief come true.

The Chicago Commission explanation was echoed by a white community leader in an interracial neighborhood in Milwaukee in 1968: "Most whites don't realize it is their panic and flight and willingness to sell cheap that causes property values to go down, not the presence of Negroes who move into the area." [23] Panic led several families in Teaneck, New Jersey, to forfeit thousand-dollar deposits on new homes when a Negro built a new home near their subdivision; other whites already living there sold their homes at "bargain prices" to whites from elsewhere who were unaware of the presence of Negro families in the community. [24] Some real-estate dealers, of course, encourage panic selling at low prices, profiting both from the commission of the sale and the increase in price when the property is resold to a black family. In 1968, *Milwaukee Journal* reporters "found hundred of examples of north-side homes sold by whites to real-estate men who resold them at much higher prices to Negroes." [25] For the whites who were stampeded into selling at panic prices, Negroes *were* associated with economic loss, but by the time Negroes were ready to buy the property, its value had miraculously increased—by 73 percent in one Chicago area studied. [26]

Given the general belief that Negro occupancy causes a decline in property values in a neighborhood, finding even some exceptions to the belief can be important. Additional evidence, however, is available from a comprehensive study by Laurenti of nearly 10,000 real-estate transactions over the period of 1943 to 1955 in three cities—San Francisco, Oakland, and Philadelphia. [27] A total of 20 racially mixed "test area" neighborhoods were compared with "control" neighborhoods that had remained white during the study period, each test neighborhood being matched with one or more control neighborhoods in the same city on factors likely to affect property values—such as age and type of building, land uses in the area, topography, and income-occupational characteristics of its residents. Local real-estate men helped to determine the area boundaries so that the only major difference betwen the test and control neighborhoods would be that the former were up to 75 percent Negro. The paired-comparison method also corrected for price changes in the real-estate market as a whole over the time period of the study.

A total of 34 paired comparisons were possible. In contradiction to the common belief, Laurenti found that the largest number of comparisons (15, or 44 percent) were in the category of *increase* in property values in the test neighborhoods, with values being as much as 26 percent higher than in the control neighborhoods. The next largest category (14, or 41 percent) was of test areas in which prices remained unchanged, varying by no more than 5 percent either way from their control areas. Only 5 comparisons (15 percent) showed a decline in values in the test areas, and the largest decline was only 9 percent. Thus, in 85 percent of the cases, prices in interracial neighborhoods either remained stable or increased; in only 15 percent did they decrease.[28] Except for white panic and the self-fulfilling prophecy, there is neither theoretical nor empirical evidence to support the belief that blacks lower property values.

REAL-ESTATE BROKERS

● BELIEFS AND POLICIES. Theoretically, the real-estate broker is a neutral intermediary who makes his services available to both buyer and seller in the interest of arranging a deal maximally satisfying to both. As such, one might not expect real-estate brokers to have an interest in determining the patterns of racial occupancy of urban neighborhoods, but in practice it seems that they do. Real-estate associations around the country have generally favored segregation and opposed measures such as open-housing legislation, which are intended to reduce housing segregation.[29]

In 1924 the *Milwaukee Journal* reported that: "Milwaukee will have a 'black belt' if the Real Estate Board can find ways and means to make it practicable . . . members say that the Negro population of the city is growing so rapidly that something will have to be done." [30] During the same year the National Association of Real Estate Boards adopted as part of their "Code of Ethics" Article 34, which stated: "A Realtor should never be instrumental in introducing into a neighborhood . . . members of any race or nationality . . . whose presence will clearly be detrimental to property values in that neighborhood." In 1950 the wording was changed, dropping reference to race and nationality, so that it read: "A Realtor should not be instrumental in introducing into a neighborhood a character of property or use which will clearly be detrimental to property values in that neighborhood." [31] In interviews that included officials of the Chicago Real Estate Board, however, Helper found that the meaning of the provision remained the same "and that 'a character of property or use covers the introduction of Negroes.' " [32]

Helper commented: "One basis on which Article 34—original and revised, and including all local variations of it—was established is the assumption that property values are lowered when Negroes and members of other minority groups enter a neighborhood; the duty of the Realtor follows from this belief." [33] We have just reviewed material showing that Negro occupancy does not ordinarily lower property values, but Helper found that realtors, whose expertise one would expect to include this knowledge, generally assumed that introducing *any* Negro family into *any* white neighborhood would lower property values and interpreted their Code of Ethics so as to obtain maximum segregation.

The policies of both the National Association of Real Estate Boards and the local real-estate boards become a little more understandable when it is realized that they are practically all white. Although there are black real-estate brokers, they have been, with few exceptions, excluded from membership in real-estate boards and have formed their own association, the National Association of Real Estate Brokers. As McEntire commented, "there are two NAREB's, separate but far from equal." [34]

Extreme in its practices, and one of the earliest to institute segregationist policies, is the Chicago Real Estate Board. In 1917 the Chicago Board established a policy stating that "it is desired in the interest of all that each block shall be filled solidly [with Negroes] and that further expansion shall be confined to contiguous blocks." [35] Thus, expansion of the Black Belt area was to take place solidly block by block, with no homes sold to whites in a block that blacks had started to move into. The system is the most effective possible for ensuring maximum residential segregation. Data such as that of the Taeubers show that it works.

At the time the Chicago policy was adopted the Black Belt was far from being solidly black. In 1920 the "oldest and densest" part of the Black Belt was only slightly more than half Negro, many whites continuing to live there for reasons of sentiment, business, or convenience.[36] With the brokers' policy of not selling homes to whites in areas in which there were already *some* Negroes living, the proportion of whites could only decline toward the zero point. One wonders whether a solidly black Black Belt would ever have developed in Chicago and other cities in the absence of a deliberate block-by-block policy imposed on Negro ghetto expansion.

Land-usage policies of one of America's greatest cities were thus determined for at least the 20th century by a relatively small group of men who had motives of personal profit and whose decisions were not subject to the normal checks of the democratic political process. The Chicago policy was important in that it provided an example of black housing for Northern cities generally.

A thorough study of the policies and practices of members of the Chicago Real Estate Board was made by Rose Helper in the late 1950s, with a follow-up study in 1964–1965 that ascertained that practices and their "supporting ideology had remained substantially unchanged." [37] Helper's study was concerned with both the ideology of real-estate brokers and the practices which resulted from following the ideology. There is a very real relationship between practices and ideologically determined policies, however, in that a realtor who violates the policies established by the real-estate board is subject to expulsion from the group, with all the economic and professional disadvantages that would entail. [38]

Helper's interviews led her to conclude that real-estate brokers' "racial practices are the logical outcome of a group of related ideas, values, beliefs, and principles—that is, the real estate ideology. Most respondents' racial real estate ideology was largely unfavorable to Negroes and supported exclusion of Negroes from white areas." She designated this the "exclusion ideology." [39]

What Helper calls "the broker's conception" of racial factors related to real estate supports the ideology of brokers. Most of them recognized that there were social class and behavioral differences within the Negro group that ranged from well-educated professionals to the ignorant poor, but maintained that on the average or as a group they were less responsible both toward property and as members of a community. Many brokers spoke of Negro attempts to obtain housing in white areas as calculated efforts to "scare white people" and to force them to move out of an area, apparently overlooking the causative role of restrictive segregation in producing such behavior. [40] The brokers seemed strongly in agreement that there was white opposition to having Negroes as neighbors and that whites seemed anxious to move out of areas that were "turning," and used terms such as "forced out," and "driven from" to describe their moving. Whites have resisted ghetto expansion and the brokers have seemed willing to cooperate.

Regarding the possibility of residential integration, more than 90 percent of the brokers interviewed by Helper judged that it was "impossible in Chicago at present." [41] Responses as to when integration might work included "never," when Messiah will come," "fifty years from now," "I don't think it'll be too soon," and "in a couple of generations, probably." [42] Brokers recognized that blacks had to have housing, but the only pattern they could realistically conceive of was more of the same block-by-block expansion, with all the resultant mutual hardships and animosities.

It was quite evident that the refusal of brokers to sell property in white areas to blacks arose not just out of a perfunctory compliance with a set of regulations but out of a strongly internalized set of attitudes and beliefs. Central to their position was the belief that blacks collectively were not as "good" for an area as were whites. This belief did not appear generally to be based on a racist assumption of inborn inferiority, but rather on differences in cultural opportunities and economic level. Given the set of factors related to restrictive segregation and the brokers' concept of an area as either all white or all black, it is easy to see how they could develop the view that to admit one is to admit all. They would thus refuse to sell a well-educated black professional man a home in a white middle-class neighborhood because they would see this as being the cause of the neighborhood going all black. Brokers believed that if they assisted in such a sale, they would be contributing to lowering both the economic and social level of the neighborhood. Refusal to sell property in white areas to blacks would accordingly be viewed by brokers as an ethical or moral obligation arising out of a responsibility to the whites in the neighborhood.

Helper even noted: "Several respondents invoked God or the Constitution of the United States as the source of their authority for their restrictive policy. They argue that God did not intend the races to mingle and therefore made them distinctive." [43] Brokers can thus view themselves as carrying out His will and helping to establish His kingdom on earth by their mediating in property exchanges. "The Constitution, [brokers] point out, ensures certain rights to citizens and the right to choose neighbors is one of them." [44] But the brokers are thinking only of the rights of the white man to choose *his* neighbors; it would seem just as constitutional for the black man to exercise a choice, including the choice to reside in an area where whites live (even if his main basis for choosing is the type of house or the convenience of the location within the city).

Principles invoked to justify segregation seem to have been given a one-sided interpretation by brokers. "It is not democratic," says one, "to force white people to live with neighbors they do not want." [45] Yet, it is presumably just as undemocratic to force blacks to live with neighbors *they* do not want in ghetto areas. Another argues: "It is not necessary to mix groups and to forget one's cultural heritage in order to be a good American." [46] Although, of course, it is not *necessary* to mix groups, there is nothing in the American creed that prevents it. American traditions recognize *both* the rights of groups to live in such a way that they retain their separate identity *and* the rights of individuals to separate themselves from their groups if they wish.

Helper reports that some brokers "speak also of the immigrants who came here from Europe and worked their way up. . . . The implication is that Negroes should build their own housing in their own areas instead of forcing themselves with police protection into white areas and forcing thrifty, self-reliant homeowners out of their homes and neighborhoods." [47] She notes that brokers tend to overlook the differences between immigrants and blacks. An extremely important difference is that when immigrants had become more successful and were ready to move out into the larger native, white community, brokers did not refuse to deal with them, insisting that they stay within the ghetto for reasons ascribable to God, the Constitution, morality, and so forth. The broker who talks of black-immigrant similarities might well be asked whether he has dealt with both in the same way.

Brokers made it clear that they believed most whites did not want black neighbors and felt that "the real estate man, as a good American, is bound to respect their wishes" by not "forcing" unwelcome neighbors upon them.[48] There was no evidence that blacks were rejected as neighbors on the basis of their personal characteristics, that the broker ascertained the characteristics of, say, John Jones, and went around and described his likes and dislikes, hobbies, tastes in music, religion, politics, and so forth to residents to find out if they would like such a person in their neighborhood.

Helper found that "In each area a majority of the respondents consider that the Negro owner cares for his home as well as or better than the white owner." [49] Thus, given the possibility of a neighbor who is financially responsible enough to be able to buy a home and who will then care for it at least as well as they would themselves, whites still reject it, considering such a person an unwanted intruder. It is a thesis of this work that much of the resistance of whites to having blacks as neighbors in modern times has arisen *because of the practice of segregation itself;* that keeping the black equivalent of the Americanized immigrant from moving out of the ghetto has resulted in conceiving of all blacks as unworthy neighbors, so that even the thought of their presence calls forth visions of the ghetto-slum in white minds.

Helper found several respondents who argued that because whites had built up the city they had prior rights, which should be recognized. She points out the ironical fact that they "were apparently unaware that the first settler was a Negro trader who built his log house at the mouth of the Chicago River in 1779 and lived there for more than 16 years." [50] Furthermore, there are records of Negroes owning property in Chicago since the city was incorporated in 1837.[51]

Most brokers saw a number of undesirable consequences to themselves and to the community that would result from their dealing with blacks and selling them property in white areas. These included the loss of business and potential clients as well as the goodwill of property owners, the public, and other realtors. "You become a social outcast among other real estate brokers." [52]

Helper sums up the view of most brokers. "The practitioners of exclusion see as the outcome for themselves a clear conscience, peace of mind, and personal satisfaction in knowing that they are not hurting people by lowering the value of their property, giving them unwanted neighbors, or starting their neighborhood on the downgrade, and also contentment in knowing that their reputation, their status in the community, and their business itself will not be harmed." [53] The brokers' contentment resulted from looking at the situation from the standpoint of whites. If blacks had their property values lowered or their neighborhood downgraded through ghetto congestion or if they had to put up with unwanted neighbors, these factors did not enter the equation.

● PRACTICES.   The practices of real-estate brokers derive naturally enough from their beliefs and policies. Most brokers simply would not sell property in a white area to blacks. If confronted by a black who wished to buy such property they would take one of several courses of action: "give a blunt refusal without explanation; say no, accept the blame, and admit the racial difficulty; warn the Negro he will be unwelcome in such an area and advise him not to try to buy; and deceive the Negro—misrepresenting in one way or another to avoid a direct refusal." [54]

Testimony to the Civil Rights Commission about Cleveland pointed to the same type of misrepresentation. A Superintendent Engineer with the Cleveland Metropolitan Housing Authority who was black and was trying to buy a home reported that "there were a lot of excuses given . . . usually the house was sold or something happened and it was transferred to another real estate company. . . ." As a professional in housing he knew property values, but he found that a house worth $18,000 would be quoted to him as $23,000 or $24,000. Another witness was told by a real-estate broker that the owner would not sell to a Negro. When the buyer confronted him with the fact that the broker himself owned the house he was told: "You wouldn't be happy in this neighborhood." Other testimony indicated that telephone inquiries from areas in which blacks live concerning homes in white areas are simply not answered.[55] Something must be going on in Cleveland to account for the fact that in 1965, although more than a third of the population of the city lived west of the Cuyahoga River, more than 99 percent of the Negroes lived east of it, a figure even higher than the 98 percent found in 1910.[56]

Hecht reports on various deceptions and misrepresentations used in Buffalo. Negro families seeking apartments have been told that they were already rented or that the tenant would have to pay large utility bills not mentioned in the ad. A black doctor, a cancer-research specialist, was told that the apartment he sought to rent was not available and referred to a low-income housing project. In other cases, agents "were unable to find the keys" to houses or apartments, sellers took their homes off the market or refused to answer the door, appointments were broken without notice, and so forth. As Hecht commented: "Details varied, but to Negroes looking for a place to live they all conveyed the message, 'We don't want any niggers here.' " [57]

Misrepresentation is probably the most damaging method for handling the situation because it reduces the amount of honest communication between the races. The misrepresentation is recognized as such by both parties. "I tell them the property has been sold. *They usually understand.*" "I say a contract is already under way, in the making. *He usually catches on.*" [58] Some brokers reported that lending agencies also give false reasons or use subterfuges in refusing loans for property. [59] Dishonesty by whites supports a belief held by many blacks that whites cannot be trusted and are "running a game" on them. Such practices make it difficult to argue otherwise. Yet brokers resent it if blacks make misrepresentations to them about property arrangements. One broker said: "They keep telling you so many stories, just lies. I just got sick and tired of it." [60]

A black who wishes to buy property in any area not already an established part of the black ghetto is obviously going to encounter difficulties even in getting the broker to show him property which is for sale. There are some ways in which this hurdle may be overcome. A white willing to sell to a black may choose to handle the sale of his property himself without the services of a broker. The black may have a white buy the property for him and transfer it to him after the sale is completed. In some cases whites have listed property with black brokers who deal with black buyers. The seller may deal with one of the few white real-estate men who will sell property in white areas to blacks—probably a "blockbuster" (see Chapter 6).

An additional point needs to be made regarding brokers and black residents. Although the preceding discussion has been concerned with buying rather than with the rental of property, a significant part of the business of real-estate agents involves the management of rental property, such as apartments. Because it is steady income, real-estate men consider property management as the "backbone of their business." The beliefs and attitudes of real-estate brokers that have been discussed above are applied to rental property as well as to property for sale. Consequently, rental practices have tended to parallel those that apply to sales. Apartment houses tend to be thought of as either all-white or all-black, as "turning" from one to the other, as being in either black or white areas, and so forth. A black tenant is more likely to be asked to give a security deposit and to supply references as a condition of occupancy. [61]

Although this discussion has drawn heavily upon Helper's study in Chicago, additional evidence indicates that her findings are probably typical of most cities. The Ohio Civil Rights Commission found similar practices in Ohio.[62] In Teaneck, New Jersey, no broker in the town would deal with Negroes; Negroes who bought houses in Teaneck had to do so through real-estate agents outside the town. In 1962 the Teaneck Fair Housing Committee "proved that the discrimination against Negroes was one hundred percent," by staging "walk-ins" on brokers. First a Negro couple would visit a broker and ask to see certain houses he had advertised for sale. The broker would not show it to them, claiming he did not have the key for a house, that it had already been sold, and so forth, evading in a manner similar to that of the Chicago brokers. Very shortly afterwards a white couple would call on the broker and ask to see the same houses, and would be shown them. In 33 such paired comparisons with nine different brokers, in no case was a Negro couple shown a house in an area other than the northeast section, in which there were some Negroes already living.[63] Paired-comparison tests similarly demonstrated broker discrimination in Philadelphia.[64]

The Teaneck brokers did not limit themselves to making racial distinctions. In the 1950s, when the town was still predominantly Protestant, its brokers concluded that it was turning Jewish and thereafter started showing Protestants homes in other towns and resisted selling them homes in Teaneck, leading Damerell to comment: "Yet without special knowledge or training, without accountability or responsibility, realtors as a group wield a social power so tremendous that it is probably second to none. They steer Protestants, Catholics, Jews, and Negroes into their respective ghettos, depriving individuals of the diversity and even friction that make life stimulating." [65]

The importance of the real-estate broker with regard to discrimination was also recognized by the United States Commission on Civil Rights, which called the broker the "key man in the majority of housing transactions," and noted that he influenced "where the various racial or religious groups will live." On the basis of "considerable testimony" the Commission concluded in 1961: "Discrimination is often the rule rather than the exception." [66] Despite an increase in the number of state and local fair-housing laws banning racial discrimination by those in the real-estate business during the 1960s, the Advisory Commission on Civil Disorders reported in 1968 that usually "real estate agents simply refuse to show homes to Negro buyers." [67] The 1968 federal fair-housing act now prohibits discrimination by real-estate brokers. There are indications that this act, plus the 1968 *Jones* v. *Mayer* Supreme Court decision, may really decrease racial residential discrimination.[68] This will be discussed in the final chapter.

LENDING AGENCIES

Few people can pay cash for their homes, so the policies and practices of the lending agencies that control mortgage financing are crucial in determining who can buy what kind of property and where, and what kinds of major improvements, if any, can be made on property. The U.S. Civil Rights Commission endorsed as "twin truths" the statements: "Mortgage financing is considered to be the fountainhead of the housing industry" and "Banks dictate where the Negroes can live." The Commission received evidence "from many parts of the country, [that] these institutions are a major factor in the denial of equal housing opportunity." [69]

Lending agency practices became important with the onset of the Great Migration. Although DuBois found that only about 5 percent of Philadelphia Negroes owned property in 1898, he did not attribute the small percentage to discrimination by lending institutions.[70] The fact that whites in Harlem in the early 1900s campaigned against banks lending money to blacks buying property there both indicates that blacks were being financed and suggests a reason for institutions becoming restrictive in lending.[71] Since the Great Migration, although borrowing has generally been more difficult for blacks than for whites, the greater importance of lending-agency policies and practices undoubtedly lies in their influence on *where* blacks can buy property rather than in their ability to keep them from buying property at all.

Because brokers and lending agencies regularly work together they seem to exert an influence on each other. Weaver wrote in 1948 that brokers discouraged financial institutions from making loans to Negroes on property in white areas.[72] Helper found in her more recent studies that the opposite situation prevailed, that brokers complained about the greater reluctance of lending agencies to provide financing to blacks than to whites, which led to the broker having to try several lending agencies before he could find one that would arrange a mortgage. All of the brokers interviewed by Helper considered that a loan from a standard lending agency to enable a black person to buy property in a white area would be "out of the question." Brokers felt that because of their continuing dependency on the services of lending agencies, they dared not risk alienating them by trying to arrange loans for blacks in white or nearly all-white areas.[73]

Lending institutions can have reasons of their own for having policies that reinforce restrictive segregation. One such reason is the desire to protect property values in white areas in which the bank already has investments. Given the common belief that Negro occupancy lowers property values, the lending agency would fear not just a loss in value on the particular property under consideration but on other property in the neighborhood on which it might also have mortgages. A second reason relates to the possible reactions of whites toward the bank if it financed a property purchase by a black in a white area. Not only would there be a loss of "goodwill," in the abstract sense, but a lending agency would fear that whites would withdraw savings and transfer their financial business elsewhere. Bankers in both Chicago and Cleveland mentioned "public relations" specifically as a reason for not lending to the *first* black to buy in a white block, the banker in Chicago saying that "the first two or three sales to Negroes in any block should be financed between the parties." [74] That public relations, rather than financial considerations, is an important factor is suggested by the fact that some agencies have taken over mortgages from "blockbusters" after other blacks have moved into an area, and that loans have been made with the proviso that the lender not be publicly recognized until after a certain period of time. Some lending agencies, however, made public statements of nondiscrimination in their lending policies even before 1960.[75]

In addition to lending money for the purchase of homes, lending agencies also perform another important function: making loans for the maintenance and improvement of property already owned by an individual. If the owner is unable to obtain adequate financing to replace leaking roofs and sagging stairs and to modernize plumbing, heating, and electrical systems, for example, the building will deteriorate, becoming less and less desirable as a residence. Yet it is in areas of deteriorated housing that legitimate lending institutions have been least likely to make loans for home improvements because of the presumably greater risk involved.[76] Thus the urban areas most in need of maintenance and modernization have been the least successful in obtaining the necessary moderate-cost financing.

Although the reluctance to lend money on property in these areas is not a matter of race as such (whites living in such areas have also been unable to obtain financing), the combination of residential segregation and economic differences confines blacks to such areas to a greater degree than whites; a policy of "red lining," or not lending money in blighted areas, becomes in effect one of not lending money for improvements to property in much of the black ghetto. Having defined the area as blighted, the policies of lending institutions have assisted in pushing the area into further decline, thus providing another example of a self-fulfilling prophecy. The resident of such an area could seek financing from sources that charge high rates of interest, but the extra interest money that he must then pay could better be used for other home improvements or for the general living expenses, that his modest income probably has difficulty in meeting anyway. Meanwhile, the well-to-do suburbanite is getting the benefits of the lowest financing costs possible.

In a study in San Francisco the investigators found that banks reported they lent "freely" to Negroes providing: (a) they lived in "an established Negro neighborhood" and (b) the property was in a "good" area. These two restrictions would effectively reduce the number of blacks to whom the financial institutions would lend money to a small minority of the total. McEntire reported the situation was similar throughout the country.[77]

In summary, mortgage financing for blacks has tended to have the following characteristics: restriction to certain areas of the city, higher interest rates, greater difficulty in obtaining, higher lending-agency charge, shorter time in which to pay off loan, larger monthly payments, greater tendency for property to be underappraised.

All of these practices are now prohibited under the 1968 fair-housing law. Discrimination could be difficult to prove in individual cases because of differences in credit judgment, but patterns of discriminatory practices of a lending institution on an overall basis would be quite evident. The U.S. Civil Rights Commission points out that agencies supervising mortgage-lending institutions have been more likely to criticize for loans made to poor risks than for loans denied to good risks. Supervisory agencies could require lending institutions to maintain adequate records so that discrimination could be detected and corrected.

The Commission concludes: "Thus the supervisory agencies could play a key role in assuring that the Nation's mortgage lending community serves to promote the cause of equal housing opportunity. It is a role they have been reluctant to assume." [78] Given the role of the government in regulating the operations and insuring the deposits of banks and savings-and-loan associations, there is no question about the ability of the government to prevent racial discrimination in lending practices. Any government-insured institution is subject to cease-and-desist orders by the insuring agency. A bank or savings-and-loan association that practices discrimination could have its deposit insurance terminated. This would cause a national bank to be dropped from the Federal Reserve, which would force it into receivership.[79] The means available for preventing racial discrimination are quite powerful.

FEDERAL HOUSING ADMINISTRATION

Although a number of different federal agencies have been involved to some extent in housing activities, the Federal Housing Administration (FHA) has undoubtedly been the most important in terms of both length of time and influence of its program. The FHA was established in 1934;

its program provides guarantees to lending institutions that the federal government will pay off housing loans on which the borrower defaults. A lender making an FHA-guaranteed loan for either home purchase or improvement is assured, therefore, that it will get the money back either from the borrower or from the FHA. Such a program could have become the means for an unprecedented rehabilitation of the nation's cities, with an increase in living standards and a decrease in segregation—possibly even at a "profit"—in that improved properties would have started yielding more tax revenue from as early as the mid-1930s. Actually, traditional real-estate interests obtained control of the program so that it became an extremely conservative one, tending to benefit the white suburbanite and to offer little to the dweller of the inner city.

Abrams commented: "One reason public agencies veer toward discrimination is the enlistment of 'experts' from private fields where bias is taken for granted. Unfamiliar with the ethical responsibility of government, these men insinuate their own biases upon the public agency." [80] Regarding the FHA, Weaver pointed out that most of its key officials were recruited from "the very financial and real estate interests and institutions which led the campaign to spread racial covenants and residential segregation." [81] Thus it can happen that a government officially committed to equality and democracy can spawn an official agency which can use governmental resources to further unequal, racially oriented treatment of its citizens.

FHA policies established in the 1930s were basically those of people then in the real-estate business, whose views and practices have already been referred to above. Real-estate textbooks in the 1920s and 1930s recommended racial segregation to protect property values. The functional similarity of black and foreigner is indicated by the fact that of two texts on real estate, both brought out in 1923, one considered the Negro the greater threat while the other considered it to be the "foreigner." Residential segregation was recommended in each book as the remedy for the situation.[82]

The basic guide that sets forth the criteria to be used in determining whether to grant an FHA-insured mortgage is the FHA *Underwriting Manual*. Although the *Underwriting Manual* is an official federal government publication, it was compiled and has been revised primarily by people engaged in the teaching and practice of real estate and has reflected their orientation. Until the late 1940s the *Manual* in effect required segregation (to prevent the intrusion of "inharmonious racial groups") as a condition for an FHA-insured mortgage and encouraged the use of restrictive covenants to prohibit "occupancy of properties except by the race for which they are intended." In so doing, the FHA "put the Federal Government's stamp of approval upon residential segregation and restrictive covenants." [83]

Abrams wrote in 1955: "Since almost every recent rental project and most individually owned homes have been built under FHA supervision and received their racial rating in accordance with its manual, the real estate group may be credited with shaping the racial and social patterns of American neighborhoods in the last generation." [84] Because land-use patterns tend to persist in cities, the neighborhood patterns so shaped could endure for the rest of the century.

Abrams maintained that FHA espousal of the restrictive covenant helped spread it throughout the country and encouraged even non-FHA property to become "restricted" because the owner might at some future time want to be eligible for an FHA loan. "Builders, seeing the covenant as an inexpensive sales tool, began to sell 'homogeneity' and freedom from . . . 'inharmonious social groups' . . . for all these phrases were worth." FHA policy thus became a major justification in itself of racial restrictive covenants. In addition, because FHA policies were "official" and widely practiced, they fed back into a new generation of real-estate textbooks the doctrines of racial segregation.[85]

FHA policies remained little changed throughout most of the 1940s. In November of 1948 the FHA was still able to claim that it "never had a housing project of mixed occupancy." [86] Some changes were made, however. The FHA stopped recommending restrictive covenants in 1947 (only a year before they were declared unenforceable by the Supreme Court). The 1947 *Underwriting Manual* also dropped references to "racial" groups or elements, referring instead to "user groups" in neighborhoods. The 1949 *Manual* specified that occupancy of an area by a different race should not *in itself* be considered to affect property values, but added, however, that "local real estate market reactions and the attitudes of borrowers" needed to be taken into account in evaluating mortgage risk.[87] Thus the expected negative reaction of whites to a black neighbor, *as judged by a real-estate broker or mortgage lender,* could take away what the FHA *Manual* finally gave in 1949.

The real-estate textbooks of the 1950s again followed the FHA lead. Although they did not state specifically that Negro occupancy in itself would lower property values, they tended to emphasize that neighborhoods should be "homogeneous" and be protected from "infiltration of inharmonious influences." Helper, who quotes this in a discussion of real-estate textbooks, states: "As in the later revisions of the *Underwriting Manual,* there seems to be an underlying meaning in this phrase, and though Negroes are not mentioned, the expression can be seen as a way of referring to Negroes or other racial or ethnic groups without mention-them." [88]

In December 1949 the FHA announced that beginning in February 1950 it would no longer insure mortgages on property covered by restrictive covenants, a move it could have taken in 1934. "With this regulation," McEntire commented, "a procedure once virtually mandatory was now prohibited." [89] In the early 1950s the FHA also started moving toward greater support of open-occupancy housing developments. It was not until 1962 that the FHA started requiring nondiscrimination pledges from loan applicants, that step being taken only as a result of President Kennedy's Executive Order 11063.[90]

FHA-insured mortgages declined during the 1960s to a point where most homes are financed by conventional mortgages.[91] This development increases the importance of the policies and practices of lending institutions in regard to all home mortgages, not just FHA-insured ones. Furthermore, recent federal programs relating to housing (to be discussed in a later chapter) are leading to FHA support for home financing in deteriorated inner-city areas—in many cases the same areas that had been "red-lined" in the past. The 25 years between the end of World War II and the beginning of the 1970s thus saw a complete reversal in FHA policies.

PUBLIC HOUSING

The term *public housing* refers to housing, generally in the form of housing projects, built with funds provided by government and rented out at less than cost to low-income families. Public housing began in the United States in 1932 with an ill-fated program that produced only two developments, which charged higher rents than could be afforded by the families for which they were intended. In 1933 legislation made possible the creation of the Public Works Administration, which built housing projects in 37 cities, although mainly for the purpose of providing jobs for the depression-unemployed; the resulting housing was a convenient bonus. The present concept of public housing was developed in the United States Housing Act of 1937, which provided for the federal government to furnish loans and financial assistance to locally established housing authorities, who would plan, build, and manage housing projects subject only to overall federal policies and regulations. Subsequent legislation and administrative reorganization have not drastically altered the original concept. Some state programs, particularly those of New York, have also provided for public housing.[92]

Two major questions may be raised about race and public housing. The first relates to possible discrimination in the allocation of housing units; that is, are blacks given a fair share of whatever housing is provided? There seems to be general agreement that there are no serious problems of racial discrimination in the number or share of total units available that are provided to blacks.[93] On the contrary, because public housing is limited to those with low incomes and because of the total social and economic situation of Negroes, they have a higher proportion of their numbers eligible for public housing; it is not uncommon to find that despite the fact that they are a minority in a population they constitute a majority of those in public housing projects. This, however, is a condition that leads to a *Yes* answer to the second question: is there residential segregation in housing projects so that projects tend to be either black or white and to be located accordingly in either black or white areas?

One can see here the same mechanism that functions in areas of private residential housing. Because a project is predominantly black it tends to be defined as, or to become, all black, possibly because of racial change in the surrounding neighborhood. Thus the mental picture the average person has of a project may be very little different from that of the slum-ghetto, with the difference that the buildings are newer. Project residents, then, would be conceived of as having ghetto characteristics because the project is viewed as equivalent to a slum-ghetto, and outsiders would then try to maintain segregation.

Before World War II, public housing did little to alter existing patterns of residential segregation. Then, as now, "the federal policy, or lack of policy," as McEntire puts it, has been influenced by national political considerations. "As the least popular and politically most vulnerable of the federal housing programs, public housing has particularly needed to hold the support of southern representatives in Congress." [94] In order to do this, and to have the support of segregationists from other parts of the country, federal policy could not be strongly nonsegregationist. A nonsegregationist policy would have meant no public housing. All regions of the country benefitted from federal aid in providing housing for their poor, however, and were happy to have it providing it did not alter their local racial housing patterns. Rather than confront the segregation issue, federal policy finessed it by giving much latitude to local housing authorities. They, in turn, "sided with the white segregationalists." [95]

Public-housing policy in the 1930s generally called for building projects in cleared slum areas and taking as occupants people who had been in that neighborhood. As such areas were frequently interracial and as there were many whites eligible for public housing because of the depression there was a certain amount of genuine residential integration in at least some early northern housing projects. Weaver mentions a number of cases of nonsegregated housing before and during World War II. [96] A serious difficulty is that patterns of restrictive segregation in private housing and the resulting block-by-block expansion of black areas have resulted in a tendency for interracial neighborhoods to become solidly black—with the result that white tenants in housing projects in such neighborhoods also tend to move away.

Since World War II the trend seems to have been in the direction of greater segregation in public housing. McEntire quotes a conclusion by Sterner that public housing had strengthened rather than weakened residential segregation and commented: "This judgment was even more accurate in 1957 than when it was made in 1942, notwithstanding the adoption of nonsegregation policies by a considerable number of local housing authorities." [97] We shall consider some aspects of the more recent situation below.

It should be noted that some factors that help to create increased racial separation in public housing are beyond the control of housing authorities. One factor is the higher proportion of blacks who are eligible for public housing. This means that a substantial part of the public-housing population will be black and that there will be proportionately fewer whites for them to be housed with. The greater availability of private housing for whites means that even low-income whites may have an easier time finding suitable private housing; this will further reduce the number of whites seeking public housing.

Because the surrounding private housing tends to be either white or black, with few stable interracial neighborhoods, there is a tendency for projects to take on the racial makeup of the adjacent neighborhood. This process is accelerated by the tendency of whites to move from an almost solidly black neighborhood, but has a parallel in the reluctance of blacks to live in a project in a white area. "Negroes will hesitate to go where they might find hostility, or they may not like to be separated from their churches, friends, and associations in existing Negro areas." [98] The overall result is usually a higher proportion of blacks in public housing than their proportion in the population would indicate, and a tendency for many public projects to be almost solidly black. "Public housing" and "low-income housing" are thus terms that in northern cities have become largely equivalent to "black housing."

Since shortly after World War II the most sharply fought battles over public housing have been waged not over whether or not there should be public housing—there has been little serious opposition to public housing in the abstract—but over the locations of sites. More specifically, upon the assumption that many of the occupants will be black, there has been strong opposition from residents of white areas to having new public-housing sites located there.

Meyerson and Banfield have presented a detailed study of the developments in Chicago in the early 1950s that concerned the location of sites for new projects. While most of the members of the city council favored public housing in general, it seems clear from the evidence that they wanted to have public housing for blacks in black areas and public housing for whites in white areas. Even earlier, in the 1940s, Weaver had commented on the reluctance of the Chicago Housing Authority to attempt to alter through public housing the "entrenched acceptance of residential segregation in the city." [99] The Housing Authority itself, however, as studied by Meyerson and Banfield, was less interested in maintaining segregation and more concerned with technical housing considerations (such as site factors) than the city councilmen, who seemed to perceive the situation mainly in terms of race and political considerations, including the possibilities that various decisions would have for rewarding friends and embarrassing enemies. The Chicago Housing Authority was eventually forced by city councilmen to accept a more segregated and less extensive program than it had originally proposed.[100]

A similar situation developed in Philadelphia. In 1956 the local housing authority proposed to build 21 small-scale projects scattered on vacant sites throughout the city. Such small projects are favored by most housing experts as not overloading any one neighborhood and not concentrating solid masses of low-income families in large developments. In addition, Philadelphia has had a particularly good reputation for its handling of residential race relationships.[101] In such a favorable environment the proposal might have been expected to produce a minimum amount of opposition. In fact, there was a great deal.

McEntire judged that there was "strenuous opposition" to the program from residents in areas where the small project sites were to be located. The mayor, who supported the program strongly, and housing authorities participated in a series of neighborhood meetings to try to defend and explain the program, "but they found the opposition in no mood to be reasoned with." "At one meeting, when a speaker began to talk about the need for public housing, the Chairman reminded him that 'this meeting was to protest the housing, not to debate it.' " One city councilman promised he would see that no streets or sewers would be provided. In the end the city council approved only 14 instead of 21 sites, a number of these different from those originally proposed.[102]

Fourteen years later, in Toledo, the Philadelphia scenario was re-enacted. The Toledo Metropolitan Housing Authority (TMHA), in accordance with its agreement with the federal government, was due to start construction of 400 units of public housing by the end of June 1970. Like Philadelphia, the development was to consist of a number of small-scale projects scattered on several sites in different parts of the city. The proposed buildings would have resembled private homes and small apartments rather than the massive institutional-looking buildings which have been characteristic of some public-housing projects. The first step involved 199 units on four different sites. The sites were on vacant land so there were no existing residents to be displaced.

Nevertheless, opposition to the housing developed in areas adjacent to each of the four proposed sites. At a meeting of the city council in May, 250 people crowded into the council chamber and corridors of the city hall, while an additional 100 picketed outside; almost everyone opposed the planned housing, one picketer's sign even proclaiming that the TMHA was "communistic." At the meeting, spokesmen from areas near the various sites called for the city council to renounce the entire 1968 agreement with TMHA, which provided for a total of nearly 2,000 units including those on the four sites in question. While the council did not go this far, it did veto all four sites by an 8 to 1 vote. (The one vote opposing the action was cast by a black councilman.) [103]

The situation was not quite that simple, however. The agreement that provided federal money to enable the housing authority to construct the projects was part of a larger grant that supported a number of improvements within the city that were unrelated to public housing. If the city refused to proceed with public housing it could face a loss of $15 million in federal funds. Furthermore, there was a serious legal question as to whether the council had the authority to renounce the 1968 agreement. The city council met again a week later, and by this time, aware of the possible loss of the $15 million in funds if it did not go ahead with the proposed housing, voted again to veto it in a stormy three-and-a-half-hour meeting. The 30th of June passed and with it went the $15 million in federal funds, plus an additional $1 million that would also have been available from a budget surplus. [104]

During June a U.S. District Court Judge ruled that the city council did not have the legal authority to void its 1968 contract with TMHA, and issued an injunction ordering TMHA to proceed with letting contracts for construction of the housing. While a rig was at one of the sites to make test borings of the soil in August someone exploded its gasoline tank, doing more than a thousand dollars damage. Demonstrations taking place nightly at this site a year later led city officials to threaten a curfew for the area.

Public-housing opponents have stated they would take court action to seek the voiding of the 1968 agreement, a move unlikely to succeed because the agreement stipulates that it cannot be voided without the consent of the U.S. Department of Housing and Urban Development, one of the parties to the agreement. City action would still be required for proper zoning or platting of the sites, and at least one city councilman said he would "never" vote for this, and other councilmen were also known to share his view. Residents near at least one of the four sites were publicly reported to be considering legal action to "end all public housing in the city," by means of a city-wide referendum if the 1968 agreement could not be voided.

Is there a need for public housing in Toledo? A spokesman for TMHA stated on a television program in June 1970 that they had a waiting list of 2,400 families and that the list would probably be considerably longer but that names were no longer being taken and that many families probably did not apply because they knew the waiting list was so long. It was also reported on the same program that one of the (white) opponents of the public-housing projects had himself lived in TMHA housing earlier! Five thousand inner-city residents had been displaced by urban renewal and expressway construction, yet only 500 housing units had been made available to house them.

Why such bitter opposition to public housing? The fact that a substantial number of public-housing residents in most cities are black has been referred to earlier. Scattering them in small projects throughout the city is therefore a step in residential desegregation. Yet, because it is "public" housing and not just "black" housing, an opponent can maintain that it is not a matter of race or prejudice, but that he is against public housing because people in such housing projects are of a lower socioeconomic level than those in adjacent neighborhoods and introduce different standards into a neighborhood, and that public housing lowers property values. It is not surprising to find that those who oppose public housing generally tend to deny that there is a racial motivation to their opposition, while those who support public housing are likely to charge that racism is a factor.

After the first veto by the Toledo city council, the Toledo Area Council of Churches passed a resolution favoring the principle of scattered low-cost housing and presented it to the city council at the second meeting; during this meeting the Executive Director of the Council of Churches charged that "the overriding issue in the [City] Council's decision was racial." The mayor retorted: "This is not a racial issue, but a people issue. . . . I'm sick and tired of ministers and others saying this is a racial issue, and I don't intend to take it." A resident of one area near a proposed site also denied racial bias, insisting: "We're afraid of a loss of property values when public housing moves in."

The court action referred to above challenging the legality of the city-council veto was initiated by a number of individuals and groups, including the NAACP, and charged that the city-council action was "racially motivated." Even if racism is not a factor it might just as well be, for the effect is the same—if small, scattered, public-housing sites are blocked, then so is any desegregation that might result from them. The Advisory Commission on Civil Disorders reported in 1968: "To date, housing programs serving low-income groups have been concentrated in the ghettos." [105] It recommended that low-income housing be on sites scattered around the city in nonghetto areas, which was the very thing attempted by the housing authorities in both Philadelphia and Toledo. The difficulties encountered in those cities indicate that the Commission's recommendation will not be an easy one to implement.

The extent to which theoretically nonsegregated "public" housing in Chicago actually is segregated was revealed in a lawsuit initiated in 1965 that finally came before a U.S. Federal District Court in February 1969. The system in Chicago under which a city councilman could informally veto any public-housing site in his ward was declared to be invalid by Judge Richard B. Austin. The judge noted that in the few cases in which an alderman failed to veto a public-housing site in a white area the site was later rejected formally by the city council.

Evidence in the hearing showed that there were 54 housing projects in the city. In 50 of them 99.5 percent of the tenants were Negro (a higher percentage, incidentally, than the advertised purity of a well-known brand of soap). The four remaining projects ranged from 1 to 7 percent Negro. Judge Austin commented: "It is incredible that this dismal prospect of an all-Negro public housing system in all-Negro areas came about without the persistent application of a deliberate policy to confine public housing to all-Negro or immediately adjacent areas." [106]

"The suit contended that during the consideration of each of Chicago's five major housing programs since 1954, white sites meeting all appropriate criteria were rejected for racial reasons." [107] The judge concluded that racial factors were the most important consideration in rejecting many sites. The evidence in this suit, going back to 1954, which was the most recent year included in the Meyerson and Banfield study cited above, can be considered as updating that study and showing that the same practices that existed in the early 1950s were continued into the late 1960s. The Philadelphia and Toledo evidence suggests that such practices are not confined to just one city.

In the summer of 1969, following the court hearing, Judge Austin issued a set of rules to the Chicago Housing Authority designed to correct the racial imbalance in Chicago's public housing. One provision of the order was that three dwelling units must be constructed in white neighborhoods for each unit constructed in a black neighborhood. The order also set density limits that would result in scattered small-scale projects rather than in the massive concentrations which have been characteristic of Chicago public housing.[108] It remains to be seen if some means will be found to evade these orders and maintain racial segregation in public housing in Chicago.

Three months after Judge Austin made his decision, however, it was cited as a precedent by a U.S. District Court Judge in Louisiana, who granted an injunction that would reduce segregation in public housing in Bogalusa.[109] Such rulings conceivably could have a considerable effect. There are a number of cities in which they might be used, including Newark, Cleveland, and Boston. Each of these cities was found by the U.S. Civil Rights Commission to have projects with from 90 to 100 percent occupancy by one race or the other. One project in Cleveland had never had a Negro assigned to it in its 20-year history. A project in Boston was divided so that there were no Negroes among over 1,000 families on one side of the street and mostly Negro families on the other side. A Boston clergyman described the dividing street as "like the Berlin Wall" and testified that even small children distinguish between the "white and Negro projects." [110]

1. Charles S. Johnson, *Patterns of Negro Segregation* (New York: Harper & Row, Publishers, 1943), pp. 173–76; Gunnar Myrdal (with the assistance of Arnold Rose and Richard Sterner), *An American Dilemma* (New York: Harper & Row, Publishers, 1944), pp. 623–24; Jack Greenberg, *Race Relations and American Law* (New York: Columbia University Press, 1959), pp. 276–77.

2. Johnson, *Negro Segregation*, p. 177; Robert C. Weaver, *The Negro Ghetto* (New York: Harcourt Brace Jovanovich, Inc., 1948), pp. 232, 246.

3. Charles Abrams, *Forbidden Neighbors* (New York: Harper & Row, Publishers, 1955), pp. 218–19.

4. Weaver, *The Negro Ghetto*, p. 232.

5. *Ibid.*, pp. 247–48.

6. St. Clair Drake and Horace R. Cayton, *Black Metropolis* (New York: Harper & Row, Publishers, 1962), p. 79.

7. Drake and Cayton, *Black Metropolis*, p. 185.

8. Myrdal, *An American Dilemma*, p. 624.

9. Leon F. Litwack, *North of Slavery* (Chicago: University of Chicago Press, 1961), p. 169.

10. Harry M. Rosen and David H. Rosen, *But Not Next Door* (New York: Ivan Obolensky, Inc., 1962), pp. 23–24.

11. Litwack, *North of Slavery*, p. 169.

12. Chicago Commission on Race Relations, *The Negro in Chicago* (Chicago: University of Chicago Press, 1922; reprinted by Arno Press, Inc., New York, 1968), pp. 194–95.

13. *Ibid.*, pp. 118–19; Roi Ottley and William J. Weatherby, eds, *The Negro in New York* (New York: The New York Public Library; Dobbs Ferry, N.Y.: Oceana Publications, Inc., 1967), p. 185.

14. Drake and Cayton, *Black Metropolis*, p. 185.

15. Norris Vitchek (pseudonym), "Confessions of a Block-Buster," *Saturday Evening Post*, July 1962, pp. 15–19.

16. Rose Helper, *Racial Policies and Practices of Real Estate Brokers* (Minneapolis: University of Minnesota Press, 1969), pp. 120 ff., 201, 223.

17. Drake and Cayton, *Black Metropolis*, p. 185; Allon Schoener, ed., *Harlem on My Mind* (New York: Random House, Inc., 1968), pp. 28, 51.

18. Ottley and Weatherby, *The Negro in New York*, p. 186; *see also* Gilbert Osofsky, *Harlem: The Making of a Ghetto* (New York: Harper Torchbooks, 1968; copyright © Harper & Row, Publishers, 1963), p. 136.

19. Drake and Cayton, *Black Metropolis,* p. liii.
20. Osofsky, *Harlem,* p. 109.
21. Chicago Commission, *The Negro in Chicago,* p. 608.
22. *Ibid.,* p. 211.
23. *Milwaukee Journal,* April 28, 1968.
24. Reginald G. Damerell, *Triumph in a White Suburb* (New York: William Morrow & Co., Inc., 1968), p. 31.
25. *Milwaukee Journal,* April 28, 1968.
26. James L. Hecht, *Because It Is Right* (Boston: Little, Brown and Company, 1970), p. 72.
27. Luigi Laurenti, *Property Values and Race* (Berkeley and Los Angeles: University of California Press, 1960).
28. *Ibid.,* p. 47.
29. Davis McEntire, *Residence and Race* (Berkeley and Los Angeles: University of California Press, 1960), p. 244 ff.
30. Quoted in McEntire, *Residence and Race,* p. 244.
31. Quoted in Helper, *Real Estate Brokers,* p. 201.
32. *Ibid.,* p. 201.
33. *Ibid.,* p. 235.
34. McEntire, *Residence and Race,* p. 249.
35. *See* Helper, *Real Estate Brokers,* p. 225.
36. Chicago Commission, *The Negro in Chicago,* pp. 108–9.
37. Helper, *Real Estate Brokers,* p. xii.
38. *Ibid.,* pp. 23–24.
39. *Ibid.,* p. 56.
40. *Ibid.,* pp. 68–73.
41. *Ibid.,* p. 103.
42. *Ibid.,* pp. 103–7.
43. *Ibid.,* pp. 124–25.
44. *Ibid.,* p. 125.
45. *Ibid.*
46. *Ibid.*
47. *Ibid.,* pp. 125–26.
48. *Ibid.*
49. *Ibid.,* p. 45.
50. *Ibid.,* p. 126.
51. Chicago Commission, *The Negro in New York,* p. 139.
52. Helper, *Real Estate Brokers,* p. 137.
53. *Ibid.,* p. 140.
54. *Ibid.,* pp. 42–43.
55. U.S. Civil Rights Commission, *A Time to Listen . . . A Time to Act* (Washington, D.C.: Government Printing Office, 1967), pp. 61–62.

56. Karl E. Taeuber, "The Effect of Income Redistribution on Racial Residential Segregation," *Urban Affairs Quarterly,* IV, No. 1 (September 1968), 8.

57. Hecht, *Because It Is Right,* pp. 9–10.

58. Helper, *Real Estate Broker,* p. 43 (emphasis added).

59. *Ibid.,* p. 168.

60. *Ibid.,* p. 62.

61. *Ibid.,* pp. 46 ff.

62. Ohio Civil Rights Commission, *A Survey of Discrimination in Housing in Ohio* (Columbus, Ohio, January, 1963).

63. Damerell, *White Suburb,* pp. 37, 171–73.

64. National Committee Against Discrimination in Housing, *How the Federal Government Builds Ghettos* (New York: February 1967), p. 27.

65. Damerell, *White Suburb,* p. 80.

66. U.S. Civil Rights Commission, *Housing* (Washington, D.C.: Government Printing Office, 1961), pp. 122–23.

67. *Report of the National Advisory Commission on Civil Disorders* (Washington, D.C.: Government Printing Office, 1968), p. 119.

68. U.S. Civil Rights Commission, *Federal Civil Rights Enforcement Effort* (Washington, D.C.: Government Printing Office, 1971), chapter 3.

69. U.S. Civil Rights Commission, *Housing,* pp. 28–29, 141.

70. W. E. B. DuBois, *The Philadelphia Negro* (1899; reprint ed., New York: Benjamin Blom, Inc., 1967), pp. 180–81.

71. Schoener, *Harlem on My Mind,* pp. 24–25.

72. Weaver, *The Negro Ghetto,* p. 215.

73. Helper, *Real Estate Brokers,* pp. 45, 71.

74. McEntire, *Residence and Race,* pp. 224–26.

75. *Ibid.,* pp. 227–28.

76. Jane Jacobs, *The Death and Life of Great American Cities* (New York: Random House, Inc., 1961), chapter 16; *see also* McEntire, *Residence and Race,* pp. 222–24.

77. McEntire, *Residence and Race,* pp. 222–24.

78. U.S. Civil Rights Commission, *Federal Civil Rights Enforcement Effort,* p. 167.

79. *Ibid.,* pp. 165–67.

80. Abrams, *Forbidden Neighbors,* p. 239.

81. Weaver, *The Negro Ghetto,* p. 70.

82. Abrams, *Forbidden Neighbors,* pp. 158–59.

83. Weaver, *The Negro Ghetto,* pp. 72–73.

84. Abrams, *Forbidden Neighbors,* p. 162.

85. *Ibid.,* pp. 163, 234–35.

86. *Ibid.,* p. 233.

87. McEntire, *Residence and Race,* pp. 302–3.

88. Helper, *Real Estate Brokers,* p. 203.

89. McEntire, *Residence and Race,* p. 303.

90. U.S. Civil Rights Commission, *Federal Civil Rights Enforcement Effort,* p. 139.

91. U.S. Civil Rights Commission, *Federal Civil Rights Enforcement Effort,* p. 165.

92. Glenn H. Beyer, *Housing and Society* (New York: The Macmillan Company, 1965), pp. 462–67.

93. McEntire, *Residence and Race,* p. 319.

94. *Ibid.,* pp. 319–20.

95. Myrdal, *An American Dilemma,* p. 626.

96. Weaver, *The Negro Ghetto,* chapter 11.

97. McEntire, *Residence and Race,* p. 321.

98. Abrams, *Forbidden Neighbors,* p. 312.

99. Weaver, *The Negro Ghetto,* p. 194.

100. Martin Meyerson and Edward C. Banfield, *Politics, Planning and the Public Interest: The Case of Public Housing in Chicago* (Glencoe, Ill.: The Free Press, 1955).

101. *See* Abrams, *Forbidden Neighbors,* p. 315; McEntire, *Residence and Race,* p. 327.

102. McEntire, *Residence and Race,* pp. 326–28.

103. Material documenting the discussion of Toledo in this section may be found in the Toledo *Blade,* May 18, 28, 29, 31; June 4, 8, 12, 30; July 8; August 11, 15, 1970.

104. Arrangements for restoration of the funds were eventually worked out.

105. *Report of the National Advisory Commission on Civil Disorders,* p. 263.

106. *Civil Liberties,* April 1969, p. 5.

107. *Ibid.*

108. *Civil Liberties,* October 1969, p. 8.

109. *City,* October 1969, p. 3.

110. U.S. Civil Rights Commission, *A Time to Listen,* pp. 64–65.

6 | Maintaining Segregation, II

QUASI-INSTITUTIONAL MEANS

BLOCKBUSTING

The large aerial bombs used during World War II were called block-busters because one of them could destroy an entire city block. Since then the term has come to be applied to real-estate agents and speculators who specialize in expanding the black area by selling to blacks property in nearby white blocks.

The white community can expand with ease; both more intensive use of land within the city and new suburban building on the fringe constantly make additional housing available to whites. Newspaper real-estate sections continually run ads to try to entice whites to help fill up the latest apartment buildings and housing developments. The black, on the other hand, finds no such pull outwards but, instead, restrictive segregation pushing inward. The blockbuster may be viewed as the counterpart of the suburban land developer in that he makes additional housing available to those who need it. In doing this he is performing a needed public service, but because of the brokers' interpretation of their Code of Ethics it is considered unethical for a real-estate broker to sell to a black property in a block that is all-white. The blockbuster is thus "unethical." [1]

An "ethical" real-estate broker is not likely to serve a black in such an instance. Furthermore, the broker will justify his behavior by reference to God, conscience, the American free-enterprise system, the U.S. Constitution, loyalty, and "principle with a capital P," as well as ethics.[2] Many of our laws are not supported by as powerful an ideology as this. Just as the person seeking illegal goods or services finds that they are denied him by legitimate society and turns to the underworld, so the black seeking property in a white area finds that it is denied him by the "ethical" brokers and lenders and turns to the "unethical" block-buster. Just as an illegal system which arises to supply legally forbidden goods and services creates problems of its own for society, so the system used by the blockbuster creates long-range problems by increasing the already generous supply of fear and hostility between the races.

In one sense, the blockbuster is only the person who arranges for the sale to a black of the first house in a white block. After the block has been "busted" it becomes a foregone conclusion in most situations that it will eventually become all-black. An isolated case of a black moving out into a white area as an individual and not as the vanguard of a nearby expanding ghetto would not be considered blockbusting. The essence of "busting" a block is not just the moving in of one black family, but rather the following through to pressure as many whites as possible to sell their homes and move out, so that blockbusting is best viewed as the entire process of directing pressures at the white residents. This is in accord with the legal definition of blockbusting in the 1968 fair-housing act:

> For profit, to induce or attempt to induce any person to sell or rent any dwelling by representations regarding the entry or prospective entry into the neighborhood of a person or persons of a particular race, color, religion, or national origin.[3]

As the existence of a legal definition might imply, blockbusting was prohibited by the fair-housing act, but, of course, behavior does not always stop with the passage of a law against it. In any event, the effects which past blockbusting have had on race relationships will undoubtedly continue for many years into the future. Although involuntary racial residential segregation may be viewed as a result of racial attitudes, its role as a cause of increased prejudice and hostility needs emphasis. Whites get panicked into selling immediately, thinking that if they do not do so they will be at an even greater disadvantage later. Their fears and resentments over the "forced" sale then are directed toward the blacks, whom they feel to be at the root of the problem, rather than toward the real-estate practices that have produced the situation.

The white homeowner is sacrificed, the black gets the blame, and the blockbuster makes the money ($100,000 a year in one reported instance).[4] Putting the situation this way makes the blockbuster a villain, yet he is practically the only one who is making an appreciable effort to increase the housing supply for blacks. He is performing an essential public service that the "ethical" brokers and lending institutions frequently have not performed. If the blockbuster is to be judged negatively, it might better be on the basis of the methods used to accomplish the job and not on the service he performs. White aversion to living in predominantly black neighborhoods and a belief that black occupancy of a neighborhood lowers property values have provided the twin supports for a system that shows a profit on the books of the speculator while it produces a loss in the race relationships ledger. The practice of blockbusting (although not by that name) was evident in Chicago even during World War I.

> There were tremendous profits to be made by both colored and white realtors who could provide houses. And so the spread of the Negro areas of residence began, with the whites fleeing before them. Artificial panics were sometimes created in white areas by enterprising realtors who raised the cry, 'The Negroes are coming.' " [5]

Descriptions since then and in other cities show only small variations in what seems to have become a highly standardized process. One aspect of it is simply the amount of attention given by real-estate dealers to a block which is "turning." It was reported that in Chicago as many as thirty brokers and speculators might work such a block at the same time.[6] A homeowner in New York City started receiving telephone calls from real-estate dealers on the same day that a black family moved in across the street.[7] A family living in an interracial area in Milwaukee told of people collecting "soup plates full of real estate men's cards." [8] Homeowners with no thought of selling and moving find themselves repeatedly being pressured to do so by door-to-door solicitation, phone calls, and "a steady flow of mail." [9] It appears that a block that is mixed racially has a powerful attraction for real-estate dealers, who attempt to unmix it by making it solidly black—which may be why researchers like the Taeubers find so few stable interracial neighborhoods.

The basic message of the blockbuster is quite simple: the neighborhood is becoming Negro, the homeowner should sell his house as soon as he can, and the longer he waits the worse off he will be. In actual practice it is not likely to be phrased this directly. A homeowner in New York City commented: "In most cases more was hinted than actually spoken. But every word, every gesture, was designed to make us feel we were idiots if we didn't sell immediately." [10] There need not even be any reference to race but only to "something like this happening in the neighborhood," "what is happening in the neighborhood," or that the "neighborhood is changing," phrases reported to have been used in, respectively, San Francisco, Chicago, and the New York area." [11]

To motivate the homeowner to sell, the real-estate dealer invokes either directly or indirectly the double threats of reduced value of property and social isolation. As in Teaneck, New Jersey, the owner may be told: "You should sell now while you can still get a good price." [12] A dealer may make a specific offer with a statement that the price will be lower later: "I'll give you $20,000 . . . next week I won't pay 18." [13] To a homeowner's fear of financial loss if he delayed in selling, the blockbuster could add—by his offer to make a "quick cash deal"—fears of Negro financial irresponsibility and their difficulty in finding financing.[14] If monetary considerations prove insufficient to induce the owner to sell, the real-estate dealer can bring in the additional threat of being "the last [white] on the block." [15]

A Chicago blockbuster reported: "The moment I make a deal, I always place a 'Sold by' sign in front of the building. A few such signs—the gaudier, the better—show that events are moving." [16] A Baltimore blockbuster induced panic in the neighborhood by "putting up a large luminescent 'sold' sign even though the house had not been sold." [17] The use of "For Sale" and "Sold" signs as a technique of "psychological warfare" in Teaneck, New Jersey, is described by Damerell:

> The 'battle of the signs' was in progress. Real estate agents erected FOR SALE signs in letters as high as three feet, on the front lawns of homes listed with them. After a sale, they would replace it with a gigantic SOLD, that might remain for several weeks until the new Negro took possession. It was a psychological warfare technique designed to panic whites into selling. . . . One could measure the tension of a street by the number and size of its signs.[18]

Finally the city council felt it necessary to pass an ordinance limiting the size of signs, whereupon the "real estate agents complained bitterly that their constitutional rights were being violated." [19] The Teaneck brokers apparently saw no threat to the constitutional rights of the Negroes they refused to deal with or to the whites they would not show homes in areas they defined as going black.[20]

We noted earlier that lending agencies have generally not made loans to the first one (or first few) blacks who buy in a white area. Some lending agencies also will not lend money to a white on property in a white area that is expected to become black soon.[21] Given this situation, *neither* black nor white could borrow from customary lending sources. A successful blockbuster will have access to sufficient capital, however, so that he can finance the first few transactions in a block. After this, lending agencies will be willing to become publicly involved. As blacks tend to be handicapped in obtaining larger amounts of capital, most of the large-scale blockbusters are white.[22] When the banker quoted earlier said that "the first two or three sales in any block should be financed between the parties," [23] he was referring indirectly to the blockbuster. Note again the self-fulfilling prophecy: if a bank believes that an area will "go black," and refuses loans to whites in the area, it forces buyers to turn to lending sources such as the blockbuster—which produces the expected result.

The "threat" of even the physical presence of blacks has been used as a "scare technique" by both blacks and whites. Around the turn of the century one New York City Negro made a regular practice of buying a lot in a white area through a white intermediary. Showing up at the site and announcing he was going to build his home there quickly led to "a handsome profit," as a white would then buy up the property to keep the area all-white.[24] By the 1920s both whites and blacks were making a considerable amount of money through the "Negro scare racket," in which property owners moved black tenants into their buildings so that the surrounding white owners would buy up the property at a good price in order to evict the blacks and keep the area all-white.[25] Blacks thus found themselves inconvenienced as well as "used" for the purpose of "scaring" the whites in order to make money. In more recent years white aversion to having black neighbors has been exploited by real-estate agents of both races, who have employed such devices as driving Negroes (preferably dark in color) around in neighborhoods, stopping outside of houses and pointing, having Negroes walk or drive up and down streets making noises and attracting attention, and so forth.[26]

The fact of blockbusting has been documented in the United States literally from coast to coast. The occupation of real-estate broker is a legitimate one in our society, of course, and there is no criticism of a broker who renders a genuine service by handling a transaction for a family that definitely wishes to move. Blockbusting goes far beyond this, though, in trying to generate movement where there is no desire, and in areas where both blacks and whites would prefer to live in a truly interracial neighborhood. In some cities whites have formed organizations to fight off the real-estate men whom they have accused, as in Milwaukee, of "unfair exploitation" and using "panic selling tactics" to "prey on residents' fears." [27] Combined with the reluctance of "ethical" brokers to sell homes in interracial neighborhoods to whites, what could be a stable biracial area comes to be thought of as one which is "turning" or "changing" and which should be speeded as quickly as possible to its ultimate destiny of being all-black.

The blockbuster thus performs his necessary task of providing additional housing for blacks, but given the existing system of racial restrictive segregation, the job is performed at the price of local social instability, psychological strain, and a greatly increased hostility between the races. Helper has commented on the tendency among brokers to apply terms of military warfare to the blockbusting process. "They speak of a 'threatened area,' as if an enemy were coming to devastate it . . . the softening-up period—an expression used at times to describe the bombardment of a place before ground forces attempt to capture it." They speak of the "target neighborhood" and "planning the attack. . . . When Negroes are attempting to enter an area, it is 'under fire.' Then, when they enter, the 'invasion' takes place, and the block is 'broken.' " [28] The warfare image is unique neither to Chicago nor to recent years. Regarding Harlem in the early 20th century Osofsky commented: "The language used to describe the movement of Negroes into Harlem . . . was the language of war." [29] The Chicago Commission on Race Relations in 1922 also noted the same phenomenon, even to the adoption by whites of a French slogan which had become famous in World War I, "They shall not pass." [30]

Blockbusters operate in many cities. It was claimed that there were over 100 in Chicago alone and that during the 1950s and 1960s two to three blocks a week were "busted." [31] If each block had an average of 50 families, this would mean that over 70,000 white families in Chicago experienced the blockbusting process during a 10-year period. If each one felt that it had been forced to move at a great financial and personal sacrifice and that blacks were to blame, the total amount of ill-will *created* and spread to other parts of the community by the blockbusting process would be considerable indeed. Add to this the feelings of anger generated in blacks by the whites' resistance and periodic violence against them and apply this to cities all over the country and one may get some indication of the contribution to racial tensions that is made just by the practice of restrictive racial residential segregation.

OTHER MEANS

This category includes a wide variety of means by which more or less formally organized groups have sought to promote segregation either directly or by working through or influencing other social institutions. Means classified as quasi-institutional lack either the durability over a period of time or sufficiently widespread distribution within the society or the formality and degree of organization necessary for them to be considered as fully institutional. A classification of means within this category will not be attempted here, but rather a description will be given of some representative types.

One early and eventually fairly common type of organization for opposing the spread of Negro areas was made up of white property owners in areas adjacent to black areas. Frequently called "protective" or "neighborhood-improvement" associations, they fought in various ways against Negro expansion. Committees of local landlords, sometimes representing only a single block, were formed in Harlem shortly after 1900, which originally had been built as a middle-class residential area. Even this early such associations were promoting restrictive covenants, the blocks so "protected" being called "Covenant Blocks." The black area continued spreading despite the associations and their covenants.

A number of groups representing larger areas were formed in Harlem, the most forceful being the Harlem Property Owner's Improvement Corporation, which was active from 1910 to 1915. The group put pressure on banks not to lend money either to Negroes or to whites who would rent out apartments to Negroes. It held meetings to gain support for opposition to black expansion. It secured publicity in local newspapers and supported anti-Negro positions held by such papers to a point where the *Harlem Home News* used in its stories such terms as "coon," "nigger," "black plague," and "black hordes." [32]

The leader of this group even proposed at one point that a 24-foot-high fence be built, beyond which the black area would not be permitted to expand.[33] The suggestion brings to mind the walled Jewish ghettos of medieval Europe. Nor was it the last time such an idea would be advanced. In Teaneck, New Jersey, in the early 1950s, as public officials discussed how to prevent Negro expansion into the city from neighboring Englewood: "One Planning Board member proposed a high fence." [34] In the late 1960s a police official from a white Maryland suburb of Washington, D.C., suggested to one of the senators from Maryland that "if you want to help us you should build a forty-foot chain link fence along the District [of Columbia] line and put barbed wire on top." [35] If ghettos in American cities are not walled in, it is not from a lack of the possibility repeatedly occurring to people.

By 1920 a number of associations had been formed in Chicago, such as the South Park Manor Improvement Association and the Lake Front Community Property Owner's Association. Like their New York counterparts, they held meetings, distributed literature, and published newspapers. The Chicago Commission on Race Relations reported:

> Racial antagonism was strong in the speeches at these meetings and in the newspapers. . . . [In one meeting] the sentiment was expressed that Negro invasion of the district was the worst calamity that had struck the city since the Great Fire. . . . Distinctly hostile sentiments were expressed before audiences that came expecting to hear how their property might be saved from 'almost certain destruction.' [36]

The Kenwood and Hyde Park Property Owner's Association published *The Property Owner's Journal,* that contained abusive, racist, hostile articles.[37]

Almost 30 years later, in 1948, Weaver was able to find much "neighborhood improvement association" activity to document; he commented that in Chicago and Detroit "and in scores of other cities in the North, property owners' and neighborhood improvement associations have assumed the roles of vociferous and intemperate champions of racial segregation. They publicly advocate separate schools and recreational facilities." Weaver noted that their heavy emphasis on restrictive covenants (with the encouragement of the FHA) would have the effect of producing *"planned segregation."* [38]

Since the 1948 U.S. Supreme Court decision against restrictive covenants and the change shortly thereafter in FHA policy from favoring to opposing covenants, improvement associations seem to have declined in importance, in some cases apparently being replaced by more devious and less visible means of attempting to maintain segregation. As the associations were generally unsuccessful in preventing black expansion, it could well be that their greatest effect was the contribution they made to the total supply of racial prejudice and discrimination in the country. By constantly opposing residential integration, frequently with racist and militant means, the associations helped to legitimize both the idea and practice of segregation—another case in which segregation has undoubtedly been a cause in itself of increased prejudice. In recent years, however, some associations have accepted the idea of having black neighbors and have worked actively to promote stable interracial neighborhood life.

In his 1955 book Abrams described 13 ways in which segregation could be maintained without using court-enforced restrictive covenants, noting that this was only a "partial list." Common to a number of these devices is that they are simply private agreements between two or more individuals and thus do not require enforcement through public channels involving the courts.[39]

While at least some of these devices are of doubtful legality, they have been used to maintain the segregation of Jews and other ethnic groups as well as blacks. As Abrams comments: "Valid or not, they are effective as delaying tactics." [40] Even if a particular device is ruled illegal in one area it may be used in another, until finally judged by the U.S. Supreme Court. By that time, a new means could be devised. Certainly by that time the subdivision in question would have been filled with the "right" kind of people.

How builders select the "right" people for real-estate developments is indicated by an account of one black family in Milwaukee that tried to buy a new suburban home in 1965. When they visited a model home of one leading builder the salesman ignored them completely although they were the only ones there at the time. When they called to inquire about a lot in one subdivision and told the salesman they were Negro he said he had "never faced this 'problem' before" and that he would call back. He never did. Another large builder refused to sell to them, saying he "could not take the chance" because of the other lot owners. One developer said he had "no intention of selling any of the lots to a Negro." Another salesman seemed genuinely helpful in offering to try to find them a lot—but not in his own firm's subdivision. When he did find a lot for them they encountered financing problems, although they had earlier paid off a 15-year $10,000 mortgage in only eight years.[41] In Bergen County, New Jersey, an agent for a new housing development told a resident of the area that they had many Negroes stop to look at the homes, but that "We get rid of them" by using various methods.[42]

A particularly elaborate "point system" that did not rely upon legal devices came to light in 1960 in Grosse Pointe, Michigan, a wealthy suburb of Detroit. The system required close collaboration between the Grosse Pointe Brokers Association and the Grosse Pointe Property Owners Association and was described in the United States Civil Rights Commission Report of 1961 as follows:

> A private detective agency investigated prospective purchasers of Grosse Pointe homes. A committee of three [real estate] brokers then graded the information (gathered largely by talking to neighbors of the prospective purchaser) to determine whether to admit the person to the area. Fifty points was passing. However, persons 'of Polish descent had to score 55 points; southern Europeans, including those of Italian, Greek, Spanish, or Lebanese origin, had to score 65 points; and those of the Jewish faith had to score 85 points. Negroes and Orientals were excluded entirely.' Any broker selling property to a person rated as 'undesirable' was compelled to forfeit his commission to the Grosse Pointe Property Owners Association, and refusal to do so rendered him liable to expulsion from the Grosse Pointe Brokers Association. The type of information that a person could be graded upon, and found undesirable, was: whether his way of living was 'typically American'; whether his business associates and friends were 'typically American'; the degree of his 'swarthiness'; the extent to which he 'spoke with an accent'; whether his name was 'typically American'; whether he dressed 'neatly,' 'slovenly,' 'conservatively,' or 'flashy'; and how his family had been thought of in previous neighborhoods.[43]

The effectiveness of the enforcement of the Gross Pointe system is certainly one noteworthy characteristic. By making the broker's fee payable to the property-owners' association in the event that he sold property to an "undesirable," the system both punished the broker and rewarded the property-owners' association for detecting violations. There was the additional sanction of expulsion of the broker from the brokers association, which could not afford not to act in case of a violation of the system.

The criteria used in evaluating prospective residents seem to support the interpretation offered earlier that the acceptability of a neighbor to native, middle-class whites is related to the extent to which he lacks observable ghetto characteristics. Nonwhites were ruled out altogether, and the system provided that whites would not be accepted if they had too many ghetto characteristics—such as swarthy skin color, foreign accent, friends and a manner of living not "typically American," and a foreign (that is, non-Anglo-Saxon) name. The system permitted an individual to offset a swarthy complexion, for example, by dressing neatly and Anglicizing his name. Thus it was not just physical characteristics but a whole way of life that was evaluated. A person of Jewish background who was not very "typically American" would not qualify, but neither would a WASP hillbilly. Both would have ghetto characteristics that would be considered undesirable. The Grosse Pointe system was so concerned with outward appearances, however, that it failed to keep out wealthy members of organized crime.[44]

One wonders how much of the concern with neighbors' characteristics is the result of worry over what casual strangers passing by might think if they were to see a person with ghetto characteristics living in the neighborhood. One woman, discussing the possibility of a Negro doctor moving in along her street, reportedly was concerned not over the prospect of her children playing with blacks but with the possibility that someone seeing this wouldn't know that the black children came from a professional family! A New Jersey man said that although he preferred a standard American car he drove a foreign sports car because of the "image" it would create, and that his main reason for objecting to having Negro neighbors was that "his image would suffer." [45]

A study by Bressler suggests that a concern with the image or status symbolism of a community may be more important to working-class than to middle-class people. Studying the move of the first Negro family into Levittown, Pennsylvania, Bressler found that the greater opposition to the family came from working-class members of the community. He concluded that whereas middle-class people generally acquired prestige and recognition from their occupations, working-class people, even those with above-average incomes, got little status from their jobs and looked more to the status of their community to provide them recognition.[46] In these circumstances, the "threat" to the status of the community by a black family would have more personal significance to them than to middle-class people. This can explain why a working-class area or suburb can be more resistant to nonsegregation than a middle-class one.

Just as our clothing has the rough and sometimes uncomfortable edges of the material on the inside so that we can present a neat, smooth appearance on the outside, so we may be concerned with the impression our neighbors make upon others, even upon complete strangers. What sort of impression would one get of a Grosse Pointe resident if he had swarthy-skinned neighbors standing outside with their non-American-type friends, talking in a foreign language, gesturing repeatedly with their hands, and eating matzo balls or ravioli? Social status and image are probably of considerable importance in determining people's views about their neighbors.

In addition to the means described above, there are what Abrams called the "officialized oppressions." [47] These rely on the use of local governmental powers for the maintenance of residential segregation, and range from very subtle to quite obvious attempts to keep out blacks. An example of the former might be Leawood, Kansas, a high-status suburb of Kansas City. A local ordinance prohibits "For Sale" signs on houses, so the only way the typical prospective buyer can learn which houses are for sale is to work through a real-estate broker, who then can screen out the "undesirables." [48] While blockbusters might use large, gaudy signs for their purposes, the absence of signs can also aid segregation. More blatant types of officialized oppression frequently involve the use of governmental controls over land use.

The case of Deerfield, Illinois, shows how local governmental powers can be used to prevent integration. In 1959 a corporation started developing a subdivision in that Chicago suburb, with plans for 50 homes to be priced at $30,000 or more. When residents of the all-white community learned that 10 or 12 of these homes would be sold to Negro business and professional people they quickly developed opposition to the entire subdivision. Within a month the town organized an election in which a large majority of the residents authorized the Park District to spend more than a half million of their tax dollars to condemn the subdivision for building purposes and create a park on the land. Was it that the community really wanted a park and the condemnation of the subdivision that proposed to have some Negro occupants was merely a coincidence? Within the previous year two land-acquisition proposals of the Park District had been turned down by the voters. This, plus the literature circulated, the issues discussed in mass meetings, and informal conversations, makes it clear that the major purpose in creating the park was to forestall the integrated housing development.[49]

It was action of this type that Abrams had in mind when he wrote, five years before the Deerfield incident:

> But more recently it has become possible for whole races to be banned from a city. . . . After developers build communities which are then incorporated, their own police are hired, their own laws enacted, and the 'wrong kind of people' kept out.

Abrams called this "the closed city" and cited a number of communities with populations of 50,000 or more that had no Negroes.[50]

The Deerfield events are of significance because there was such strong opposition to no more than a dozen black families with above-average incomes and middle-class occupations moving into the community. There would surely be even more determined resistance to low-income housing in suburban areas. This kind of racial discrimination seems particularly difficult to prevent by means of legal action. There is nothing illegal or unconstitutional in a community acquiring land for park purposes. If some people in a community feel that a certain governmental action is detrimental to their interests, they may oppose it by legal or political means (appearing before the mayor or city council, seeking a court injunction, and so forth). But in an all-white suburban community, many of whose residents are there *because* it is all-white, blacks who are disadvantaged by the community action are not within the system, and those whites who are and would oppose the action on idealistic grounds are outnumbered.

Nevertheless, where local zoning and land acquisition practices seem to be *for the purpose of* maintaining racial discrimination, lawsuits are being instituted. One such suit, initiated in 1969 by the U.S. Department of Justice against the city of Lackawanna, New York, maintains that the city rezoned an area from *housing* to *parks and playgrounds* in order to prevent the development of a subdivision of homes for low-income families, including Negroes. A federal-court decision in 1970, subsequently upheld by the U.S. Supreme Court, found that the Lackawanna rezoning action was for purposes of racial segregation and hence illegal.[51]

On the other hand, a 1971 U.S. Supreme Court decision in the case of San Jose, California, maintained that a public-housing project may be vetoed by voters in a community referendum as long as the issue is public housing and not race.[52] In view of the fact that public housing is generally associated with racial issues, the distinction would seem a difficult one to make. California is one of only a small number of states that require voter approval for public-housing projects. Where action is taken directly by public officials apparently for racial reasons, the Lackawanna precedent would presumably apply. The National Committee against Discrimination in Housing has announced a nationwide program of opposing racial discrimination legally.[53]

The American Civil Liberties Union Foundation has also entered the scene; it filed suit in Federal District Court in St. Louis in 1971 in what might be considered an extreme case of this type—the incorporation of an area as a suburb in order to enact zoning regulations that would keep out racially mixed moderate-income housing. Early in 1970 three organizations affiliated with the Methodist Church proposed to build a 214-unit multiple-dwelling development, Park View Heights, on a 12-acre site that they already owned in an unincorporated area of St.

Louis County. The action of the nearby white residents recapitulated a number of types of opposition that have been described here. "Neighborhood associations" in the area "held mass meetings, wrote letters to the federal government and sent a delegation to Washington" to protest against federal assistance for the development.

When HUD approval was given, after an "unusual" three-month delay, residents of the area immediately began a petition campaign to have the area, ironically long known as Black Jack, incorporated as a separate city. This was accomplished in less than two months. "One of the first official acts of the Black Jack City Council was to re-zone all the land in Black Jack in a way that would forever bar multi-family dwellings—or, indeed, any moderate income housing since each housing unit must be set on a lot of at least 10,000 square feet." [54] The Black Jack case seems even more severe than that of Deerfield; at least Deerfield was already incorporated.

The situation in the St. Louis area is typical of conditions described here generally. Between 1950 and 1970 the number of blacks in the City of St. Louis doubled, while the number of whites decreased by about half. Population increases in the suburban areas have been almost entirely white. During this same period, although the number of payroll jobs in St. Louis County increased by almost 200,000, the City of St. Louis lost 37,000 payroll jobs. Even this latter figure is deceptive, because the city lost 77,000 manufacturing jobs of the type that many blacks would be qualified for.[55] That the loss in total payroll jobs was not as great as this indicates that some service and business-professional jobs were created in the city during the period. Some of these positions are very likely filled by whites living in and around Black Jack.

Whites generally, like those in Black Jack, assert that their opposition to low-cost housing is based on social and economic considerations rather than on race. This is very likely so. Matters of life style associated with social class, regardless of race, are important to many people. Here again is the situation where even if opposition is not based on race it just as well might be, if its effect is to keep blacks out of many suburbs.

It should be added that even residence by blacks in suburban areas is not necessarily an indication of decreased residential segregation. In Philadelphia, for example, two-thirds of the black suburbanites "live in all-black enclaves not too different from the inner city." [56] The 1970 census found that although there was a large increase in the number of white suburbanites during the 1960s, the increase of blacks in the suburbs of the nation's large cities was only "modest." [57] As part of this increase took place in all-black suburban areas, the contribution to desegregation by the movement of blacks to the suburbs in the 1960s was minimal.

Many of the quasi-institutional means discussed have been used primarily in new suburban housing developments. While the institution-alized means of the real-estate broker and lending agencies have helped maintain segregation in areas of existing housing, the quasi-institutional devices have done the job in new areas. Because the latter are more varied, less obvious, and not always clearly illegal, they are much harder to combat, with the result that good suburban housing is particularly difficult for the black to obtain. Abrams observed: "By 1954 a minority family was still not free to settle where it was unwelcome. The devices used to keep it out were still ample and the community bias was still strong." [58] In 1960 McEntire concluded: "Segregation is nowhere more complete than in the new subdivisions where the initial occupancy of whole areas is controlled by private builders." [59] In 1968 the National Advisory Commission on Civil Disorders, after noting a heavy move-ment of whites to the suburbs, reported regarding blacks: "Discrimina-tion prevents access to many nonslum areas, particularly the suburbs. . . ." [60] One can hardly maintain that the reduction of residential racial discrimination is proceeding at breakneck speed. Indeed the situation is little different from that observed by the Chicago Commission on Race Relations a half-century earlier when, regarding new subdivisions, it stated: "Almost without exception these sections are exclusively for whites, and usually it is so stated in the prospectus." [61]

INFORMAL MEANS

There are some ways in which segregation may be maintained that do not involve the use of laws or written agreements, organized groups, or formal action by governmental units. Such methods rely on informal social pressures on either blacks or whites, with sanctions ranging all the way from simple social disapproval or rejection to physical violence. Included in rejection is avoidance of the minority group through moving away. In the early 1940s Myrdal considered that "*informal* social pressure from the whites" was probably "the chief force maintaining residential segregation of Negroes." He noted: "Few white property owners in white neighborhoods would ever consider selling or renting to Negroes; and even if a few Negro families did succeed in getting a foothold, they would be made to feel the spontaneous hatred of the whites both socially and physically." [62] He believed that the main reason why this in itself did not keep Negroes from moving into white areas was the tremendous need for housing generated by overcrowding in the ghetto.

Myrdal's observations were reaffirmed 15 years later by McEntire:

"In most all-white neighborhoods, to sell or rent to a nonwhite would be considered a serious offense to the neighborhood. An owner, consequently, who is considerate of his neighbors or who values their good opinion would not wish to introduce a nonwhite into the neighborhood." [63] As did Myrdal, McEntire pointed out some exceptions in which individuals did not identify with their neighbors and so were unlikely to be influenced by their opinions, or even in which they sold to a black in order to spite their neighbors. Financial pressures caused by a need to sell and inability to find a white buyer (possibly in a "threatened" area where a white cannot obtain financing) may also be a factor.

In addition, there are cases in which refusal to sell to a black would be determined not by a concern for what the neighbors would think, but by the individual's own racial attitudes. An extreme case of this is a person who said: "I'm not prejudiced, but I'd burn this building down before I'd sell it to any damned nigger." [64] (One wonders what the respondent would do if he *were* prejudiced.)

Both because the white owner leaves the neighborhood and hence is no longer readily accessible, and because the Negro has traditionally been defined as a suitable victim, the black resident in a white area is more likely to receive the bulk of the animosity resulting from the change in racial occupancy. Harassment of blacks moving into white areas by threatening them (including the children), damaging the property, forming crowds to interfere with their moving in, and annoying them in more or less serious ways afterwards is reported over and over again.

One drastic means which has been used from at least the time of World War I has been the attempted destruction of the building and possible injury to its residents through bombing. There were 58 bomb explosions related to the expansion of the Chicago Black Belt between July 1, 1917, and March 1, 1921—an average of approximately one bombing every three weeks over a period of more than three-and-a-half years—with a result of two blacks killed, a number of both blacks and whites injured, and over $100,000 in property damage. [65]

Amid protests by Negro newspapers, bombings continued into the 1920s—one Negro Baptist church was bombed repeatedly in 1925—but they gradually tapered off as restrictive covenants took over the job of fighting the expansion of the Black Belt. The tradition remained, however, to be reactivated during World War II, when white Chicagoans bombed homes of their black neighbors at the same time that other Americans were bombing the cities of Nazi Germany. In June 1945 the Chicago *Defender* reported that 30 homes of Negroes had been attacked in preceding months by stoning, bombing, or burning. As earlier, the police seemed unable to stop the destruction or to capture those who committed the acts. [66]

Black occupancy of a home in a white area has sometimes led to the assemblage of mobs, frequently destructive in stoning or setting fire to the house, and sometimes to actual race riots. One such incident in Detroit in 1926 attracted considerable publicity when a new black resident, Dr. Ossian Sweet, shot a member of a white mob and was tried for murder. Clarence Darrow, the famed attorney, defended him and he was acquitted.[67] In Cicero, Illinois, in July 1951 Governor Adlai Stevenson finally had to declare martial law as a white mob of up to 4,000 rioted for four days, attacking an apartment house in which a Negro veteran had rented a unit. "Flares, bricks, and burning torches were thrown into the $100,000 apartment house; radiators and walls ripped out; furniture was thrown from windows, and trees were torn up by the roots as the mob cheered. Policemen joked with the mobsters as though it were a prank." [68]

When a few black families moved into a "white" *public*-housing project in Chicago in 1953 "a virtually continuous riot lasting more than three years" began, which at times required the services of more than a thousand policemen. Crowds threatened the first black family to move into Levittown, Pennsylvania, throwing stones and making noise at night so that the family could not sleep.[69]

The Commission on Civil Disorders reported harassment of black families during the 1960s, mentioning such additional tactics as throwing garbage on the lawn, making threatening phone calls, and the burning of crosses in yards.[70] In 1967 the home of a 61-year-old black in predominantly white Cleveland Heights, Ohio, was blasted with a time bomb containing 15 sticks of dynamite. In 1968 a racially mixed couple was forced out of the Detroit, Michigan, suburb of Warren by continual harassment. Crowds gathered in front of their house when they moved in, throwing bricks through the windows. Their eight-year-old daughter was called names, and the word "niggers" was painted on their garage. After a year of this they concluded that "there's just no chance for us in this neighborhood." [71] Warren was subsequently described by columnist Clayton Fritchey in 1970 as "America's most celebrated, blue-collar, hard-hat, lily white working class suburb . . . a community of 180,000 in the shadow of Detroit, now in the limelight because of its angry resistance to administration efforts to reduce segregated suburban housing." [72]

Also in 1968 the only Negro family in Dearborn, Michigan—a Detroit suburb of over 100,000—decided to move out. The newspaper report quoted the father as saying that he moved there originally so that he could give his children "a better education and a better place to live." Instead, he found that his children, ranging in age from 6 to 16, were constantly harassed by other children. He also claimed that school personnel did not accept them, adding: "I want to get the children out before they get hurt too bad, I can fight on any level, but these children are too young to tell what it's all about." [73]

That Dearborn, Michigan, should thus be all-white in 1968 is interesting in view of the fact that 20 years earlier its mayor, Orville Hubbard, campaigned for re-election openly on the racial issue, claiming that he had kept Negroes out of Dearborn. By 1971 Hubbard had served as mayor for 29 years. He was elected to his 13th term by 87 percent of the vote and was quoted as saying, "I have nothing against Negroes," although he "doesn't believe in integration." [74] His successive re-elections indicate that he has had the solid support of the Dearborn citizenry.

Whites who have aided integration have not been immune to danger and harassment. The home in Cleveland Heights, Ohio, mentioned just above was also bombed when it was occupied by a white who was active in Fair Housing, Inc., in Cleveland. The white who sold his home in Levittown, Pennsylvania, to the first black was fired from his job. In 1949 when a white, Jewish, labor organizer had some Negro labor representatives visit him at his home in Chicago the rumor spread that he was selling it to blacks and crowds of up to 2,000 people attacked the house and roamed the area for days beating up Jews.[75] Helper found some realtors who reported being threatened with personal or economic damage if they handled sales to blacks in white areas, a continuation of the tradition evident in Chicago by 1920 of threatening and bombing offices and property of white realtors who dealt with blacks.[76] In 1966 when the neighbors of a white owner of a $45,000 home in the New York City area thought he would sell it to a Negro, one told him, "I can't be responsible for what another person would do to your children." [77]

As McEntire pointed out, violent episodes resulting from a black moving into a white area are relatively infrequent. "But terror, to be effective, does not need to touch every individual directly." [78] Even if the black person can surmount the institutional and quasi-institutional barriers to nonghetto residence, he still faces the question of the effect his move will have in the neighborhood. Will it start a riot? Will his furniture be damaged while it is being moved in? Will crowds attack his house? Will he be awakened constantly by middle-of-the-night phone calls? Will his wife and children be safe? Or even if it is only a matter of bearing the insults and jeers of neighbors and of cleaning up garbage thrown on his lawn, is the move worth it? The writer knew a very well educated professional man who was black and who needed more adequate housing. He had a chance to buy a home in a white suburb of St. Paul, but finally decided against it because he and his family were not prepared to subject themselves to the abuse that was sure to result from such pioneering. They remained in a cramped apartment in a ghetto area.

If all else fails, the white has still another weapon with which to maintain segregation—the time-hallowed practice of withdrawal. It was noted earlier that this was the way the native whites of the mid-19th century met the influx of Irish immigrants; they simply moved away into areas accessible only to those with superior economic resources. Since then, withdrawal has been regularly employed against both immigrants and blacks. In Harlem, at about the time of World War I, whites "fled as from a deluge." [79] McEntire commented that: "Often, in the past, the anxiety of whites to get away has resembled a panic, with everyone trying to leave as quickly as possible." [80] The Commission on Civil Disorders discussed the continuing withdrawal of whites, terming it "white flight." Because of "massive racial transition" at the edges of Negro neighborhoods, whites leave and blacks take over, frequently with the encouragement of blockbusters, with segregation remaining as pronounced as before. Furthermore, because many whites flee to the suburbs which tend to be the "purest" white for reasons discussed earlier, residential segregation can tend to become even more complete. [81]

With such a variety of institutional, quasi-institutional, and informal means all working toward the maintenance of restrictive residential segregation, it is no surprise that the condition continues.

---

1. Rose Helper, *Racial Policies and Practices of Real Estate Brokers* (Minneapolis: University of Minnesota Press, 1969), p. 117.

2. *Ibid.*, pp. 124–40.

3. U.S. Civil Rights Commission, *Federal Civil Rights Enforcement Effort* (Washington, D.C.: Government Printing Office, 1971), p. 141.

4. Norris Vitchek, "Confessions of a Block-Buster," *Saturday Evening Post,* July 1962, p. 18.

5. St. Clair Drake and Horace R. Cayton, *Black Metropolis* (New York: Harper Torchbook, Harper & Row, Publishers, 1962), p. 62.

6. Vitchek, "Confessions of a Block-Buster," p. 16.

7. Ralph Bass, "Prejudice Won't Make Us Sell Our House," *Coronet,* July 1959, pp. 103–7.

8. *Milwaukee Journal,* April 28, 1968.

9. Reginald G. Damerell, *Triumph in a White Suburb* (New York: William Morrow & Co., Inc., 1968), p. 38.

10. Bass, "Prejudice," p. 104.

11. U.S. Civil Rights Commission, *A Time to Listen . . . A Time to Act* (Washington, D.C.: Government Printing Office, 1967), p. 74; Vitchek, "Block-Buster," p. 16; Damerell, *White Suburb,* p. 37.

12. Damerell, *White Suburb,* p. 37

13. Bass, "Prejudice," p. 103.

14. Vitchek, "Block-Buster," p. 16.

15. Damerell, *White Suburb*, p. 38; Bass, "Prejudice," p. 104.
16. Vitchek, "Block-Buster," pp. 16–17.
17. James L. Hecht, *Because It Is Right* (Boston: Little, Brown and Company, 1970), p. 61.
18. Damerell, *White Suburb*, pp. 160–61.
19. *Ibid.*, p. 161.
20. *Ibid.*, p. 37.
21. Vitchek, "Block-Buster," p. 16.
22. *Ibid.*
23. Davis McEntire, *Residence and Race* (Berkeley and Los Angeles: University of California Press, 1960), p. 226.
24. Allon Schoener, ed., *Harlem on My Mind* (New York: Random House, Inc., 1968), p. 22.
25. Roi Ottley and William J. Weatherby, eds., *The Negro in New York* (New York: The New York Public Library; Dobbs Ferry, N.Y.: Oceana Publications, Inc., 1967), p. 186.
26. Damerell, *White Suburb*, pp. 46–51; Helper, *Real Estate Brokers*, p. 141.
27. *Milwaukee Journal*, April 28, 1968.
28. Helper, *Real Estate Brokers*, p. 141.
29. Gilbert Osofsky, *Harlem: The Making of a Ghetto* (New York: Harper Torchbooks, 1968; copyright © Harper & Row, Publishers, 1963), p. 105.
30. Chicago Commission on Race Relations, *The Negro in Chicago* (Chicago: University of Chicago Press, 1922; reprinted by Arno Press, Inc., New York, 1968), p. 119.
31. Vitchek, "Block-Buster," p. 16; Urban America, Inc., and The Urban Coalition, *One Year Later* (New York: Praeger Publishers, Inc., 1969), p. 112.
32. Osofsky, *Harlem*, pp. 106–7.
33. Schoener, *Harlem on My Mind*, p. 25.
34. Damerell, *White Suburb*, p. 21.
35. Fred P. Graham, "Black Crime: The Lawless Image," *Harper's Magazine*, CCXLI, No. 1444 (September 1970), 71.
36. Chicago Commission, *The Negro in Chicago*, pp. 116–19.
37. *Ibid.*, pp. 121–22.
38. Robert C. Weaver, *The Negro Ghetto* (New York: Harcourt Brace Jovanovich, Inc., 1948), p. 253.
39. Charles Abrams, *Forbidden Neighbors* (New York: Harper & Row, Publishers, 1955), pp. 224–25.
40. *Ibid.*, p. 225.
41. *Milwaukee Journal*, August 22, 1965, Part 7, p. 1.
42. Damerell, *White Suburb*, p. 346.
43. U.S. Civil Rights Commission, *Housing* (Washington, D.C.: Government Printing Office, 1961), p. 126.
44. Stuart L. Hills, *Crime, Power, and Morality* (Scranton, Pa.: Chandler Publishing Company, 1971), p. 111.

45. Damerell, *White Suburb*, p. 60.
46. Marvin Bressler, "The Myers' Case: An Instance of Successful Racial Invasion," *Social Problems*, Fall 1960, pp. 126–42.
47. Abrams, *Forbidden Neighbors*, p. 226.
48. *Time* magazine, March 15, 1971, p. 16.
49. Harry M. Rosen and David H. Rosen, *But Not Next Door* (New York: Ivan Obolensky, Inc., 1962).
50. Abrams, *Forbidden Neighbors*, pp. 101–2.
51. *City*, June 1969, p. 18; *Time* magazine, September 7, 1970, p. 51.
52. AP dispatch, Toledo *Blade*, April 26, 1971.
53. *City*, June 1969, p. 18.
54. *Civil Liberties*, February 1971, pp. 1, 4; The Justice Department also filed suit later in 1971. See *Time* magazine, June 28, 1971, p. 25.
55. *Civil Liberties*, February 1971, p. 4.
56. *City*, January–February 1971, p. 40.
57. U.S. Census Bureau News Release, Washington, D.C., February 10, 1971.
58. Abrams, *Forbidden Neighbors*, p. 226.
59. McEntire, *Residence and Race*, p. 75.
60. *Report of the National Advisory Commission on Civil Disorders* (Washington, D.C.: Government Printing Office, 1968), p. 259.
61. Chicago Commission, *The Negro in Chicago*, p. 116.
62. Gunnar Myrdal (with the assistance of Arnold Rose and Richard Sterner), *An American Dilemma* (New York: Harper & Row, Publishers, 1944), p. 622.
63. McEntire, *Residence and Race*, p. 74.
64. Drake and Cayton, *Black Metropolis*, p. 188.
65. Chicago Commission, *The Negro in Chicago*, pp. 122 ff.
66. Drake and Cayton, *Black Metropolis*, pp. 79 and 213.
67. Weaver, *The Negro Ghetto*, p. 240.
68. Abrams, *Forbidden Neighbors*, p. 103.
69. McEntire, *Residence and Race*, p. 76.
70. *Report of the National Advisory Commission on Civil Disorders*, p. 119.
71. AP dispatches in *Milwaukee Journal*, May 15, 1967, and summer of 1968 (exact date uncertain).
72. Clayton Fritchey, syndicated column, August 27, 1970.
73. AP dispatch in *Milwaukee Journal*, June 10, 1968.
74. *Ibid.;* also see Abrams, *Forbidden Neighbors*, p. 100.
75. Abrams, *Forbidden Neighbors*, p. 107.
76. Helper, *Real Estate Brokers*, pp. 155–60; Chicago Commission, *The Negro in Chicago*, p. 123.
77. Damerell, *White Suburb*, p. 346.
78. McEntire, *Residence and Race*, p. 76.
79. Ottley and Weatherby, *The Negro in New York*, p. 185.
80. McEntire, *Residence and Race*, p. 77.
81. *Report of the National Advisory Commission on Civil Disorders*, pp. 119–20.

7 | The Slum

We have commented earlier on the tendency of the nonghetto native white to resist having neighbors with ghetto characteristics because he tends to equate slum and ghetto and associated ghetto social pathology —crime, vice, sexual irregularities, juvenile delinquency, and so forth —with those whose appearance or behavior suggests the ghetto to him. Here the distinction between slum and ghetto is an important one. Social pathology is not a basic problem of the ghetto as a whole but of its *slum* portion. A stable, responsible, middle-class family from the ghetto would probably be rejected because of a failure to distinguish between it and a possibly seriously deviant slum family.

Problems of the slum tend to be of two types: (1) poor quality housing facilities and factors directly associated with level of housing and (2) problems of social pathology common in slum areas that are not directly due to housing itself but to social and economic characteristics of people who live in slums. This chapter will concentrate on slum housing.

Some of the factors that determine housing quality in this context should be specified. Age in itself is not important. Some buildings a century or more old offer excellent housing; other buildings may be slums practically from the time they are built. Also unimportant for our purposes are status symbols such as walnut paneling and crystal chandeliers. Rather, our concern is with the factors that make a dwelling a safe, healthful, and comfortable place in which to live. Whatever problems nonslum residents may have, their housing does not automatically add an additional burden as slum housing does for its residents. Adequacy must be judged according to the knowledge and standards of the time, however, so that housing of a hundred years ago could not be faulted for failing to provide electricity. But as water closets were used in the ancient world and as garbage may be carried away by horse and wagon as well as by truck, inadequate sanitary provisions in the past were not due to lack of knowledge within the culture. Thus, mid-19th-century housing for the Irish in Boston that provided absolutely no toilet facilities for its residents and permitted its garbage to "decay at its leisure" was clearly inadequate and a threat to the health of those

who tried to live in it.¹ Window-making being an ancient art, a room
that did not provide its benefits could be considered inadequate even by
the standards of thousands of years ago.

Slum housing, then, is inadequate housing that adversely affects the
health, safety, and living conditions of those who live in it—in short,
undesirable housing. Because slum housing is used only by those who
have no alternative, slum areas tend to be inhabited by those at the
bottom of the social structure. The slum resident finds that in addition
to the difficulties that have resulted in his being forced to live in slums
in the first place, there are others that are the result of the inadequacy
of the housing itself and the nature of the slum neighborhood. The slum,
then, may be considered as inadequate housing inhabited primarily by
people who for economic reasons cannot live elsewhere.²

The term slum does not necessarily refer to any certain type or style
of building. At one time or another slums have included a six-story brick
tenement in New York, a two-and-a-half story frame structure in
Chicago, a converted warehouse in Boston, a former mansion in Milwaukee, an expensive apartment building in Cleveland, a single family
shack in Pittsburgh—the common element uniting them all being the
inadequate housing provided to their luckless inhabitants—whether
Negroes, American Indians, native whites "down on their luck," European immigrants, Spanish-Americans, or hillbillies. Whatever the type
of building and whoever the inhabitants, slums tend to have a logically
and operationally interrelated set of characteristics.

These characteristics will be discussed in more general terms than
those of the recent black ghetto; the slum has had a long history of
inflicting itself upon the hapless people who are forced to turn to it
seeking shelter but who frequently find instead damaged, even shortened,
lives. Comparisons will be made to earlier slums to show that the
modern black ghetto-slum is the way it is because it is a slum, not because it is black. For well over a century in America and for much
longer in Europe, poor newcomers to the city have found the slum
waiting for them, only to discover that its open arms were not the
ones of a sheltering parent but those of a consuming monster. In
describing the slum we are describing a pattern that was firmly established well before the Great Migration of blacks and that has yielded
no more to meet their needs than it did for their predecessors. Because
of the overlap of slum and ghetto areas, an understanding of the slum
is vital to an understanding of the ghetto. Part of this understanding
lies in a realization of the toughness and durability of the slum.

HIGH RENTS

Let us start with the paradox that despite the poverty of the tenants and the low level of accommodation provided, rents for slum housing are high. This is nothing new to the Western world; even the poor who lived in the tenements of ancient Rome had to pay "extortionate rents to merciless landlords." [3] During the medieval period cities were not large enough to have slums, but beginning in the 16th century, as a result of in-migration to the cities, "the ground rents rose and living conditions worsened." [4]

Concerning the mid-19th century Irish in Boston, Handlin judged: "Immigrant rents were everywhere high beyond all reason." [5] In New York City renters protested in newspapers and mass meetings.[6] A New York State legislature investigation learned that rents "in the worst slums of the lower wards" were higher by 25 percent or more than housing in better areas.[7] The situation appeared to be little different some 40 years later at the turn of the century.[8] Studies in Chicago in 1888 and in the early 1900s had similar findings; the newest immigrants were the most exploited. "They have paid the highest rents for the poorest apartments." [9]

Blacks encountered the same situation, but in even more severe form. Riis wrote of the 1880s that the Negro "has always had to pay higher rents than even [the Italians and Polish Jews] for the poorest and most stinted rooms." [10] In 1900 he observed: "The old robbery still goes on . . . he pays more rent than his white neighbor next door, and is a better tenant." [11] Meanwhile, a group that investigated housing in New York City arrived at the same conclusion.[12] DuBois made a similar discovery about Philadelphia.[13]

In Chicago blacks paid premium rents even before the Great Migration; landlords were able to take advantage of the demand for housing in Negro areas "to raise rents and postpone repairs." [14] Studies in Chicago during the World War I decade generally indicated that South Side rents were "excessive, considering the inferior dwellings." [15] In both New York and Chicago there were instances of whites being evicted from apartments so they could be rented to blacks for more money. Both blacks and whites circulated petitions of protest, the blacks complaining of high rents and the whites, as they did not mind having Negro neighbors, objecting to being forced to move. White resentment at being evicted tended to be directed towards the blacks as the "cause." Higher rents for blacks in Harlem continued during both the prosperity of the 1920s and the depression of the 1930s, as they also did in Chicago.[16]

Drake and Cayton commented on high rents in Chicago during World War II [17] and Weaver cited a case in which a real-estate agent collected in rents each year more than twice what he had originally paid for the building. In another instance a two-room apartment with shared kitchen and bath in the Black Belt was found to be renting for more than the mayor of Chicago was paying for a Gold Coast apartment.[18] Duncan and Duncan reported more recently that "Negroes pay higher rents for a given quality of housing than whites," and that "non-whites get less desirable housing for a given rent than do whites." [19] Chicago is not unique. Lee and Humphrey concluded that one of the causes of the 1943 Detroit race riot was that blacks were being charged more than whites for comparable housing.[20]

The 1968 Report of the National Advisory Commission on Civil Disorders presented evidence showing that the ancient practice of charging high rents for poor quality housing continued into the 1960s. Two types of rental pattern were noted by the Commission: "Negroes in large cities are often forced to pay the same rents as whites and receive less for their money, or pay higher rents for the same accommodations." The Commission referred to the higher rents paid by Negroes as a "color tax" on housing and estimated it to be well over 10 percent.[21] Such a "tax" of course falls on those least able to pay it, and it has continued into the 1970s.[22]

CROWDING

Crowding may occur as a result either of herding more people into each dwelling unit or of increasing the number of dwelling units in a building by subdividing its original rooms or apartments into smaller units—thus creating more units per building. Frequently the methods are used together, and the result is high population density per unit, per building, and per neighborhood.

Subdividing of units and buildings, like high rents, has a long history; it existed in ancient Rome, where "profiteering landlords . . . learned how to subdivide old quarters into even narrower cells to accommodate even poorer artisans. . . ." [23] The practice quickly returned with the rise of cities after the Renaissance; a report of the Lords of the Council of London recognized the problems resulting from "dividing up single houses meant to house a single family" in 1583.[24] Subdividing of old single-family houses to make units for immigrants was practiced in American cities even in the 18th century.[25] The mid-19th-century Irish were similarly confronted with housing units created by subdividing "old mansions and disused warehouses." [26] An 1857 investigation of housing in New York City found: "Large rooms were partitioned into several smaller ones, without regard to light or ventilation." [27]

As the reader may suspect, the same practices continued for the benefit of the turn-of-the-century new immigration. Handlin commented: "The immigrants find their first homes in quarters the old occupants no longer desire. . . . The carpenters hammer shut connecting doors and build rude partitions up across the halls." [28] Middle-class single-family homes thus became apartment houses holding many families. In some cases the partitions were not even walls but "mere boards and curtains" separating several families in one large room.[29] By means of "remodeling," a house in New Haven was increased in occupancy from one native family of 3 persons to five Italian families with a total of 30.[30] One New York City block was reported to contain 492 families, while Philadelphia, accused by Steiner of having the "most unwholesome tenements," had an instance of "thirty families numbering 123 persons occupying thirty-four rooms." [31]

Blacks similarly became subject to crowding through this practice of creating dwelling units by subdividing.[32] During the 1920s and 1930s: "For Negroes, large flats were cut up into small family units, with existing bath facilities serving a number of families in common. Beaverboard partitions were common; closets were converted into kitchens, and living and sleeping space merged." [33] The resulting "kitchenette" apartments were quite profitable for the building owner, who "could increase his income substantially by renting 'kitchenettes' to six or seven families rather than leasing flats to two families." [34] Many of the units created then are probably still in use. That the subdividing of buildings has continued into recent years is indicated by reports of both the United States Civil Rights Commission and the Advisory Commission on Civil Disorders. The report of the latter mentions both the profitability for landlords in creating more units and obtaining denser occupancy this way, and the consequent increased deterioration of buildings from heavier usage.[35]

Subdividing results in smaller-sized dwelling units and more people living in each building. The other way in which population density increases is through the crowding of more people into each room or dwelling unit. Poverty plays an important role. Whether out of a feeling of obligation to help poor kin or countrymen, or a need to add to a meager income, or out of some combination of the two, the tendency of slum families to take in others is remarkable. Given the poor quality of the typical slum dwelling unit to start with, asking that it house additional people makes its inadequacy all the greater.

The taking in of lodgers was very commonly reported among the new immigrants. An 1895 *Harper's Weekly* article about immigrants in New York City said: "Single families, inhabiting one or more rooms, generally [have] a family as sub-tenants, or a number of lodgers or boarders." [36] Handlin estimated that more than half of the immigrant families in New York City took in lodgers.[37] Fairchild considered lodgers to be "the rule rather than the exception." [38] Thomas and Znaniecki reported on the tendency of married Polish couples to take in other Poles as roomers or boarders.[39] Jane Addams wrote of "the inevitable boarders crowded into a dark tenement already too small for the use of the immigrant family occupying it." [40]

Lodgers were common to Negro slum dwellers, too. In the late 19th century DuBois observed: "The practice of sub-renting is found of course in all degrees." [41] The Chicago Commission on Race Relations considered lodgers to be "one of the most conspicuous problems in the Negro housing situation." [42] Almost 20 years later the Chicago Black Belt still showed extensive "doubling up." [43] Still more recently Duncan and Duncan concluded: "To compete more effectively with whites in a restricted housing market, Negro families are led to improvise irregular living arrangements—doubling up of families, keeping of lodgers, pooling of incomes of relatives to meet high rents." [44] Regarding Harlem in the 1960s Clark said simply: "There are more people in fewer rooms than elsewhere in the city." [45]

The extreme of crowding is reached when a bed is used in "shifts" by different people. Osofsky refers to this as the "repeating" or "hotbed" system and notes it was found in Harlem in the early 1920s.[46] It continued into the 30s, when "lucky families" could find people who would pay for the chance to occupy the "same bed, same sheets, and be bitten by the same bugs." [47] The system was also practiced in Chicago, where it was similarly attributed to economic pressures on poor families.[48] Such practices result from the nature of slums and not from the race of their occupants, as is shown by the fact that the hot-bed system has also been reported for European immigrants.[49]

The combination of subdivision and the taking in of lodgers necessarily results in high population densities for slum areas. One hundred years after the Irish made Boston's North End the most densely settled area of the city, Firey found that this "physically deteriorated" area was "by far the most congested residential quarter of Boston," with a density three times higher than the next most densely settled area.[50] But by the latter time the crowded ones were Italians rather than Irish. The same indications of high densities have been found in Negro slums. Regarding the "piling-up tracts"—the Negro ghetto areas most solidly black and thus the oldest areas with the poorest housing—Duncan and Duncan found that gross population density in Chicago increased between 1940 and 1950 by more than 7,000 persons per square mile, with no appreciable increase in the number of dwelling units.[51] At the beginning of the 1970s population density in black slum areas was considerably higher than that in middle-class urban areas, and 100 times greater than in the suburbs.[52]

MAINTENANCE

The slum also has a long history of inadequate maintenance of its buildings by their owners, the same ones who collect the high rents discussed earlier. Mumford notes that in ancient Rome Crassus made a fortune by buying up old buildings and renting them out with "meager repairs." [53] Descriptions of American slums have a startling degree of similarity, whether they are of those of the Irish around 1850, the new immigration around 1900, or the blacks in more recent years:

Mid-19th-century housing for Boston Irish:

> Rooms were unpainted; closets were rare. . . . Walls were damp, roofs leaked. Stairs were generally dilapidated, windows were often broken, and many buildings had not felt the hand of the repair man in ten or more years.[54]

Immigrant housing in Pittsburgh in 1914:

> Some of the conditions we found were as bad as could be imagined. . . . leaky roofs causing the walls and ceilings to become watersoaked, rendering the rooms damp and unhealthy; broken and worn floors; broken stair railings and worn and broken treads; plaster broken and paper torn and dirty.[55]

Chicago Black Belt slums in the 1930s:

> Housing conditions [were] so wretched as to be unfit for Chicago homes in the twentieth century . . . no attempt has been made to keep these tenements in any sort of repair. For the most part, they are frame houses, unpainted and grimy. Numerous windows have been broken and not replaced. . . . Broken doors and doorways, unsteady flooring, and general dilapidation were met by the investigators on every side.[56]

The author of the last quotation judged that the South Side area would "continue to deteriorate steadily with the passage of time." [57] But if the housing was so bad, could not the tenants have moved out and gone elsewhere? For the slum resident, white or black, there is no elsewhere except another slum with deficiencies undoubtedly equal to those of his present one. In the New York City immigrant slums: "The complaint was universal among the tenants that they were entirely uncared for, and

that the only answer to their requests to have the place put in order
by repairs was that they must pay their rent or leave." [58] Negro tenants
later in Chicago encountered the same "pay your rent or leave" philosophy, reporting that "they found it impossible to persuade their landlords either to make the necessary repairs or to release them from their
contracts." [59] They had the choice of spending their own scarce money
on the repairs or enduring the existing conditions.

Osofsky wrote of Harlem in the 1920s: "Some landlords, after opening houses to Negro tenants, lost interest in caring for their property and
permitted it to run down—halls were left dark and dirty, broken pipes
were permitted to rot, steam heat was cut off as heating apparatus wore
out." [60] The same process was documented for Cleveland in a 1967
Civil Rights Commission report. One woman testified about being one
of the first blacks to move into a good, well-maintained apartment
building. At first there were two families of custodians who worked on
shifts during the day and night to keep up the building. "They kept it
very clean . . . it was a fabulous apartment, they really kept it up."
As the number of blacks increased the quality of maintenance declined.
The two custodian families were replaced with only one family "and they
stopped keeping it up. It just went down, down until it was . . .
dilapidated." [61] Tenants, both immigrant and black, have frequently
been blamed for deterioration in buildings, but in this case it is evident
there was a decline in the maintenance provided. Riis observed, regarding a Jewish tenement area more than a half-century earlier, that the
landlord "spends nothing for repairs and lays the blame on the tenant." [62]

A case illustrating the end result of this process was given in a 1968
Life magazine article that described the situation faced by one Harlem
family:

> The whole building's crawling with roaches and rats. The plaster is
> falling down. . . . The heat had gone off the night before and three
> [goldfish] were floating on the surface, dead from the cold. 'Fishies
> dead, fishies dead,' [three-year-old Richard] kept mumbling. . . .
> 'The landlord looks and promises, but nothing happens' . . . . Norman
> Jr. and Kenneth lay on their sheetless bunks, fully clothed and under
> blankets, fighting the cold and their homework.[63]

A year later America demonstrated its ability to land a man on the
moon.

Data on housing conditions from the 1960 census show that for cities
in the East-North the percentage of nonwhite-occupied housing units
classified as deteriorating or dilapidated ranged from 28 percent in
Detroit to 49 percent in Pittsburgh. Units classified as deteriorating were
not getting sufficient repair to maintain them adequately. Units are
classified as dilapidated if they do not provide safe and adequate shelter.
If dwelling units that are in sound buildings but are without full

plumbing facilities are included in the above figures, the percentages rise to a range of from 30 to 59 percent—which might be described as the percentage of nonwhites in large Northern cities living in substandard housing.[64]

In 1965 Clark commented: "Slum landlords, ready enough when the rent is due, are hard to find when repairs are demanded." [65] A black woman from Cleveland described it more prosaically to the Commission on Civil Rights: "I'll tell you when you start complaining about that particular building no one seems to want to own the building. . . . The only time anybody really wants the building is when it is time to pay the rent and after then nobody wants the building." [66]

Her problem with the absent landlord is an old one. Ernst describes how in mid-19th-century New York City the owner of a building "was assured of an income and relieved of responsibility" by turning the management of his property over to an agent who "thought in terms of risk and reimbursement, not of tenant welfare." [67] In 1903 Riis bitterly attacked absentee landlords: "They did not fail to collect the rents. . . . No, but let us give them their due—an agent collected the rents, they did not. *They* traveled abroad; perhaps they never saw the dens upon the proceeds of which they lived at their ease." [68] More than 60 years later another writer noted: "There are many cases of 'absentee' landlords who have agents which collect the rent," and then went on to say that the "most frightening danger of these crumbling tenements is fire," and that fires were so common that "only the most spectacular" were reported in the newspapers.[69] That there is a relationship between the location of the landlord and the maintenance of his buildings is indicated by a study of the Milwaukee Inner Core area. As judged by tenants, two-thirds of the landlords who lived in the building itself did "enough" to maintain and improve the property, as compared to from one-fifth to one-fourth of landlords who lived in other locations.[70]

Yet when the question of housing conditions has arisen landlords have tended to claim that the responsibility was the tenants'. An investigation by the New York State legislature in 1857 of housing conditions in New York City slums found that landlords blamed "the filthy habits of their tenants . . . for the condition of their property.[71] At about this same time, whites in Cincinnati were justifying the "deplorable" housing conditions for Negroes with the belief that "Negroes naturally lived that way." [72] Several decades later reformers were still fighting to have landlords assume more responsibility. Riis attacked the "false plea" that the Irish preferred squalid housing and argued that slum-ghetto tenants "have been shown all along to be superior to their surroundings." [73] In 1968 attorneys (both black and white) in the Gary, Indiana, Legal Department resisted taking legal action against landlords to enforce housing codes because they considered that "the root of the city's housing problem was the indolent and malicious behavior of the tenants." [74]

SANITATION

Sanitation—the adequate disposal of garbage and human waste—can be viewed both as a matter of taste or aesthetics and in terms of health and disease prevention. As the germ theory of disease was developed only in the latter part of the 19th century we cannot fault earlier periods for not recognizing that inadequate sanitation contributed to disease. Yet the fact that the mid-19th-century Boston Committee of Internal Health concerned itself with sanitation indicates some realization of a relationship between the two. [75]

In any event, the evidence shows that landlords and municipalities did not greatly bestir themselves to provide adequate sanitation for slum residents in earlier periods. Even though ancient Rome had an elaborate water and sewer system, with waterclosets in the private homes of the more well-to-do, the sewers "were not connected to the crowded tenements at all." [76] The poor could meet their needs only through the use of public toilets, which charged a fee, or pits at the bottom of stair wells. Fifteen hundred years later, crowding in 16th-century London "caused grievous sanitary difficulties." [77]

Provisions for sanitation in the slums of the 1840s and 1850s were practically nonexistent. In Boston, one privy might be expected to serve a hundred people, in addition to the casual passerby, and as responsibility for their upkeep was not fixed they were generally "a mass of pollution." [78] The same situation existed in New York, where Ernst noted that "the privies remained a constant menace to health, and their contents, instead of being drained away, frequently overflowed to the surface and created breeding places of disease." [79] Also, water for washing and bathing was inadequately supplied and garbage went uncollected, accumulating in the narrow spaces between buildings.

By the beginning of the 20th century adequate basic knowledge about the role of sanitation in disease causation and transmission had been acquired so that the new immigrants could benefit from it. Did they? A 1901 study of Chicago's immigrant tenements found defective plumbing, large numbers of privy vaults, "as well as other types of insanitary provisions," a scarcity of bathing facilities, filthy open areas, and frequent neglect of garbage. [80] Handlin saw little disadvantage in the slum housewife's simply throwing her garbage out of the window, because the wooden garbage boxes were so broken open that they easily admitted the rats who lived off of their infrequently collected contents. [81]

Of the garbage boxes in the Hull House area of Chicago, Jane Addams wrote: "The children of our neighborhood twenty years ago played their games in and around these huge garbage boxes. They were the first objects that the toddling child learned to climb." [82]

Blacks naturally fared no better. DuBois' 1899 Philadelphia study found that only one Negro family in seven had access to bathrooms and water closets, and that even these frequently were shared with other families. What bathtubs there were usually did not have hot water and often were not connected to any water supply.[83] Some 30 years after Jane Addams had won reforms in Chicago's garbage-handling procedures Abbott found in the Black Belt area that accumulations of rubbish practically blocked the passage of large vehicles and that in some places "the odor from decaying garbage, and sometimes dead rats, was almost insufferable." [84] Blacks in Harlem complained that the rats were "better fed" and "better housed" than the people.[85]

Inadequate garbage collection invariably attracts rats. Harlem rats have prospered for decades. Two-thirds of all the rat bites in New York City in 1952 occurred in Harlem. The chairman of a civic group investigating the problem attributed the prevalence of rats in Harlem to the high proportion of absentee landlords concerned only with collecting rents.[86] In the United States as a whole in 1965 it is estimated there were more than 14,000 cases of rat-bite, almost all in slum areas.[87] As rats have been perennial slum residents, it is not surprising that both immigrants and blacks have kept dogs and cats to ward them off.[88]

A 1967 report of the United States Commission on Civil Rights quotes testimony given by a resident of the Hough area in Cleveland: "I was living in one apartment, the rats got in bed with me and my sister is still living in the same building and the rats are jumping up and down. The kids they play with rats like a child would play with a dog or something. They chase them around the house and things like this." [89] A study made in Cleveland in 1962 found that 7,000 buildings had rats on the premises. Some buildings containing rats undoubtedly escaped notice. A restudy in 1966 found that "large and widespread rat populations continued to flourish in Cleveland, particularly in substandard areas." [90] A Harris poll that sampled black Americans in general in 1970 found that 29 percent said their housing contained rats, 32 percent complained of faulty plumbing, and 38 percent indicated they had cockroaches.[91]

There is a relationship between inadequate sanitation and the high population of slum areas that is produced by subdividing units and by the crowding of individual units. The presence of large numbers of people generates a need for particularly thorough sanitation measures. Giving such areas treatment equal to middle-class detached-housing areas produces inequality. While once-a-week garbage collection may be sufficient in low density suburban areas it is likely to be completely inadequate in high density slum areas. Equality in sanitation may require garbage collection every day in the slum. Similarly, heavier usage of plumbing in slum buildings would require, in order to have equality, that it be better and easier to maintain than that in suburban homes.

INFLUENCE AND MUNICIPAL SERVICES

Much less was expected of local governments in previous centuries than at present. That this was so does not offset the fact that the slum residents bore the heaviest burden as a result of the city administration's failure to see that buildings were constructed well enough so that they did not collapse, that they provided adequate means of egress in case of fire, that they offered sufficient light and ventilation, that some reasonable portion of each lot would be reserved from building so as to provide at least a slight amount of open space, and that there was adequate provision for the removal of wastes and garbage. The more well-to-do had more living space and could see that their own needs were met simply because they had enough money to protect themselves.

The slum tenants were practically helpless in their dealings with their landlords. We have already documented the "pay your rent or leave" philosophy of slum owners. The only other realistic possibility the tenants had was the local government. By the turn of the century the obligation the city had towards ameliorating slum conditions was coming to be more commonly recognized, and cities commonly enacted legislation regulating the construction or alteration of housing and provisions regarding sanitation.

Enacting legislation is one thing, however, and following through with adequate enforcement is another. Here the same poverty which has rendered slum dwellers impotent in their dealings with landlords operates to their detriment in city hall. They have lacked the money to contribute to political campaign expenses and the skills that would make them helpful campaign workers. They have had votes, but the party or machine in power would probably have helped out in enough day-to-day minor matters (helping find a job, fixing a ticket, providing money in an emergency) so that it would command the loyalty of those in the slums.[92] Furthermore, as Clinard has emphasized, not only are many slum poor unable to exert influence but they tend to have the kind of fatalistic attitude that leads to apathetic acceptance of existing conditions. They not only tend to be ineffective, they feel that they are.[93]

On the other hand, the slum landlord is automatically a "property owner" and a "taxpayer"—statuses that have always carried weight in city hall. In addition, housing supervision and enforcement require extra money, at least on a short-run basis—and additional demands on the city budget have always been unwelcome. Also relevant is the traditional view that the poor are in that condition because they deserve to be. Add to this the common belief that the old slum buildings will soon be replaced anyway and it is not hard to see why governmental action to remedy slum conditions has been neither frequent nor vigorous. Inaction has affected both black and immigrant alike.

When Hull-House residents did a study to find out the reason for the high death rate in the area they concluded: "(1) that the uncovered privy vault, supposedly outlawed in 1897, was the source of the malady, the infection being carried by the common housefly; and (2) that the Health Department was either criminally inefficient or actually corrupt." [94] Chicago enacted legislation in 1902 and 1910 that required certification by the Commissioner of Health that certain minimum construction standards and sanitation needs had been met in the construction of new buildings. Abbott reported that although more than 24,000 tenement buildings were erected during the years from 1913 to 1916, only 91 such certification permits were actually issued.[95]

Jane Addams commented about municipal services in Chicago immigrant slum areas:

> The policy of public authorities of never taking an initiative, and always waiting to be urged to do their duty, is obviously fatal in a neighborhood where there is little initiative among the citizens. . . . The streets are inexpressibly dirty, the number of schools inadequate, sanitary legislation unenforced, the street lighting bad, the paving miserable, and altogether lacking in the alleys and smaller streets, and the stables foul beyond description. Hundreds of houses are unconnected with the street sewer. The older and richer inhabitants seem anxious to move away as rapidly as they can afford it.[96]

Things have been little better for blacks. In the early 1930s investigators doing a study of Black Belt conditions "frequently had to walk along alleys that were almost impassible with mud and filth . . . refuse and garbage, and, in most cases, the accumulation was of long standing." [97] A decade later, in 1944, a Mayor's Conference still found the same problems in slum areas—the lack of building repairs and neglect of garbage disposal and street cleaning.[98] Concerning Harlem in the 1960s Clark commented about slum landlords that "even the city cannot seem to find some of them, and when they go to trial for neglect, they are usually given modest and lenient sentences—compared to Harlem teen-agers who defy the law." [99] A series of articles in the *Milwaukee Journal* in March 1968 about violations of building and health regulations in slum areas cited such cases as that of one building in which 55 violations were found. After long legal delays the owner (who was a lawyer) was "punished" by a fine of $100. This amounted to less than $2 per violation—less than the cost of a parking ticket in many a city and far less than the cost of repairs. Under these circumstances it is cheaper to pay fines than to obey the law. The one who pays the most is the tenant.

The United States Commission on Civil Rights found a similar situation in Cleveland in 1967. Although the owner of one apartment building claimed that he had attempted to correct conditions as soon as tenants complained about them, the records examined by the Commission showed that "identical recurring violations had been reported each year since 1962." [100] It was reported as of 1967 that the New York City Building Department received some 500 complaints a day about "falling plaster, holes in walls, rats, hazardous plumbing and unsanitary facilities." There, too, the fines imposed by the Housing Court cost less than the repairs, and so corrections frequently went unmade.[101]

That such practices are common is indicated by the Report of the National Advisory Commission on Civil Disorders:

> Thousands of landlords in disadvantaged neighborhoods openly violate building codes with impunity, thereby providing a constant demonstration of flagrant discrimination by legal authorities. A high proportion of residential and other structures contain numerous violations of building and housing codes. Refusal to remedy these violations is a criminal offense, one which can have grievous effects upon the victims—the tenants living in these structures. Yet in most cities, few building code violations in these areas are ever corrected, even when tenants complain directly to municipal departments.[102]

DEATH AND DISEASE

The whole complex of slum characteristics discussed so far converges to undermine the physical well-being of slum residents. Poverty and high rents contribute jointly to limiting both the quantity and quality of the diet. Subdividing and crowding bring people closer together; this, with the aid of insufficient sunlight and ventilation, facilitates the transmission of communicable diseases. Inadequate garbage removal increases the population of rats and flies, and unsanitary plumbing adds another hazard. Poverty and lack of social status also result in inadequate care for those who need medical attention. These conditions make it natural that slum residents have higher rates of illness and mortality than others.

Poverty, inadequate housing, and disease are as old as immigration to America. The Pilgrims, in 1620, certainly experienced poverty and had poor quality overcrowded housing in the New World, and half of them died during the first winter.[103] Eighteenth-century immigrants appeared to fare little better. Concerning a yellow fever epidemic in New York City in 1795, a doctor of the time wrote that the fever was most prevalent "in that district that the greatest number of the poor, especially the immigrant poor, reside." [104]

In both England and America slum areas consistently had higher incidences of disease and death. In New York City the rate of death of children during their first year of life (the infant-mortality rate) doubled between 1810 and 1870, as population density rose rapidly and medical-sanitation knowledge increased hardly at all.[105] Ernst concluded that high disease rates in New York City were "directly related to the sanitary conditions of tenement dwellers," and that the "immigrants suffered more heavily from disease than the native population was well known." [106] The situation was little different in Boston.[107] The specific diseases common in slum areas were those due to poor sanitation—typhoid, typhus, and cholera—and the respiratory diseases associated with poor housing conditions—tuberculosis, bronchitis, and pneumonia. Both natives and immigrants were limited by the same relatively primitive medical knowledge of the time, but the slum-dwelling immigrant fared by far the worse. Seventy-one families interviewed in one New York City tenement in the 1850s were able to report experiencing a total of 138 deaths in the preceding two years, practically one death per family per year.[108]

Within a few decades, in the latter part of the 19th century, a major medical revolution took place as one breakthrough followed another to lay the foundations for modern medicine and, finally, to give man the beginnings of a solution to the mystery of the cause, treatment, and prevention of disease. How much did this medical revolution benefit slum residents?

Not much, apparently. Even though most immigrants were in the prime-of-life age range, "yet they died more rapidly than the generality of Americans." [109] Mortality in the Hull-House ward in Chicago was "very heavy." [110] In one Chicago slum area three out of five babies died during their first year of life.[111] The Tenement House Committee in New York called slum dwellings "infant slaughter houses," leading Riis to comment that one could say of a dead baby that "the house killed it." [112]

Whatever its other shortcomings, the slum is highly democratic in bestowing its effects upon its residents regardless of race. Before the Civil War mortality rates of blacks in both New York and Philadelphia were high.[113] DuBois' analysis of data for Philadelphia in the 1880s showed that although the Negro death rate was half again as high as that of the white on an overall basis, both black and white death rates varied according to housing adequacy as indicated by location within the city.[114]

Since the beginning of the modern black ghetto period, studies have repeatedly documented the fact that black families in slum housing have high rates of disease and mortality. One New York City study in the 1920s showed that the death rate in Harlem was 42 percent higher than that in the city as a whole, that Harlem mothers had a death rate from childbirth twice as high as other mothers, and that the death rate of Harlem infants was also twice that of others.[115] The Negro death rate from tuberculosis was then about four times the white rate, and the pneumonia death rate was three times as high.[116] In Chicago at this period the Negro death rate was double that of the white and the Negro tuberculosis death rate was five times the white rate. The differences in rate continued into the 1930s and 1940s.[117] High tuberculosis incidence and other health problems were noted in a 1945 study in Newark, New Jersey.[118] Similarly, Washington, D.C., blacks had a tuberculosis rate five times and a maternal-mortality rate six times those of whites.[119] Depression, war, and prosperity all seemed to have little effect on life (and death) in the slums.

In the large northern cities in the early 1960s the nonwhite infant-mortality rates ranged from approximately 60 to 100 percent higher than the white rates.[120] The 1959 infant-mortality rate for central Harlem showed an *increase* over 1958 and was three times as high as that of the lowest-rate district in New York.[121] In Chicago in 1969 one black baby in 20 died during its first year.[122] This would give a mortality rate of 50—a rate higher than the U.S. nonwhite rate for 1963 and more than twice the rate for white infants.

Only recently has another health problem that affects slum children almost exclusively come to be more generally recognized. This is the ingestion of lead from the paint used in older houses. Lead was a common paint ingredient before World War II and many older houses in the "lead belts" of cities still have such paint on their walls. Children consume the lead by eating chips of paint that have flaked from the walls, putty from around windows, and plaster that has crumbled loose. A statement by the U.S. Surgeon General and a Senate hearing in the fall of 1970 revealed that an estimated 400,000 children of from one to six years old are suffering from lead poisoning, which can cause mental retardation and even death. Possibly dietary deficiencies or socio-psychological aspects of the slum environment might make slum children more likely to eat the lead-containing substances, but poor maintenance would seem to be a crucial factor. Well-maintained buildings, even old ones, would not have any loose paint, plaster, or putty available to be consumed by children.[123]

As of 1965 the maternal-mortality rate for nonwhites was four times that of whites, with the relative gap between the two having become *greater* since 1940. Life expectancy is of course shorter for nonwhites.[124] Modern life has added a new hazard to the problems of the slum dweller: a combination of crowded inadequate housing and insufficient recreation facilities leads youngsters to play on the streets, risking the heavy traffic. As a result, the death rate of children and young adults from cars and trucks in Harlem is 60 percent higher than in the city as a whole.[125]

After surveying evidence on the housing and living conditions of European immigrants in a number of Northern cities Fairchild concluded in 1916: "It is painfully evident that conditions exist on a wide scale in these centers, which are a disgrace to any civilized country. A large proportion of the lower classes of our cities are living under conditions which render self-respect, cleanliness, and even decency almost impossible." [126] One wonders how different his conclusions would be if he were able to study the conditions faced by slum dwellers more than a half-century later.

STABILITY AND CHANGE

The slum is not a casual or transitory or unnatural phenomenon but rather a stable, enduring, social institution. Writers such as Clinard and Riemer have pointed out socially and individually useful functions that the slum has performed.[127] For most people, though, its effect has been adverse, and the slum will not readily go away just because outsiders are appalled by conditions within it. Its roots are deep. Programs for dealing with housing and the slum will be discussed in a later chapter.

The material here has implications for both blacks and whites. Living conditions in the slums are what they are not because the residents are black but because slums are slums. It appears evident that such slum housing conditions as high rents, high population densities, and inadequacies in sanitation and maintenance have their effects upon the residents—who fight a losing battle trying to contend with these conditions.

Finally, there are two differences between the modern ghetto-slum and that of the past that should be mentioned. As miserable as were the living conditions of the 19th-century urban immigrants, they were not as greatly different from those of a substantial part of the American population as today's slum dwellers' are from those of modern middle-class society. In the days of the immigrant slum a much smaller part of the total population was middle-class and a much larger part was rural. The majority of Americans at that time did not have running water, indoor plumbing, automatic heat, and so forth. The *difference,* then, between the slum dweller and the "average American" was considerably less in the past than it is today. The relative deprivation of the immigrant slum dweller was less than that of today's slum residents.

In a way the second difference between past and present is related to the first; it is a matter of the *means* the slum dweller can use to compare himself to society outside the slum. In the past, as noted earlier, the immigrant was more isolated from outside society. Long hours of work, socializing mainly within his group, and the tendency to confine his reading to a foreign-language newspaper that emphasized his ethnic group limited his perspective and kept him from being as aware of outside society as in the slum dweller of the present. Television is undoubtedly of great importance in giving the present-day slum dweller a broader view of outside society than he could attain by any other single means. This includes both program content and commercials. The slum resident, child and adult alike, can sit in his slum and see in his own living room "how the other half lives." To evaluate his own situation all he has to do is turn his eyes from the screen. In this way, not only has "outside" American society pulled away from the slum dweller, it has provided him with the means to view the distance.[128]

---

1. Oscar Handlin, *Boston's Immigrants* (Cambridge, Mass.: Harvard University Press, 1959), p. 111.

2. For two recent discussions of slums, *see* Marshall B. Clinard, *Slums and Community Development* (New York: The Free Press, 1966); David R. Hunter, *The Slums: Challenge and Response* (New York: The Free Press, 1964).

3. Lewis Mumford, *The City in History* (New York: Harcourt Brace Jovanovich, Inc., 1961), p. 221.

4. Lewis Mumford, *The Culture of Cities* (New York: Harcourt Brace Jovanovich, Inc., 1938), p. 121.

5. Handlin, *Boston's Immigrants,* p. 108.

6. Robert Ernst, *Immigrant Life in New York City, 1825–1863* (Port Washington, New York: Ira J. Friedman, Inc., 1965; copyright © 1949), p. 50.

7. Francesco Cordasco, ed., *Jacob Riis Revisited* (Garden City, New York: Doubleday & Company, Inc., 1968), p. 10.

8. *Ibid.,* pp. 16, 324.

9. Edith Abbott, *The Tenements of Chicago, 1908–1935* (Chicago: University of Chicago Press, 1936), p. 135; *see also* p. 30.

10. Cordasco, *Jacob Riis Revisited,* p. 52.

11. *Ibid.,* p. 336.

12. Gilbert Osofsky, *Harlem: The Making of a Ghetto* (New York:

Harper Torchbooks, 1968; copyright © Harper & Row, Publishers, 1963), p. 13.

13. W. E. B. DuBois, *The Philadelphia Negro* (1899; reprint ed., New York: Benjamin Blom, Inc., 1967), p. 295.

14. Chicago Commission on Race Relations, *The Negro in Chicago* (Chicago: University of Chicago Press, 1922; reprinted by Arno Press, Inc., New York, 1968), pp. 199–200.

15. *Ibid.,* p. 203.

16. Allon Schoener, ed., *Harlem on My Mind* (New York: Random House, Inc., 1968), pp. 27–28, 51, 136; Abbott, *The Tenements of Chicago,* pp. 124, 274, 282, 295–96; Weaver, *The Negro Ghetto* (New York: Harcourt Brace Jovanovich, Inc., 1948), p. 119.

17. St. Clair Drake and Horace R. Cayton, *Black Metropolis* (New York: Harper Torchbook, Harper & Row, Publishers, 1962), p. 207.

18. Robert C. Weaver, *The Negro Ghetto,* p. 104.

19. Otis Dudley Duncan and Beverly Duncan, *The Negro Population of Chicago* (Chicago: University of Chicago Press, 1957), pp. 9, 81.

20. Alfred McClung Lee and Norman Daymond Humphrey, *Race Riot* (New York: Dryden Press, 1943), p. 91.

21. Report of the National Advisory Commission on Civil Disorders (Washington, D.C.: Government Printing Office, 1968), pp. 258–59.

22. *Time* magazine, April 6, 1970, p. 53.

23. Lewis Mumford, *The City in History* (New York: Harcourt Brace Jovanovich, Inc., 1967), pp. 219–20.

24. Lewis Mumford, *The Culture of Cities* (New York: Harcourt Brace Jovanovich, Inc., 1938), p. 123.

25. Clinard, *Slums,* p. 32.

26. Handlin, *Boston's Immigrants,* p. 101; Ernst, *Immigrant Life,* p. 48.

27. Quoted in Cordasco, *Jacob Riis Revisited,* p. 8.

28. Oscar Handlin, *The Uprooted* (New York: Grosset & Dunlap, Inc., 1951), pp. 146–47.

29. Abbott, *The Tenements of Chicago,* p. 28.

30. Peter Roberts, *The New Immigration* (New York: The Macmillan Company, 1912), p. 161.

31. Edward A. Steiner, *On the Trail of the Immigrant* (New York: Fleming H. Revell Company, 1906), p. 265.

32. Osofsky, *Harlem,* p. 138.

33. Weaver, *The Negro Ghetto,* p. 68; *see also* p. 38.

34. Allan H. Spear, *Black Chicago* (Chicago: University of Chicago Press, 1967), p. 150.

35. Report of the National Advisory Commission on Civil Disorders, p. 259; U.S. Civil Rights Commission, *A Time to Listen . . . A Time to Act* (Washington, D.C.: Government Printing Office, 1967), p. 15.

36. Quoted in Oscar Handlin, *Immigration as a Factor in American History* (Englewood Cliffs, N.J.: Prentice-Hall, Inc., 1959), p. 65.

37. Oscar Handlin, *The Uprooted* (New York: Grosset & Dunlap, Inc., 1951), p. 151.

38. Henry Pratt Fairchild, *Immigration* (New York: The Macmillan Company, 1913), p. 239.
39. William I. Thomas and Florian Znaniecki, *The Polish Peasant in Europe and America* (Boston: Gorham Press, 1920), V, 31.
40. Jane Addams, *Twenty Years at Hull-House* (New York: The Macmillan Company, 1910; reprinted, 1960), p. 295.
41. DuBois, *The Philadelphia Negro,* p. 290.
42. Chicago Commission, *The Negro in Chicago,* p. 158.
43. Weaver, *The Negro Ghetto,* p. 111.
44. Duncan and Duncan, *The Negro Population of Chicago,* p. 19.
45. Kenneth B. Clark, *Dark Ghetto* (New York: Harper & Row, Publishers, 1965), p. 30.
46. Osofsky, *Harlem,* p. 139.
47. Schoener, *Harlem on My Mind,* p. 138.
48. Abbott, *The Tenements of Chicago,* p. 264.
49. Fairchild, *Immigration,* p. 247; Roberts, *The New Immigration,* pp. 130–31.
50. Handlin, *Boston's Immigrants,* p. 109; Walter Firey, *Land Use in Central Boston* (Cambridge, Mass.: Harvard University Press, 1947), pp. 171–72.
51. Duncan and Duncan, *The Negro Population of Chicago,* pp. 16, 238.
52. *Time* magazine, April 6, 1970, p. 52; Urban America, Inc., and The Urban Coalition, *One Year Later* (New York: Praeger Publishers, Inc., 1969), pp. 49–50.
53. Lewis Mumford, *The City in History* (New York: Harcourt Brace Jovanovich, Inc., 1961), p. 220.
54. Handlin, *Boston's Immigrants,* p. 113.
55. Quoted in Clinard, *Slums,* p. 36.
56. Abbott, *The Tenements of Chicago,* pp. 121–23 passim.
57. *Ibid.,* p. 121.
58. Cordasco, *Jacob Riis Revisited,* p. 6.
59. Abbott, *The Tenements of Chicago,* p. 123.
60. Osofsky, *Harlem,* p. 140.
61. U.S. Civil Rights Commission, *A Time to Listen,* p. 15.
62. Cordasco, *Jacob Riis Revisited,* p. 324.
63. *Life* magazine, March 8, 1968, pp. 49–61 passim.
64. Report of the National Advisory Commission on Civil Disorders, pp. 257–58.
65. Clark, *Dark Ghetto,* p. 30.
66. U.S. Civil Rights Commission, *A Time to Listen,* p. 14.
67. Ernst, *Immigrant Life in New York City,* p. 50.
68. Jacob A. Riis, *The Peril and the Preservation of the Home* (Philadelphia: George W. Jacobs Co., 1903), p. 76 (italics in original).
69. Schoener, *Harlem on My Mind,* p. 12.
70. Charles T. O'Reilly, Willard E. Downing, and Steven I. Pflanczer, *The People of the Inner Core—North* (New York: Le Play Research, Inc., 1965), pp. 68–69.
71. Cordasco, *Jacob Riis Revisited,* p. 8.

72. Richard C. Wade, *Slavery in the Cities* (New York: Oxford University Press, Inc., 1964), p. 170.

73. Cordasco, *Jacob Riis Revisited*, p. 8.

74. Edward Greer, "The 'Liberation' of Gary, Indiana," *Trans-action*, VIII, No. 3 (January 1971), 30–63.

75. Handlin, *Boston's Immigrants*, pp. 111, 329.

76. Mumford, *The City in History*, pp. 215–16.

77. Mumford, *The Culture of Cities*, p. 122.

78. Handlin, *Boston's Immigrants*, p. 111.

79. Ernst, *Immigrant Life in New York City*, p. 51.

80. Abbott, *The Tenements of Chicago*, p. 59.

81. Handlin, *The Uprooted*, p. 152.

82. Addams, *Hull-House*, p. 282.

83. DuBois, *The Philadelphia Negro*, p. 292.

84. Abbott, *The Tenements of Chicago*, p. 121.

85. Osofsky, *Harlem*, p. 140.

86. Schoener, *Harlem on My Mind*, p. 208.

87. Report of the National Advisory Commission on Civil Disorders, p. 138.

88. Roberts, *The New Immigration*, p. 147; *Life* magazine, March 8, 1968, p. 147.

89. U.S. Civil Rights Commission, *A Time to Listen*, p. 16.

90. *Ibid.*, p. 17.

91. *Time* magazine, April 6, 1970, p. 53.

92. *See* Robert Merton, *Social Theory and Social Structure* (New York: The Free Press, 1968), chapter 3, *esp.* pp. 126 ff.

93. Clinard, *Slums*, pp. 14–15.

94. Abbott, *The Tenements of Chicago*, p. 63.

95. *Ibid.*, p. 66.

96. Addams, *Hull-House*, p. 98.

97. Abbott, *The Tenements of Chicago*, p. 121.

98. Drake and Cayton, *Black Metropolis*, p. 202.

99. Clark, *Dark Ghetto*, p. 30.

100. U.S. Civil Rights Commission, *A Time to Listen*, p. 14.

101. Schoener, *Harlem on My Mind*, pp. 12–13.

102. Report of the National Advisory Commission on Civil Disorders, p. 259.

103. George F. Willison, *Saints and Strangers* (New York: Reynal & Company, 1945), pp. 166–67.

104. Quoted in Clinard, *Slums*, p. 32.

105. Mumford, *The Culture of Cities*, p. 171.

106. Ernst, *Immigrant Life in New York City*, pp. 52–53.

107. Handlin, *Boston's Immigrants*, p. 114.

108. Clinard, *Slums*, p. 37.

109. Handlin, *The Uprooted*, p. 155.

110. Abbott, *The Tenements of Chicago*, p. 63.

111. Handlin, *The Uprooted*, p. 156.

112. Cordasco, *Jacob Riis Revisited*, pp. 304, 341.

113. Leon F. Litwack, *North of Slavery* (Chicago: University of Chicago Press, 1961), p. 169.

114. DuBois, *The Philadelphia Negro,* pp. 149 ff.

115. Osofsky, *Harlem,* p. 141.

116. Schoener, *Harlem on My Mind,* p. 81.

117. Drake and Cayton, *Black Metropolis,* pp. 202–5.

118. Weaver, *The Negro Ghetto,* p. 118.

119. National Committee on Segregation in the Nation's Capital, *Segregation in Washington* (Chicago, Ill., 1948), pp. 48–53.

120. U.S. Department of Health, Education and Welfare *Indicators,* "Mortality" (Washington, D.C.: Government Printing Office, January 1966).

121. Michael Harrington, *The Other America* (New York: The Macmillan Company, 1962), p. 146.

122. *Time* magazine, April 6, 1970, p. 48.

123. AP and Reuters dispatches in Toledo *Blade,* September 30, 1970, and November 8, 1970, respectively. The *Baltimore Sun* called attention to lead poisoning in 1954, stating that there were 102 cases of lead poisoning in Baltimore since 1931, 85 percent of them in blighted areas. *See* Reuel Hemdahl, *Urban Renewal* (New York: Scarecrow Press, Inc., 1959), pp. 19–20.

124. Report of the National Advisory Commission on Civil Disorders, p. 136.

125. Clark, *Dark Ghetto,* p. 31.

126. Fairchild, *Immigration,* pp. 237–38.

127. Clinard, *Slums,* pp. 16 ff.; Svend Riemer, *The Modern City* (Englewood Cliffs, N.J.: Prentice-Hall, Inc., 1952), pp. 139 ff.

128. Cf. Report of the National Advisory Commission on Civil Disorders, p. 92.

8 | Slum Pathology

There is one especial disadvantage suffered by blacks that was not encountered by the various immigrant groups in the past. Although immigrants in general were continuously associated with the slum, no single immigrant nationality group long remained in the worst slums at the bottom of the social hierarchy; this was because of the operation of an "immigration ladder," by which each wave of immigrants tended to come from a particular area or country in Europe within a relatively narrow span of time and to take over the bottom rung of the social ladder by virtue of being even rawer and less knowledgeable than the group that preceded it. Thus each group in succession was automatically raised in status by a later arriving one.

Riis emphasized that the "German ragpicker" of 1860 was "quite as low in the scale as his Italian successor" was in 1890, and Steiner recalled just after the turn of the century: "Many of us remember when the German and the Scandinavian immigrants who came, received no heartier welcome than we now give the Slav, the Italian and the Jew." [1] The latter were then pushed upwards by the arrival of the "Greeks, Syrians, and allied races." [2] These were in turn elevated by the arrival of the Great Migration blacks, who took over the bottom position—only to find that no group came afterwards to displace them. Thus while the slums themselves remained the immigrant nationality groups within them regularly changed so that no single group remained long enough to become closely identified with the slum—until the blacks. This has made it easier for the white to equate slum and black than was the case for any immigrant nationality. Native whites were at one time quite concerned about the "dark people" from southern Europe, but the arrival of the black in the city made the issue relatively unimportant. The black has had no other race do for him what he did for the Sicilian. Even so, the handicap of being the last group aboard might have been overcome but for the elaborate system of racial restrictive segregation that was documented earlier.

Why, if the Negro has been in this country for more than 300 years, should his status be lower than that of groups here only about 60 years? It is because the status of any racial or ethnic group has been determined not by simple presence in the country but by that group's becoming a significant factor in America's major cities. The status of the southern European was determined not by Christopher Columbus and the early Spanish conqueror-explorers, the status of Jews not by the fact that some were here during the Colonial period, but by the new-immigration masses that poured in around the turn of the century. In Banfield's opinion, had the bulk of the migration of blacks to the Northern cities taken place in the period between the Civil War and World War I, which would be prior to or at the same time as the new immigration, "most Negroes would long since have entered the middle class." [3]

The passage of time has made the immigration-ladder status differences less important than they used to be. Nevertheless, as of 1968 America had never elected a president from a new-immigration background, and the only non-Protestant president, John F. Kennedy, was of Irish descent—and the Irish preceded the new immigration by a half-century. The 1968 election was notable, however, in that the vice-presidential candidates of both major parties had new-immigration nationality backgrounds. It has taken the new immigration the better part of a century to obtain high status and influence at the national level.

That blacks have not had another group come to push them up does not mean that they can not or will not rise in status, it only means that it has not happened to them automatically as it has to the various immigrant-nationality groups. The resulting continued occupancy of the ghetto-slums by blacks, aided by the exclusionary practices of the whites, has tended to perpetuate the identification of ghetto with slum with black just as ghetto and slum and immigrant were identified with each other in the past.

It was mentioned earlier that slum problems of physical housing should be distinguished from the problems of social deviance commonly found in slum areas. Perhaps the materialistic emphasis in American culture is responsible for the long-held belief that curing the problems of physical housing will automatically correct problems of social deviance. A close student of New York's slums says:

> Once upon a time we thought that if we could only get our problem families out of those dreadful slums, then papa would stop taking dope, mama would stop chasing around, and junior would stop carrying a knife.[4]

Evidence from recent decades indicates that adequate physical housing is not a cure-all for problems of social deviance, and that one can find stable, well-organized neighborhoods in areas of relatively low quality housing and high rates of social deviance in physically good housing.[5]

It seems plausible, for instance, that a crowded, uninviting, tenement apartment might drive a young person out onto the streets, where he is more likely to get involved with a juvenile gang and become delinquent, but the crowded housing might equally well drive him into a library or a church youth group. We cannot attain "salvation through bricks," as Reinhold Neibuhr has put it; human beings and societies are more complicated than that. Social pathology is a matter of the total social environment.

SOCIAL EFFECTS OF SLUM HOUSING

The overcrowding of rooms and dwelling units, which is so common in slum areas, can in itself increase social deviance through its moral, social, and psychological effects. A mid-19th-century investigation of Irish living conditions in Boston described the area as a "perfect hive of human beings . . . in many cases, huddled together like brutes, without regard to sex, or age . . . sometimes wife and husband, brothers and sisters, in the same bed." [6] Some 60 years later Jane Addams found similar conditions among the new-immigration foreigners and commented on "the surprisingly large number of delinquent girls who have become criminally involved with their own fathers and uncles" as a result of congested housing.[7]

The taking in of lodgers, which was common in slum areas, further complicates problems related to crowding. DuBois was referring to lodgers when he wrote: "In such ways the privacy and intimacy of home life is destroyed, and elements of danger and demoralization admitted." [8] In the 1930s Abbott found numerous cases of heavy occupancy, about which she concluded: "One of the worst features of this overcrowding is the demoralizing lack of privacy." [9] She found cases of physically mature brothers and sisters sharing the same room, with problems further increased by the frequent presence of lodgers. Abbott's study included both black and immigrant slum areas, and the similarities were far greater than the differences.

With lodgers or without, cases of seven, eight, or more people living in two- or three- or four-room units are not at all hard to find at the present time. The National Advisory Commission on Civil Disorders found that nonwhite housing units were more likely to be both crowded (more than 1 person per room) and overcrowded (more than 1.5 persons per room) than white housing units in the same city. For the 10 cities studied the highest percentage of white units that were crowded was not as great as the lowest percentage of nonwhite crowded units.[10]

PSYCHOLOGICAL ABNORMALITY

Aside from matters of sex and morality, the difficulties of living with other people constantly underfoot must create a psychological strain that would not be encountered by those who have more room and consequent opportunity for privacy. Add to this the difficulties arising from poverty and low social status and it is not hard to see why slum residents have been more prone to mental illness than people living in other parts of the city.

Until the Irish started arriving in Boston in large numbers in the 1840s, caring for the mentally ill "was neither financially nor medically serious," but it soon became a serious problem because of the high incidence of mental illness among the Irish immigrants.[11] In New York City in the 1850s more than three-fourths of those admitted to the "city lunatic asylum . . . were of alien birth; two-thirds of these were natives of Ireland." [12] It is not that the Irish had any greater inborn propensity for mental illness than other groups; the demoralization, poor health, and destitution that resulted from the famine and privations of their voyage—plus their slum living conditions after arrival—can account for their having rates higher than other immigrant groups. Immigrants in general consistently showed higher rates of mental illness than the native whites. In the early 20th century the slum-dwelling immigrants were still disproportionately represented among the mentally ill.[13]

A study of insanity rates in Chicago in the 1930s showed that the highest incidence of schizophrenia, the most common type of functional mental illness, was in the slum areas, especially the Black Belt.[14] More recently, Harlem in the early 1960s had the highest rate of admission to state mental hospitals of any area in New York City—a rate more than three times the city average.[15] A recent description in *Life* magazine of a slum family offers an insight. The family of 10 lives in a Harlem slum apartment. The mother is described as a "strong woman" of 39. "As the day wears on, she seems to age with it. By nightfall she has crumpled into herself. 'All this needing and wanting is about to drive me crazy,' she said." [16] The statistics show that for many people it does.

FAMILY DISORGANIZATION

Closely related to the psychological demoralization of individuals is the disorganization of family relationships as a result of the total situation confronting slum residents. Family disorganization was a major theme in much of the literature concerned with the immigrants and is mentioned in various places in this work. Problems of poverty, slum living conditions, and generational cultural differences all acted to weaken immigrant slum families.

Present-day black slum families also face problems. The father of the Harlem family referred to above was described as being conscientious in trying to provide for them but his lack of education resulted in his being able to find only unskilled, irregular employment. When not able to work his depression led him to drink, which made him abusive to members of his family. One such time, after he had beaten up his wife ("He gave me a going-over last night. My ribs feel like they're broken"), she poured sugar and honey into a boiling pan of water ("To make it stick and burn for awhile") and threw the mixture into his face. He had to be hospitalized and was described as being so badly burned as to be hardly recognizable.[17]

Piri Thomas has given a particularly vivid and personal account of disorganization in a Puerto Rican family—the fight between his father and himself that led to his leaving home:

> Pops dropped me and swung out. I felt his hard fist on my face and the cutting edge of his ring. My head rocked. I felt my face and the blood on it, and everything got red with hate. I ran to the kitchen 'cause I didn't want to hit Pops; I wanted to kill him. . . . Sis was hysterical, José was stone-quiet and James was standing there white with fright. I grabbed a kitchen knife and met Pops running into the kitchen with a baseball bat, and measured."
>
> 'Stop it! Stop it!' Sis screamed, and jumped in between us. Her voice was way out. 'Stop it, do you hear? I'm going crazy and you're the cause of it. Oh God! Mommie, what's going to happen to us?' [18]

Family disorganization is frequently associated with a variety of types of social deviance, which will be discussed below.

ALCOHOL AND DRUGS

The depressing effects of both the slum environment and the low social status that results from poverty tend to generate a desire for escape, even if only temporary. That desire has frequently been met through alcohol although in recent decades drugs have become more common. Actions while under the influence of alcohol or drugs or crimes committed to obtain money for their purchase have frequently brought the individual to the attention of the police. Although the early Irish immigrants in Boston did not generally commit major crimes, they acquired a "reputation for criminality" as a result of their frequent drinking.[19] Drinking was not confined to the Irish but, regardless of nationality, the consequences were similar: "Under the influence of drink, desperate and reckless individuals forgot their sufferings and sorrows, committed assault or robbery, and wound up in jail." [20]

Writing of the 1850s Ernst describes immigrant tenement areas in New York in which drinking "was encouraged . . . by innumerable bartenders." [21] The new-immigration foreigners found conditions little different, leading Riis to comment about the drinking place, "where is it not next door in these slums?" [22] In another work Riis cited drunkenness as destroying eight families in one week: "the suicide of four wives, the murder of two others by drunken husbands, the killing of a policeman in the street," and the torture and eventual murder of an elderly woman by her drunken son.[23]

The extremity of such behavior can only suggest the great desperation of the slum residents. Riis saw the reasons for turning to drink: "Man is a social animal, whether he lives in a tenement or in a palace. But the palace has resources; the tenement has not. It is a good place to get away from at all times. The saloon is cheery and bright, and never far away. . . . The saloon has had all the monopoly up to date of all the cheer in the tenements." [24] The one who dispensed the liquid cheer was, however, likely to be an outsider—a native who could "reap a golden harvest" by supplying the immigrants with drink.[25] The pattern would be repeated later when, around 1930, practically all of the night clubs in Harlem would be owned by whites who, in another example of the immigration ladder, were frequently new-immigration people who had by this time moved up to be the exploiters instead of the exploited.[26]

Regardless of who did the dispensing, the slum environment generated the need for drink. Even a clergyman was reported in 1900 to have said that he could not blame residents of the Negro slums for drinking if that helped to ease the hardships of their living conditions.[27] Handlin recognized the value of alcohol for the immigrant slum dweller: "It was relief a man needed as much as the eyes in his head. . . . In the good company, as his burdens lightened, he discovered in himself altogether unexpected but exhilarating powers, acquired daring and self-confidence beyond any sober hope." [28]

Cocaine is even more effective. As described by Malcolm X, who used it when he was young: "Cocaine produces, for those who sniff its powdery white crystals, an illusion of supreme well-being, and a soaring overconfidence in both physical and mental ability. You think you could whip the heavyweight champion, and that you are smarter than everybody." [29] Heroin does even more. Regarding the effects of heroin a black addict from Toledo said: "It was beautiful, just beautiful. . . .

Man, when you shoot H, you're no longer in the ghetto. You are in your own world. You can't see the rats. You can't see the roaches. You can't smell the garbage. You're no longer hungry. The holes in your shoes don't bother you. It's your own heaven, and you want to stay there. As long as you stay high, nothing bothers you." [30] Is it any wonder that people feeling hopeless and living in squalor turn to alcohol or drugs?

The last sentence in his statement offers a clue, however—as long as you stay high. In order to stay high over the 15 years he had been an addict, he had committed crimes totaling an estimated $500,000 and had spent five years in prison. Married, with a seven-year-old boy, he said: "I'm scared he'll be in some kind of drug scene in a year or two." Describing himself as dying because of drugs, the man pleaded: "I want to live! I don't want to die! Can't somebody please help me?" [31] Escape from the ghetto-slum through drugs comes at a high price.

Although drugs were less common in the past and consequently their use was not as prevalent in white slum areas as it is now in the black, they were by no means unknown. Zorbaugh wrote of a white slum area in Chicago in the 1920s and commented on the number of drug addicts who lived there. He went on to say: "It has since been cleaned up. But 'dope' is still liberally peddled in the slum." [32]

Narcotic drugs were not uncommon in Harlem even in the 1920s,[33] but beginning in the early 1950s they practically engulfed it. Of this period Claude Brown writes:

> Heroin had just about taken over Harlem. It seemed to be a kind of plague. Every time I went uptown, somebody else was hooked, somebody was strung out. People talked about them as if they were dead. You'd ask about an old friend, and they'd say, 'Oh, well, he's strung out.' It wasn't just a comment or an answer to a question. It was a eulogy for someone. He was just dead, though. . . . It was like a plague, and the plague usually afflicted the eldest child of every family, like the one of the firstborn with Pharaoh's people in the Bible. Sometimes it was even worse than the biblical plague. . . . It was a disheartening thing for a mother and father to see all their sons strung out on drugs at the same time. . . . Guys who were already strung out were trying to keep their younger brothers away from stuff. . . . Cats were starving for drugs; their habit was down on them, and they were getting sick. They were out of their minds, so money for drugs became the big thing . . . this desire for money was wrecking almost all family life. Fathers were picking up guns and saying, 'Now, look, if you fuck with that rent money, I'm gon kill you,' and they meant it. Cats were taking butcher knives and going at their fathers because they had to have money to get drugs. . . . Harlem was a community that couldn't afford the pressure of this thing, because there weren't many strong family ties anyway. . . . If the plague didn't hit you directly, it hit you indirectly. It seemed as though nobody could really

get away from it. There were a lot of guys trying to get young girls started on drugs so they could put them down on the corner [as prostitutes]. . . . Most girls [who were addicts] would start selling their body.[34]

Only very recently has drug usage among middle-class white youth come to be considered a serious social problem. Many blacks say cynically that nobody worried about drugs as long as they only affected poor ghetto blacks.

GAMBLING

The systematic widespread distribution of an illegal substance or service—alcohol during prohibition, narcotic drugs, gambling on the numbers—requires a substantial organization of distributors and dealers who in turn encourage the use of their products or services. This organization itself provides a means for some slum residents to earn considerable money—that is, to become "successful"—through supplying wants that have been declared illegal. Organized crime thus finds a strong base in the slums by supplying its most commonly used service— numbers or "policy" gambling.

If alcohol and drugs offer one means of escape from the slums, another is by suddenly winning a relatively large amount of money by "hitting" on a number. In one common form a person may bet a nickel or a dime or even a penny and be paid back 600 to 1 if he wins. His odds of winning are 1,000 to 1, the 40 percent difference being the "take" of the organization. Policy gambling existed in New York at least as far back as the 1830s, even though it had been outlawed in 1832. Natives, immigrants, and Negroes all participated, although it appeared that "Negroes were the main victims of this numbers racket." [35] Numbers gambling was common in the slums of the new immigration, so that by 1900 "Al Adams, the New York policy king, had a widespread network." [36] Riis cited the case of a "poor Irish tenement ward" in New York in which hundreds of dollars were spent daily on policy gambling, the betting frequently being handled by the local saloonkeeper, who "got his share." [37] Things were little different in Boston in the 1940s, when Firey reported that gambling was common in the Italian area, with local businessmen acting as "bookies" and with the inevitable bribery of local officials.[38]

Policy playing was popular with blacks in Northern cities around the turn of the century, with the winning numbers generating "intense excitement" in Negro areas in New York.[39] Policy playing was also rampant in Philadelphia, leading DuBois to observe: "Gambling goes on almost openly in the slum sections," and in the worst slum sections, "policy shops abound." [40] Although illegal in Chicago, policy gambling as well as other types were conducted quite openly in the Black Belt during and after World War I.[41] That the gambling was not concealed despite publicity given it by the local press strongly suggests police payoffs, a natural consequence of organized illegal activity. In Harlem in the 1920s: "The poorest of the poor sought instant riches through the numbers racket. . . . The odds were thousands to one against success, yet the smallest hope for a richer life was better than none and Negroes continued to play 'policy' avidly." [42]

Gambling on the numbers is not considered sinful or improper by many in the Negro slum areas. Malcolm X told of how in his early days in New York in the 1940s he would gamble as much as $15 and $20 a day and dream of what he would do when he "hit" on a number. "Practically everyone played every day in the poverty-ridden black ghetto of Harlem. Every day, someone you knew was likely to hit and of course it was neighborhood news; if big enough a hit, neighborhood excitement." [43] A friend of his was able to buy a musical instrument with money from a hit in numbers and went on to form a dance band, with which he earned his living.[44] Even the loser had the excitement of waiting to see if his number were lucky and dreaming of what he would do if it were. Thus gambling may be viewed as entertainment. The person who pays money for a theater ticket gets no more.

In 1954 the *Amsterdam News* conducted an extensive investigation of the numbers game. It concluded that 75 percent of the adult residents of Harlem played the numbers, but that the practice had spread so that more whites were playing than blacks. The employment possibilities on the inside of the policy operation are indicated by the estimate that more than 20,000 people, most of them black, were earning their livelihood from organized policy activities. It was reported that four hours of work would make a good runner from $30 to $100, far more than the average black could earn in a "legitimate" job. The big money —about two-thirds of the total—went outside the black area to white organization "bankers." Nevertheless, because policy is against the whites' laws and the ones easiest to catch breaking the law are those on the lower rungs of the organization ladder, each year more than 7,000 blacks, some of them innocent, were arrested and acquired police records.[45] Of course a police record makes it more difficult for a person to get "legitimate" employment and thus makes it more likely that he will continue in the rackets.

In his later years, after his conversion to the Black Muslims, Malcolm X referred to those who bet on the numbers as "my poor, foolish black brothers and sisters." [46] Kenneth Clark said: "Even the numbers racket, a vital and indestructible part of Harlem's economy, is controlled by whites. Here is unproductive profit-making at its most virulent, using the Negro's flight from despair into the persistent dream of quick and easy money as the means to take from him what little money he has." [47] Both Malcolm X and Clark thus echoed what Riis had written about Negro policy playing some 75 years earlier: "the wages of many a hard day's work are wasted by the negro; but the loss causes him few regrets. Penniless, but with undaunted faith in his ultimate 'luck,' he looks forward to the time when he shall once more be able to take a hand at 'beating policy.' " [48]

An additional consequence of policy is that the necessary bribery of police that illegal gambling produces helps to decrease respect for law in the slum area and to substantiate the common slum belief that "everyone has a racket," which becomes a justification for engaging in crime and delinquency.

VICE

Vice has also long found a home in the slums. Girls whose slum backgrounds did not adequately prepare them to get ahead in society had little to lose in social status and a great deal to gain economically by prostitution. This is aside from the prostitution that is almost the inevitable result of drug addiction. The earlier Irish immigrant girls had the reputation of being relatively strict sexually, "but by 1860 illegitimate births were probably more frequent among them than among any other nationality." [49]

A slum area is a natural place for houses of prostitution because the slum resident lacks sufficient influence or social status to keep prostitution out. This has long been true. Wirth reports that in earlier centuries in Europe: "In some cities the houses of prostitution were transferred to the [Jewish] ghetto, because the ghetto was a fitting place for an institution of ill repute . . . the location of the quarter was usually in the least desirable region of the city." [50] Just after World War I the Chicago Commission on Race Relations criticized "the city's tolerance of gambling and immorality in and near areas of Negro residence," and added: "Little consideration is given to the desire of Negroes to live in untainted districts, and they have not been able to make effective protest." [51]

During the 1920s Harlem was a leading center of prostitution in Manhattan. As with alcohol, drugs, and gambling, though, the big money went to the whites; most of the houses of prostitution in both New York and Chicago were owned and managed by whites.[52] The tendency for houses of prostitution to be located in Negro slum areas was also evident even before World War I in Philadelphia, Boston, and Cincinnati.[53] In 1912 the Chicago Chief of Police informed prostitutes that as long as they were located in a Negro area they would not be disturbed by the police.[54] Thus the same powerlessness that has saddled the slum resident with his miserable housing has also made him more likely to be both a neighbor and victim of organized crime and vice.

Organized houses of prostitution and red-light districts have become less common generally in our society in the past few decades so that they are now less relevant to the slums than in the past. Prostitution still exists, however, and just as in earlier years immigrants were more likely than the natives to be prostitutes, now blacks constitute a disproportionate share of prostitutes.[55]

TRADITIONAL CRIME

In addition to organized crime there is another category—traditional crime—which includes the common types of crime and delinquency such as robbery, burglary, assault, rape, and murder, engaged in by individuals or small gangs. We know of no study on the spatial distribution of crime within cities that does not show that the incidence of such crime is highest in the most deteriorated areas of cities.

In New York immigrant tenement areas there were "serious problems of juvenile delinquency as early as the 1820s." [56] The Irish reputation for criminality has already been alluded to. The Secretary of the Prison Association of New York reported to a legislative committee in the 1860s: "The younger criminals seem to come almost exclusively from the worst tenement-house districts." [57] In the 1880s the Jewish ghetto on the West Side in Chicago "was a place of filth, infested with the worst element any city could produce. Crime was rampant. No one was safe." [58] A police superintendent in New York in 1890 told Riis that the fourth ward, a particularly deteriorated area, "has turned out more criminals than all the rest of the city together." [59]

In the 1920s crime was also common in the Sicilian slum area of Chicago, which came to be known as "Little Hell." According to Zorbaugh: "The corner of Oak and Cambridge streets long ago became known throughout the city as Death Corner, because of the frequent feuds that were settled there by shootings or stabbings. Little Hell has been long notorious for its unsolved murders." [60]

In the immigrant slums, in general, it was not the immigrants themselves who were most likely to engage in crime, but their children. The children faced problems of poverty (which seemed greater to them, judging by American standards, than it did to their parents, who had the norms of European peasant society) and the culture conflict of American vs. European ways, which alienated them from their parents. The generation gap is not new.

In the early years of the 20th century Jane Addams observed: "Four-fifths of the children brought into the Juvenile Court in Chicago are the children of foreigners. The Germans are the greatest offenders, Polish next." [61] Thomas and Znaniecki, who studied the Polish immigrant, also called attention to the "well-known fact that even the number of crimes is proportionately much larger among the children of immigrants than among immigrants themselves." [62] Using 1910 census data, Commons showed that in the North Atlantic states the children of the foreign-born had a delinquency rate more than twice that of children of native-born parents. Similarly, Northern Negroes had a rate of criminality twice as high as that of Negroes in the South. [63]

There was considerable agreement among the explanations offered by these various workers; all of them emphasized the difficulties faced by unacculturated recent migrants to the city in trying to bring up their children in an unfamiliar environment. Jane Addams said: "Many of these children have come to grief through their premature fling into city life, having thrown off parental control as they impatiently discarded foreign ways." [64] Thomas and Znaniecki explained that "the children brought up in American cities have more freedom and less respect for their parents." [65] Commons similarly concluded: "This amazing criminality of the children of immigrants is almost wholly a product of city life, and it follows directly upon the incapacity of immigrant parents to control their children under city conditions." He also accounted for the higher rate of Negro criminality in the North as being due to the "degenerating effects" of the city, because most Northern Negroes were urban while most Southern Negroes were rural. [66]

In a classic study Shaw and McKay compiled data on juvenile delinquency in Chicago from 1900 to 1940. Their data showed that over the entire period the highest delinquency rates were in the areas that can be described simply as slum areas, and that these same areas also had the city's highest rates of truancy, families on relief, tuberculosis, infant mortality, mental illness, and so forth—in short, the highest rates of the various types of social pathology. The time span of the study permitted observation of delinquency rates for the same areas as they were inhabited successively by different ethnic groups. It also enabled them to study the delinquency rates of an ethnic group whose members were located in different parts of the city. They found that some areas of the city (the slum areas) had high rates of delinquency regardless of the ethnic group living there, while other areas had low rates no matter which ethnic groups lived there. [67] Thus Germans living in high-rate areas showed high rates of delinquency. Germans in low-rate areas showed low rates, while the Italians, for example, who replaced them in the high-rate areas had high rates. It is not surprising to find that Negroes who lived among or replaced the immigrants in high-rate areas showed high rates themselves.

DuBois found that there was considerable crime, delinquency, and vice in the Negro slum areas in the 1890s.[68] Delinquency increased considerably in Harlem between 1914 and 1930 as inundation by the Great Migration turned it into a slum.[69] Drake and Cayton similarly found high crime and delinquency rates in Chicago in the 1930s and early 1940s.[70] Data compiled for various Northern cities in the early 1960s regularly showed Negro delinquency rates that were from two to four times the rates for their cities as a whole.[71] Most recently, the National Commission on the Causes and Prevention of Violence reported that violent crime was disproportionately concentrated "in the ghetto slums where most Negroes live." [72]

The data studied by Shaw and McKay led them to conclude that "the conduct of children, as revealed in differential rates of delinquents, reflect the differences in social values, norms, and attitudes to which the children are exposed . . . delinquency has developed in the form of a social tradition, inseparable from the life of the local community." [73] Out of this view has developed the concept of the delinquent subculture or contraculture.

Briefly described, theories of this type maintain that in high-rate areas there will be a substantial part of the youthful population that will be able to maintain a separate subculture or way of life that opposes conforming to society and offers rewards and social status (of the gang) to group members who conform to the gang. To the lower-class slum youth, the chance of "making it" in outside society can seem very remote indeed, so that the ideology of the gang ("Everybody's got a racket anyway") and the social acceptance and rewards of gang membership and delinquency can seem quite attractive.[74]

That crime and delinquency are still found in the ghetto-slums makes one question whether culture conflict over foreign vs. American ways was as important a causative factor as was earlier thought. An explanation in terms of "city life" also seems too simple, as many areas of the city have low incidences of crime and delinquency. Variations in rates of crime for each minority group over a period of time rule out an explanation of "natural" or "racial" factors. Finally, the physical conditions of slum housing in themselves seem inadequate to explain social deviancy.

We are left with the way of life within slum areas and the characteristics of the people who live there, with race or color in itself of little importance. Social status certainly seems to be relevant. Residence in a slum is both evidence of relative ineffectiveness in society and an indication of low social status, which is exemplified by the physical environment. Many slum parents probably lack the influence and ability to be an effective force. The child can think: "If doing things your way results in being in a crummy place like this, I won't follow your way. I'll try something (anything) else." He has little to lose by becoming socially deviant.

THE CHILD IN THE SLUM

In thinking back over the various types of social pathology discussed in this chapter, let us keep in mind that the majority of adult slum residents are trying to be law-abiding, responsible members of society and to bring up their children to be the same. However, in addition to the difficulties that result from the low social status of even the responsible slum parent, there is the additional burden of raising his children amid the crime, vice, and corruption that he is unable to keep out of his neighborhood. His children are growing up in a neighborhood which makes successful growing-up far more difficult than that it is in the typical middle-class area. Clark has written that given the amount of social pathology in Negro slum areas, it is surprising that so many youths manage *not* to come into conflict with the law.[75]

DuBois commented on the mixture of respectable and criminal elements in Negro slum areas in Philadelphia in the 1890s: "Investigators are often surprised in the worst district to see red-handed criminals and good-hearted, hard-working, honest people living side by side." [76] Only a few years later Riis wrote of the immigrant slums: "The most terrible of all the features of tenement-house life in New York, however, is the indiscriminate herding of all kinds of people in close contact; the fact that, mingled with the drunken, the dissolute, the improvident, the diseased, dwell the great mass of respectable workingmen of the city with their families." [77]

In 1916 the *Chicago Daily News,* after describing crime and vice in the Negro area, went on to say: "These are some of the influences which the colored population is forced to combat in its fight for decency and good citizenship. A few secure political preferment and others profit by catering to the city's vices, while the rank and file are hedged around by demoralizing influences and the race is discredited unjustly." [78] A half-century later, mothers from Gary and Cleveland testified before the Civil Rights Commission about the difficulties of raising their children in a slum environment. A mother from Gary told of people who sat in their cars drinking liquor "because this is just a slum and who cares. And all this, your children see all this. They have to grow up right with all this." The Cleveland mother feared that her son, seeing pimps "with $125 suit and a big car" would "want to do criminal things . . . he may want to leave school for this easy life." [79]

James Conant tells of the junior high school principal who distributed a questionnaire asking students what their biggest problem was. The answer given by a majority of the junior high school girls, whose ages would be mostly between 12 and 15, was that their biggest problem was to get from the front door of their buildings to their tenement apartments without being molested in the hallways. [80]

A vivid account in an issue of *Look* magazine describes the same phenomenon. The article presents the case of José Rivera, age 14, who was born in Puerto Rico but who lived in New York City for the preceding seven years, "most of that time in a crumbling three-room flat on West 84th Street, with nine members of his family." The article was concerned with the "struggle between two sets of values—the social vs. the antisocial—for the future of José," although it stated: "Given the intolerable living conditions, the corruption of some politicians, the community's prejudice and indifference, and the awesome malevolence of the slums, the wonder is that there is any struggle."

> The street rather than the home becomes a growing boy's basic training ground. From the age of seven on, there has been virtually nothing that José hasn't seen. A man was murdered on the sidewalk 50 yards from his front door a few years ago. He has seen prostitutes soliciting and drug addicts 'on the nod' in hallways; the moonshiner shuffling along with a jug in each hand; the sharpies in the numbers racket passing folded bills back and forth. José knows the woman with eight children who keeps boiling water on the stove to fend off night intruders, and the hard-working father with a machete under his bed for self defense. . . . What he sees on West 84th Street day by day seems the only way of life. [81]

José was described as a fair student, but said he didn't like school very much except for the lunch. When asked about the future, he replied: "Tomorrow? I don't think about tomorrow." School probably offered his best chance for escape from the slums, but if he didn't think about tomorrow how would he do on an assignment due the next week? By now José is an adult. One wonders which set of values won.

José was lucky that so far he had not become more personally involved. Claude Brown also grew up in the New York slums, and although he went on to law school and wrote his autobiography, he did not escape the violence of the slum while younger. He begins the story of his life:

> I could hear Turk's voice calling from a distance, telling me not to go into the fish-and-chips joint. I heard, but I didn't understand. The only

thing I knew was that I was going to die. I ran. There was a bullet in me trying to take my life, all thirteen years of it.

While in the hospital he learned that a woman had shot him as his gang was taking some bedspreads off her clothesline, thinking that they were "winos or dope fiends." [82]

The article about José also reported that in his neighborhood an Episcopal minister, the Reverend James Gusweller, was conducting a "David-and-Goliath campaign" to improve the slums but that he was having "only middling success" in the face of opposition from slum landlords and inaction by public officials. "Short of a major effort to meet the needs of the underprivileged," the article concluded, the story of New York's West Side slums "will never have an ending." [83] This recalls another housing crusader of an earlier era, Jacob Riis, who also had middling success battling slum landlords and municipal inaction, and who concluded in 1890 that "the tenements will exist in New York forever." [84]

If our description of slums is accurate, almost any individual case of a slum should have most of the major characteristics discussed. Here is one example of a New York Puerto Rican slum area described in 1958 by Harrison Salisbury:

> I have visited the places where these families live. These are not tenements. These are the dregs of tenements. A hundred years ago they were accurately described by Charles Dickens. Indeed, he may have had some of these very places in mind when he wrote. . . . A fifteen-by-twenty room in a hundred-year-old house is rented to a family of four for twenty dollars a week. Slightly smaller rooms cost fifteen dollars. There is no water. Little heat in winter. A gas plate for cooking. No refrigerator. No icebox. No bath. No shower. A dirty toilet and a single faucet down the hall. There were six cubicles to a floor. By renting each at $15 a week the thieving landlord was taking more than $1,000 a month out of a rat-infested building in which a farmer would not think of housing goats.

> 'Walk down our streets of a summer evening,' Father Hoodak said, 'say at eleven or twelve o'clock. You will see little children three and four years old sitting on the stoops or playing under the lights. Why are they on the streets? A very simple reason. They can't go to bed. Someone is sitting on it. Until the adults are ready for bed there is no place for the children to sleep.' The children have no privacy. There is no place for them to study.*

> 'Yesterday,' said Father Hoodak, 'I saw a twelve-year-old girl hanging out in a candy store near here. I know the dope users hang out here.

---

* Almost 50 years earlier in Chicago Jane Addams wrote of "the school children who cannot find a quiet spot in which to read or study and who perforce go into the streets each evening." [85]

She is a good girl and she comes from a good family. . . . I asked her if she didn't know it was a bad place where they used dope. She said she didn't know.' 'Someone put some sneezing powder under my nose,' the girl told Father Hoodak. Sneezing powder is heroin. The vice business is an ally of the dope business. The two go hand in hand. First the girl is 'hooked' to drugs. Then, she is put into prostitution to earn to pay for her drugs. . . . Dope is not the only illicit product of the neighborhood. This is also an area of moonshine whiskey, cheap synthetic liquor made from industrial alcohol in tenement back rooms and sold in plain jugs for Friday-night parties and weekend jags. . . . Sometimes, the maker is careless or ignorant. Then his customers may die.[86]

This one case contains almost every element discussed here concerning slums—high rents, crowding and subdividing, deteriorated buildings, inadequate sanitation, rats, alcohol and drugs, crime and vice, and the problems of a good family trying to bring up children in such an area.

THE SIMILARITY OF THE SLUMS

Throughout these two chapters on the physical and social characteristics of the slum, striking similarities have been evident between slums of different periods, slums in different cities and even different countries, and slums occupied by peoples of a variety of ethnic and racial backgrounds. Others have called attention to the resemblances between slums. Remarking that while the physical form of the buildings varied between different European and American cities, Mumford still concluded that "they are united by certain common characteristics." [87] Although Jacob Riis' efforts were largely confined to New York, he considered it "typical of most of the large cities of our country," and said: "We struggle with the same evils in Boston, in Chicago, in Buffalo, in St. Louis, in Washington." [88] Clinard also has written of the similarity of descriptions of the immigrant slums, "all making much use of the words 'miserable,' 'squalid,' 'filthy,' 'foul,' 'deplorable,' . . . and other words of similar connotations." [89] The similarity of Negro areas was also pointed out by Drake and Cayton: "Understand Chicago's Black Belt and you will understand the Black Belts of a dozen large American cities." [90]

---

1. Francesco Cordasco, ed., *Jacob Riis Revisited* (Garden City, N.Y.: Doubleday & Company, Inc., 1968), pp. 20–21; Edward A. Steiner, *On the Trail of the Immigrant* (New York: Fleming H. Revell Company, 1906), p. 94.

2. Henry Pratt Fairchild, *Immigration* (New York: The Macmillan Company, 1913), p. 235.

3. Edward C. Banfield, *The Unheavenly City: The Nature and Future of Our Urban Crisis* (Boston: Little, Brown and Company, 1970), p. 69.

4. Daniel Seligman, "The Enduring Slums," in *The Exploding Metropolis,* by the editors of *Fortune* (Garden City, N.Y.: Doubleday and Company, 1958), p. 106.

5. *See,* for example, William Moore, *The Vertical Ghetto* (New York: Random House, Inc., 1969); Lee Rainwater, *Behind Ghetto Walls: Black Families in a Federal Slum* (Chicago: Aldine Publishing Company, 1970); Herbert J. Gans, *The Urban Villagers* (New York: The Free Press, 1962).

6. Quoted in Oscar Handlin, *Boston's Immigrants* (Cambridge, Mass.: Harvard University Press, 1959), pp. 113–14.

7. Jane Addams, *Twenty Years at Hull-House* (New York: The Macmillan Company, 1910; reprinted, 1960), p. 296.

8. W. E. B. DuBois, *The Philadelphia Negro* (1899; reprint ed., New York: Benjamin Blom, Inc., 1967), p. 194.

9. Edith Abbott, *The Tenements of Chicago, 1908–1935* (Chicago: University of Chicago Press, 1936), p. 264.

10. *Report of the National Advisory Commission on Civil Disorders* (Washington, D.C.: Government Printing Office, 1968), p. 258.

11. Handlin, *Boston's Immigrants,* p. 122.

12. Robert Ernst, *Immigrant Life in New York City, 1825–1863* (Port Washington, N.Y.: Ira J. Friedman, Inc., 1965; copyright © 1949), p. 54.

13. Oscar Handlin, *The Uprooted* (New York: Grosset & Dunlap, Inc., 1951), p. 159; Fairchild, *Immigration,* p. 339.

14. Robert E. L. Faris and H. Warren Dunham, *Mental Disorders in Urban Areas* (Chicago: University of Chicago Press, 1939).

15. Kenneth B. Clark, *Dark Ghetto* (New York: Harper & Row, Publishers, 1965), p. 82.

16. *Life* magazine, March 8, 1968, p. 52.

17. *Ibid.,* p. 61.

18. Piri Thomas, *Down These Mean Streets* (New York: Signet Books, The New American Library, 1968; copyright © 1967), p. 194.

19. Handlin, *Boston's Immigrants,* p. 121.

20. Ernst, *Immigrant Life in New York City,* p. 57.

21. *Ibid.*

22. Cordasco, *Jacob Riis Revisited,* p. 26.

23. *Ibid.,* p. 403.

24. *Ibid.,* p. 404.

25. Peter Roberts, *The New Immigration* (New York: The Macmillan Company, 1912), p. 161.

26. Allon Schoener, ed., *Harlem on My Mind* (New York: Random House, Inc., 1968), p. 126.

27. *Ibid.*, p. 21.

28. Handlin, *The Uprooted*, p. 160.

29. Malcolm X, *The Autobiography of Malcolm X* (New York: Grove Press, Inc., 1965), p. 134.

30. Toledo *Blade*, October 11, 1970.

31. *Ibid.*

32. Harvey W. Zorbaugh, *The Gold Coast and the Slum* (Chicago: University of Chicago Press, 1929), pp. 135–36.

33. Gilbert Osofsky, *Harlem: The Making of a Ghetto* (New York: Harper Torchbooks, 1968; copyright © Harper & Row, Publishers, 1963), p. 148.

34. Claude Brown, *Manchild in the Promised Land* (New York: The Macmillan Company, 1965), pp. 187–92 passim.

35. Ernst, *Immigrant Life in New York City*, p. 58.

36. Handlin, *The Uprooted*, p. 163.

37. Cordasco, *Jacob Riis Revisited*, p. 403.

38. Walter Firey, *Land Use in Central Boston* (Cambridge, Mass.: Harvard University Press, 1947), p. 190.

39. Cordasco, *Jacob Riis Revisited*, p. 57.

40. DuBois, *The Philadelphia Negro*, pp. 265, 294.

41. Chicago Commission on Race Relations, *The Negro in Chicago* (Chicago: University of Chicago Press, 1922; reprinted, Arno Press, Inc., New York, 1968), p. 344.

42. Osofsky, *Harlem*, p. 47.

43. Malcolm X, *Autobiography*, pp. 84–85.

44. *Ibid.*, p. 44.

45. Schoener, *Harlem on My Mind*, pp. 209–11.

46. Malcolm X, *Autobiography*, p. 85.

47. Clark, *Dark Ghetto*, p. 28.

48. Cordasco, *Jacob Riis Revisited*, p. 57.

49. Handlin, *Boston's Immigrants*, pp. 122–23.

50. Louis Wirth, *The Ghetto* (Chicago: University of Chicago Press, 1928, 1956), p. 35.

51. Chicago Commission, *The Negro in Chicago*, p. 201.

52. *Ibid.*, p. 344; Osofsky, *Harlem*, p. 146.

53. John R. Commons, *Races and Immigrants in America* (New York: The Macmillan Company, 1916), p. 57.

54. Chicago Commission, *The Negro in Chicago*, p. 343.

55. Marshall B. Clinard, *Sociology of Deviant Behavior* (3rd ed.) (New York: Holt, Rinehart & Winston, Inc., 1968), pp. 377–79.

56. Ernst, *Immigrant Life in New York City*, p. 59.

57. Cordasco, *Jacob Riis Revisited*, p. 4.

58. Wirth, *The Ghetto*, p. 180.

59. Cordasco, *Jacob Riis Revisited*, p. 33.

60. Zorbaugh, *The Gold Coast and the Slum*, pp. 170–71.

61. Addams, *Hull-House*, p. 252.

62. William I. Thomas and Florian Znaniecki, *The Polish Peasant in Europe and America* (Boston: Gorham Press, 1920), V, 189.

63. Commons, *Races and Immigrants*, pp. 170–72.

64. Addams, *Hull-House*, p. 252.

65. Thomas and Znaniecki, *The Polish Peasant*, p. 189.

66. Commons, *Races and Immigrants*, pp. 170–72.

67. Clifford R. Shaw and Henry D. McKay, *Juvenile Delinquency and Urban Areas* (Chicago: University of Chicago Press, 1942), *esp.* pp. 150–55.

68. DuBois, *The Philadelphia Negro*, pp. 294, 312–13.

69. Osofsky, *Harlem*, p. 147.

70. St. Clair Drake and Horace R. Cayton, *Black Metropolis* (New York: Harper Torchbook, Harper & Row, Publishers, 1962), p. 204.

71. Clark, *Dark Ghetto*, pp. 86–87.

72. National Commission on The Causes and Prevention of Violence, *To Establish Justice, To Insure Domestic Tranquility* (Washington, D.C.: Government Printing Office, 1969), p. 23.

73. Shaw and McKay, *Juvenile Delinquency*, pp. 435–36.

74. For a brief discussion, *see* Clinard, *Deviant Behavior*, pp. 229–43.

75. Clark, *Dark Ghetto*, p. 87.

76. DuBois, *The Philadelphia Negro*, p. 81.

77. Jacob A. Riis, *The Peril and the Preservation of the Home* (Philadelphia: George W. Jacobs Co., 1903), p. 33.

78. Quoted in Chicago Commission, *The Negro in Chicago*, p. 202.

79. U.S. Civil Rights Commission, *A Time To Listen . . . A Time To Act* (Washington, D.C.: Government Printing Office, 1967), p. 10.

80. James B. Conant, *Slums and Suburbs* (New York: Signet Books, The New American Library, 1964), p. 25.

81. *Look* magazine, February 16, 1960, pp. 23–25.

82. Brown, *Manchild*, pp. 9, 11.

83. *Look* magazine, February 16, 1960, p. 27.

84. Cordasco, *Jacob Riis Revisited*, p. 15.

85. Addams, *Hull-House*, p. 296.

86. Harrison E. Salisbury, *The Shook-up Generation* (New York: Harper & Row, Publishers, 1958), pp. 92–97 passim.

87. Lewis Mumford, *The Culture of Cities* (New York: Harcourt Brace Jovanovich, Inc., 1938), p. 168.

88. Riis, *Peril and Preservation*, p. 70.

89. Marshall B. Clinard, *Slums and Community Development* (New York: The Free Press, 1966), p. 32.

90. Drake and Cayton, *Black Metropolis*, p. 12.

9 | *Relieving Slum Problems*

It has been shown here that many of the problems of both involuntary ghetto segregation and slum housing have existed and been reported on, only to be rediscovered and recalled to attention years, decades, even a century or more later. The durability—the toughness—of the types of problem that have been discussed here can hardly be overestimated.

This chapter will cover some aspects of the improvement of housing quality. This does not imply that recent programs will quickly and miraculously accomplish what generations of reformers have failed to do in the past, but neither does it suggest that hopeless resignation is in order. Rather, a realistic perspective recognizes that problems of slum and ghetto will not be eliminated easily, but only through strenuous and persistent effort. This view is supported by a conclusion stated in a study made a year after the report of The National Advisory Commission on Civil Disorders: "Black and white Americans remained far apart in their perceptions of slum-ghetto problems and the meaning of civil disorders. The gap probably had widened by the end of the year." [1]

HOUSING AND THE SLUM

The problem of the slum is primarily one of the adequacy, in quantity and quality, of housing; the problem of involuntary ghetto segregation is mainly one of attitudes and practices regarding human relations. Theoretically, either problem could be solved without having an appreciable effect on the other. Immigrants eventually solved their slum problem by moving out one-by-one into nonslum areas; because of segregation most blacks have been confined to ghetto areas, many of which are also slum areas. In practice, then, the two types of problem are likely to be related.

Many writers over the years have commented on the effect of housing upon people. Regarding Negroes in 1900, one writer marveled that they were "as good as they are," considering "they are compelled to live in places where health, decency and privacy are all but impossible." [2]

145

Twenty-two years later the Chicago Commission on Race Relations reported: "Our inquiry has shown that insufficiency in amount and quality of housing is an all-important factor in Chicago's race problem. . . ." [3] Another 22 years went by and Myrdal, after noting that housing "provides the setting for the whole life of the family" and calling attention to the relationship between poor housing and social pathology, stated: "Nothing is so obvious about the Negroes' level of living as the fact that most of them suffer from poor housing conditions." [4]

In 1948 Weaver also observed: "There is hardly an aspect of minority-group problems in the North that is not related to housing." [5] Two more decades passed and the Advisory Commission on Civil Disorders found the same conditions—physical inadequacy, overcrowding, higher rents, decay and poor maintenance, and so forth—and arrived at the same old conclusion: "The result has been widespread discontent with housing conditions and costs. In nearly every disorder city surveyed, grievances related to housing were important factors in the structure of discontent." [6] After 70 years of such findings one begins to conclude that housing for Negroes may be inadequate and an important source of discontent.

Some workers have commented upon the social-psychological implications of housing and neighborhood. Firey wrote: "*Where* a person lives 'places' him in the eyes of others, because space so readily lends itself to representing social affiliations." He found that successful second-generation Italians tended to move out of the Boston Italian slum colony and explained: "In this respect they are conforming to the typical urban residential pattern of western society in which place of residence is an objective symbol of personal achievement rather than of in-group identity." [7] Kenneth Clark has also emphasized the subjective aspect of housing for the individual.

> Housing is no abstract social and political problem, but an extension of a man's personality. If the Negro has to identify with a rat-infested tenement, his sense of personal inadequacy and inferiority, already aggravated by job discrimination and other forms of humiliation, is reinforced by the physical reality around him. If his home is clean and decent and even in some way beautiful, his sense of self is stronger. A house is a concrete symbol of what the person is worth.[8]

Psychiatrist Robert Coles arrived at similar conclusions as a result of studies in which he asked children in Boston and Cleveland to draw pictures of familiar things. Describing a picture a Negro boy drew of his home, Dr. Coles observed:

> This house is a shambles. . . . He has much better drawing ability. The house is deliberately ramshackled. There is a black sky. . . . The

ground is brown and not green, and there are no flowers. It is a dismal place. . . . The child told me that the property was condemned.[9]

It is not just that the child lives in such a house; he thinks of it that way. It is *his* house; *he* lives in it. It is easy for him to come to think of *himself* as ramshackled, dismal, and condemned.

MEETING HOUSING NEEDS

The problem of slum housing is primarily the problem of providing adequate housing for the poor.

One may ask whether our society has ever met the need for adequate housing of its urban poor. The inadequate housing of immigrants in the past was described earlier. Both in this country and in Europe housing reformers in the 19th century constructed "model tenements" to demonstrate the kind of housing considered to be minimally acceptable for the time. The lead generally was not followed up, one reason being that even this minimal housing proved to be too costly for the tenants it was intended for.[10] History may repeat itself. By the end of the 1960s many local public-housing authorities had encountered such increased operating costs that they found themselves in severe financial straits and could "see no alternative but to raise rents beyond the reach of those for whom the program was intended." [11] At the beginning of 1971 the New York City Housing Authority was operating at a $20-million-a-year deficit.[12]

In the middle of the depression 30s Abbott concluded: "Evidently the provision of modern housing at a rent within the grasp of the unskilled wage-earner is beyond possible attainment in the immediate future and the problem can scarcely be met by private ownership or private philanthropy in the tenement districts." [13] Despite two subsequent decades of prosperity, conditions remained so little changed that McEntire judged in 1960 that housing for low-income families and minority groups had "proved most difficult to supply." [14] On the basis of more than a century of inadequate housing for low-income families one might conclude that the private housing market is simply unable to provide minimally adequate housing for such families. Indeed, by 1970 Herbert Gans was maintaining that private enterprise was not able to provide new housing even for middle-income families.[15] Evidence that supports his opinion will be presented below.

THE "TEMPORARY" SLUMS

Despite the persistence of slum housing in American cities our society has tended to view slums as a temporary phenomenon, which would soon pass away naturally. After all, slum buildings are old and decrepit and we know that automobiles and refrigerators whose time also has come do disappear from the scene. Certainly, people may think, the same thing happens with buildings, aided perhaps by programs of "slum clearance" and "urban renewal." This has not been the way, however.

New York, whose slums are a match for practically any city in the Western world, has had a slum clearance law since 1895.[16] Jane Addams recognized by the turn of the century the effect that society's view of the slum as being only transitory had on efforts to improve housing. She wrote:

> Many unsavory conditions are allowed to continue which would be regarded with horror *if they were considered permanent.* Meanwhile, the wretched conditions persist until at least two generations of children have been born and reared in them.[17]

Material reviewed here indicates that many of these conditions have continued to endure for more than two additional generations.

How stable is the slum? Consider the following:

1. Writing of his "ten years' war," which began in 1890, against the New York slum Jacob Riis stated:

> The slum is as old as civilization. . . . The battle with the slum began the day civilization recognized it as her enemy. . . . When common sense and the golden rule obtain among men as a rule of practice, it will be over. Justice to the individual is accepted in theory as the only safe groundwork of the commonwealth. When it is practiced in dealing with the slum, there will shortly be no slum. We need not wait for the millennium to get rid of it. We can do it now.[18]

2. Twenty-three years after Riis began his battle, Henry Pratt Fairchild was able to note:

> Up to the present the slum, in spite of all the attacks upon it, has maintained itself as a permanent feature of most of our large cities.[19]

3. More than 50 years after Fairchild's statement, David Hunter concluded:

> Slums are one of America's major social and economic problems in the 1960's. This in spite of the fact that we live in an 'affluent society'; in

spite of the fact that we have had housing and slum clearance programs for many years. . . . The slums are still with us.[20]

It is material such as this that compels the conclusion that the slum should not be viewed as a passing phase, which will soon automatically correct itself. Despite the prevalence of slums in cities of America and other countries, neither should slums be viewed as inevitable in Western urban society. Colean has noted concerning Sweden that "the old and crowded buildings and the narrow streets of Stockholm obviously would lend themselves to slums equally as well as those of New York's Lower East Side." He writes, however: "It has often been noted that Stockholm, despite the antiquity of much of the city and the obsoleteness of many of the buildings, has no slums." [21] He argues that slums exist not because buildings are old, but because there are "landlords who are indifferent to their property" and communities which permit slums to develop and persist through inadequate enforcement of decent standards. A large city does not have to have slums.

Twenty-five years after completing his monumental study of the American racial situation, *An American Dilemma,* Gunnar Myrdal testified in Congress, in 1969, that he had been wrong in his expectation that racial relations would improve in the Northern cities after World War II. He explained: "I could not foresee that the United States, with all its expert knowledge in the social field . . . would permit the worsening of the slum situation, the decay of the cities which was so clearly on the cards 25 years ago." [22] His opinion was that any program of "amelioratory building" in the slums that did not make substantial provision for permitting blacks to become more spread out in the whole metropolitan area (that is, eliminate restrictive involuntary segregation) would not solve the slum problem.

THE HOUSING SUPPLY

It is difficult to separate the problem of slum housing from that of the total housing supply in the country. If the total supply of housing were plentiful, then rents would be more reasonable, overcrowding would be reduced, and maintenance would be more extensive as landlords actually competed to attract tenants. Buildings unable to offer minimally adequate housing would go unoccupied, forcing either their improvement or their replacement. In practice, urban population growth seems to have outstripped housing production almost continuously since about 1840, when, in New York, "serious housing problems began . . . when the first tenements were built." [23] Periods of slackened urban growth caused by economic recession have usually been accompanied by slowdowns in building construction, so that housing scarcity has tended to be perennial.

In 1965 Beyer made an "Estimate of Attainable Housing Need, 1965–75." Taking into account the number of new households formed, migration to the city, and dwelling units added or lost through conversions or demolitions, he concluded that between 1.6 and 2.1 million nonfarm dwelling units would have to be constructed each year of the period simply to keep housing at the 1965 level of adequacy.[24]

If housing quality or adequacy is to be raised, rather than simply maintained, a higher rate of housing construction is necessary. How much higher a rate is needed depends upon assumptions and judgments that must be made about imponderables, with the additional complication that much of the basic data are inadequate. Some of these difficulties are discussed in a report about future housing needs by The National Commission on Urban Problems (The Douglas Commission).[25] A working estimate of the construction needed to improve housing adequacy appreciably might be the 2.6 million units per year during the 1970s set forth by Congress in the Housing and Urban Development Act of 1968. As well as being an officially established goal, the 2.6 million figure is about midway between the high and low estimates of housing needs recommended by three responsible housing groups.[26] This latter figure would represent more housing construction per year than at any time in American history. For the period 1965–1970, the total number of actual housing units started averaged approximately 1.4 million per year[27]—well below even Beyer's minimum need estimate and only about half that considered necessary by Urban America to improve housing quality significantly. As Beyer notes, however, the number of housing starts is influenced primarily by financial circumstances and not by the amount of actual need for housing.[28]

Real-estate interests have generally taken the position that housing for low-income people should be met by the "filtering-down" process by which new housing is built for higher-income groups, who eventually move out into more desirable housing, leaving their old dwellings to be occupied by families with less income, so that as buildings become older and less desirable they progressively house those with less and less income. The concept tends not to work in practice.[29] Even if people were willing to change their dwellings regularly according to their changed economic circumstances, an inadequate total supply of housing would interfere; if a sufficient amount of new housing is not fed into the system from the top, then there is not enough to filter down and the whole arrangement will not work.

To provide adequate housing for low-income families, the filtering down process requires that even old buildings receive enough maintenance so that they are not hazardous to the health or safety of their occupants. We have seen, though, that maintenance in slum areas has been inadequate, with enforcement by city officials lax. If too many demands for maintenance are made—with the substantial costs involved in making major improvements—the landlord may simply abandon the building rather than upgrade it. By 1969 in New York City some 15,000 buildings, containing 150,000 dwelling units, had been abandoned— with the rate of abandonment estimated at 1,000 per week.[30] It has been estimated that 20,000 buildings nave been abandoned in Philadelphia, 5,000 in Baltimore, 1,500 in Detroit, and 1,000 each in Boston and Washington.[31] An abandoned building has reached the end of the filtering down process before it has been able to provide adequate housing for the lowest income levels. Given a sufficient input of new buildings, abandonment of old ones would be a sign of healthy functioning of the housing system, but with insufficient new construction, abandonment intensifies the problem by further decreasing the total housing supply. An inadequate housing supply also tends to discourage enforcement of housing and sanitation codes by city officials because of the lack of places to which a tenant could move were he evicted from an unsafe unit.

LOW-INCOME HOUSING

Low-income housing may be defined as non-slum housing for families whose incomes are too low to cover the cost of minimally adequate housing in the normal housing market. Public housing, begun in the United States in the 1930s, was the first widespread attempt to provide adequate housing for low-income families, with rents based not on the actual cost of providing housing but upon the ability of the family to pay. Most of such housing was in the form of large-scale projects, in some cases providing for thousands of families.

Not only have such projects tended to segregate racially, as has been discussed earlier, but by forcing out the more economically successful, whose incomes rose above the project's income limits, they evicted those who could provide leadership and stability, thus concentrating within the project only those who were the least capable. Regarding massive public-housing projects Harrison Salisbury said:

> They spawn teen-age gangs. They incubate crime. They are fiendishly contrived institutions for the debasing of family and community life to the lowest common mean. . . . Some projects seem more like Golgothas designed to twist, torture and destroy the hapless people condemned to their dismal precincts than new homes for unfortunates.[32]

Rainwater called the Pruitt-Igoe project in St. Louis a "federal slum." [33] The dream in the 1930s of good housing for the poor had turned into a nightmare even by the 1950s. The project buildings may last well into the 21st century.

At the time of this writing, however, the federal government is still trying to decide whether or not to tear down the Pruitt-Igoe housing project in St. Louis. The high-rise federal project was built in 1955 at a cost of $36 million to accommodate 2,800 families, but it has consistently been plagued with high vacancy rates, crime, and vandalism. Even by 1959 it had become a "community scandal." [34] In 1969 the project saw 10 murders and 14 rapes. With less than one-fourth of its units occupied, it would cost more than the original construction to rehabilitate the buildings in the project. One HUD investigator said he had never before seen such "complete and total alienation" as was shown by the Pruitt-Igoe residents.[35] This is further evidence that it takes more than buildings to deal with social pathology; it does not mean, however, that physically adequate housing is not important in its own right.

HOUSING-PROGRAM POSSIBILITIES

Recent years have seen an increase in the variety of types of low-income housing. Once it is recognized that low-income families may be housed other than in large-scale public projects, a number of possibilities occur. Some major ones will be briefly described.

● SMALL-SCALE SCATTERED SITES. This approach involves scattering public-housing projects about the city, with each project containing a relatively small number of families. What would be considered a small size would vary according to the size of the city and the scale of standard housing in the area. In some instances a site might contain a dozen or so families, in others it could be considerably larger. Regardless of race it probably would not be advisable to build public housing in a high-status neighborhood simply because social-class differences in housing and style of life could lead to friction. Earlier discussion pointed out, however, how opposition to small-site housing developed even in average neighborhoods.

● "TURNKEY" PUBLIC HOUSING. This term designates not the form of a housing project but the manner in which it is developed and built. New housing units are planned and built by private builders who have an agreement with a local housing authority to purchase the buildings when they are completed. The builder then turns the key over to the authority. Such housing tends to be more varied architecturally and less "institutional-looking" than earlier government housing projects. Turnkey housing can also include older buildings purchased from private owners, with rehabilitation, if necessary, being performed before their acquisition by the housing authority. The turnkey program is well adapted to small-scale scattered-site housing.

● LEASED HOUSING. Authorized by Congress in 1965, the leased-housing program authorizes HUD to reimburse local housing authorities who lease existing, privately-owned dwelling units for rental to low-income families. The families pay rent according to their income, the difference between what they pay and the actual rental cost being made up by the housing authority, which is compensated in turn by the federal government. This plan lends itself well to small-scale scattered sites. One important advantage of this system is that a family is not forced to move out if its income increases; it can simply pay a higher rent and continue living there, even if its income rises to the point where it can assume the full cost of the rent. As only a portion of the increase goes for rent there is still an incentive for the family to earn a higher income. As of June 1969 there were approximately 70,000 dwellings receiving support under the leasing program. In only four years leased housing came to include almost 10 percent of the total amount of publicly supported low-income housing.[36]

● RENT SUBSIDIES. This program was established in 1965 in the same legislation that authorized leased housing. It provides that a family pay one-fourth of its income for rent, with a federal subsidy making up the difference between that and the actual market rental of the property—which must be new or in good repair and owned by a nonprofit, limited-dividend, or cooperative organization. Like leased housing, rent subsidy permits the use of small scattered sites. It has proven more difficult to develop and administer, however, so that only 12,500 units were covered by the program in June 1969, only about one-sixth the number of leased-housing units. Both leased-housing and rent-subsidy programs have another advantage in that the units in the programs remain privately owned and pay local taxes.[37]

● MORTGAGE-SUBSIDY RENTAL PROGRAM. Initiated in 1961 and revised in 1965, this federal program makes available mortgage money at 3 percent interest to nonprofit, cooperative, or limited-dividend sponsors who will build rental housing for families whose incomes are above the public-housing range but insufficient to allow them to secure adequate housing in the private-housing market. The favorable mortgage-interest terms make it possible for such housing to be economically self-sufficient, to charge rents that cover all expenses and yet are about one-fourth less than rents on the open market. The program has not proven to be very popular, however, with housing starts under it accounting for only 5 percent of all rental housing starts in 1967.[38]

● MORTGAGE-SUBSIDY HOME-OWNERSHIP PROGRAMS. Included in this category are programs of various government agencies that are designed to permit low- and moderate-income families to buy homes or to rehabilitate their present homes. There are programs that provide for low-interest-rate mortgages for the purchase of rehabilitated, single-family homes for families with relatively low incomes. One part of the urban renewal program provides for low-cost loans for rehabilitating dwellings in urban renewal areas. By arresting deterioration and bringing existing buildings up to minimum health and safety standards, the quality of housing provided by older buildings can be improved considerably.[39]

A number of the above types of housing program involve financial guarantees by the FHA. "The Federal Housing Administration, traditionally most active in the suburbs, is now loosed in the slums, equipped with a wide range of guarantees and incentives." [40] As a corollary of these new FHA activities, the "red lining" or banning of loan guarantees in older areas of the city has decreased, a practice that was noted earlier as speeding the decline of those neighborhoods that needed the most financial support. The FHA has thus undergone a tremendous change since its early days in the 1930s when it concerned itself almost entirely with middle-class homeowners and actively encouraged residential segregation.

The federal programs discussed above provide assistance in the form of direct or indirect subsidies for housing to low-income families. People who work hard and save in order to buy decent homes sometimes resent it when poor families are subsidized by the government and live in housing just as good. Alvin Schorr, an official of the Department of Health, Education and Welfare, has pointed out, though, that middle- and high-income families also receive subsidization for their housing in the form of income-tax deductions. Whereas in 1962 the federal government expended $820 million in subsidizing housing for the poor, it spent three-and-one-half times that much in the form of income-tax deductions for housing for those with middle-level incomes and above. The top 20 percent of families according to income received a housing subsidy that amounted to twice as many dollars as that of families in the lowest 20 percent. In discussing this, Urban America cautions: "This policy will not build a sense of community, nor will it build the housing that is needed." [41]

The increase in the variety of ways of providing housing for those with low incomes means that one can no longer accurately assess the extent to which low-income housing needs are being met simply by determining the number of public-housing units provided. Public housing is no longer the only type of low-income housing. In order to begin meeting the needs of low-income families the Advisory Commission on Civil Disorders recommended that 6 million new units be provided in 1969 for low- and moderate-income families and 6 million during the succeeding five years.[42] The magnitude of this recommendation can best be appreciated by considering that for the entire 18-year period from 1950 to 1968 only 543,000 low-rent public-housing units were made available for occupancy.[43]

The Housing and Urban Development Act of 1968 accepted the goal of 6 million low-income housing units but increased to 10 years the time period during which it would be achieved, making an average of 600,000 units per year. During the first two years, however, less than half this number of units was achieved.[44] Enacting legislation to set up housing programs and establish housing goals is one thing, but the actual appropriation of money to operate the programs and achieve the goals is, of course, another. Appropriations sufficient to implement the 1968 Housing Act were not made even for its first year.[45] Heavily unbalanced federal budgets, plus an economic slowdown at the beginning of the 1970s, do not offer promise of full implementation of the Act during at least the early 1970s.

The 1968 Housing Act also projected 20 million conventionally built, unassisted, housing units over a 10-year period. In 1970 the administration started including mobile homes in housing totals,[46] thus in effect decreasing the number of conventionally built housing units to be provided, as mobile homes had previously not been counted as part of the regular housing supply. Peak levels of housing construction are certain to be needed during the 1970s, if for no other reason than that new-family formation will reach a peak as a result of the marriages of those born during the peak birth-rate years of the 1950s.

As mentioned above, low-income housing cannot be considered independently of the question of total housing supply available. Two factors seem to be particularly relevant in influencing total housing supply through their effect upon the amount of new housing started. One factor is interest rates, which in 1969–1971 have been near 8 percent. At this rate a family that carries a $20,000 mortgage over a 30-year period would pay a total of almost $60,000—twice as much interest as the value of the mortgage itself. Such a family would require a gross annual income of at least $13,000 and have to pay $266 a month for housing costs, including mortgage payments, taxes, maintenance, and insurance.[47] Furthermore, a $20,000 house is about at the bottom of the new-home market in most cities. The median value of new houses offered for sale in 1970 was $27,000.[48] From one-half to two-thirds of the American population is priced out of the market for new homes. The housing problem is not just the concern of those at the bottom of the economic heap.

The other factor is that of the cost of housing itself. Unlike almost any other product commonly used in America, housing still tends to be produced by antiquated methods unaffected by the industrial revolution. Extensive use of modern materials and factory methods of production could lower housing costs considerably (which in turn would lower the amount of money one would need to borrow and pay interest on). "Prefabricated" housing is thought of by many as being cheap and unattractive. Modern materials and designs, however, make possible the construction by efficient factory methods of housing that is durable and attractive and that can have a conventional appearance.

It was recognized in the 1940s that eliminating much expensive hand-type work on the building site in favor of efficient factory methods could contribute to an increased housing supply.[49] Although there was little evidence of much actual change up to 1970, a number of manufacturers have developed products and techniques that can lower costs by making construction more efficient. Manufacturers of conventional building products and the building-trades workers have not been in the forefront of those working for modernization.[50]

URBAN RENEWAL

Urban renewal is a broad topic; here the concern will be only with its direct relationships to housing and racial residential segregation. "The first laws specifically designed to encourage the revitalization of deteriorated areas" were passed in the states of New York and Illinois in 1941 and provided a precedent for the federal program, which came to be referred to as urban renewal, that was established in the 1949 Housing Act.[51] The program provides federal financial assistance to communities for improvements, generally in blighted areas.

Bollens and Schmandt emphasize that from its very beginning there has been a division of opinion over the primary goal of the program. Some advocates of urban renewal have argued that its basic function should be economic, that it should try to clear land and develop it in such a way that it produces the maximum revenue in taxes; other proponents have viewed its major purpose as being the social or moral one of improving the housing quality and living conditions of those who live in poor quality housing. Bollens and Schmandt comment that in practice: "Whatever the motives of those who have promoted urban renewal, the economic rather than the social or moral appeal has sustained the program. Given this emphasis, it is understandable that the plight of low-income families has not been of high priority in the renewal plans of municipalities." [52]

Although, accordingly, there has been much "slum clearance" under urban renewal, the land thus cleared has generally not been put back into use for housing low-income families but instead has been developed for the housing of middle- or upper-income families or for business and commercial purposes.[53] Aiken and Alford recently stated flatly: "There seems to be little doubt that the main effect of the program has been to reduce the stock of low-cost housing. . . ." [54] Furthermore, although there are differences between various cities in the extent to which the families evicted from to-be-demolished homes have been aided in finding suitable shelter, there has been general criticism to the effect that displaced families have usually not been given much useful assistance in relocating. Bollens and Schmandt cite conflicting evidence concerning the extent to which families have been able to locate in standard quality housing, but nevertheless conclude: "Whatever the validity of these various figures, relocation has been one of the weak features of the renewal program, a fact acknowledged by federal officials." [55]

Although slums have been cleared under the program, in some cases urban renewal has destroyed nonslum areas of older housing inhabited by stable, nondeviant, working-class families. Gans has given a detailed account of one such instance in Boston, where a cohesive Italian neighborhood in the West End was demolished in the late 1950s after years of vacillation by public officials. Such was the attachment of the residents to the area that "before the West End was totally cleared—and even afterwards—West Enders would come back on weekends to walk through the old neighborhood and the rubble-strewn streets." [56] Gans concluded that the West End was not a slum but a "low-rent district," that the planning had not taken into account the needs of the residents, and that the quality of their housing was not improved by the program.[57]

In a later article, significantly titled "The Failure of Urban Renewal," Gans cited additional evidence and studies indicating that the program generally had had an unfavorable effect on residents of urban renewal areas.[58] He noted, however, that books and articles critical of the program were based on its early years and that there were some highly successful programs. Such critical works themselves have pointed to ways in which urban renewal can be improved. Also, renewal need not require the demolition of housing, but can also provide for upgrading of older housing (as mentioned earlier in this chapter). Given the tension between economic and social goals in the context of the desperate economic plight in which many cities find themselves, it seems unlikely that social goals will take complete precedence over achieving an adequate central-city tax base. It should be possible, however, to achieve some blend of the two goals so that the considerable promise of urban renewal, a promise largely unfulfilled at least up to recent years, will be realized.

SELF-HELP PROGRAMS

One type of housing problem that is a result of racial segregation is that most black homebuyers have had access only to older homes. Unlike new suburban housing, such buildings generally require relatively large down payments and short periods for paying off the mortgage. One means for making homebuying possible for the family that does not have the substantial amount needed for a down payment is the purchase of a land contract. The buyer occupies the house, but the title to the property remains in the name of the seller.

An equitable contract arrangement makes it possible for many people to buy homes who would otherwise be unable to afford them. In practice, the system has frequently seen abuses develop, often by sellers who have charged high interest rates on inflated prices to blacks who have had few other alternatives. A side-effect of overly high house payments is that the family does not have sufficient money left over to maintain the house adequately, and it tends to deteriorate.

A case in Chicago shows how the contract system has worked for blacks; it also throws additional light on real-estate and blockbuster practices. A real-estate speculator (or blockbuster) bought a house in 1960 in an area that was just "changing" for $15,250. By claiming a value of $21,000 for the house he was able to get $17,300 on a mortgage, thus getting his money back plus $2,000. He soon sold it on a contract to a black family for $26,500, which, although $11,000 more than he had paid for it, was about average for houses sold to blacks in the neighborhood. (Who says black occupancy lowers property values?) The contract was for 20 years, during which time the buyer would not have title to the property, and if he missed only one monthly payment even after he had paid, say, $45,000, he could be evicted and would have nothing.[59] The speculator could use the payments he received to pay off his own mortgage, also profiting on its smaller amount and lower interest rates. He could use the money from the mortgage itself to buy another house and repeat the process.

To combat unreasonable contract provisions the Contract Buyer's League was formed in Chicago early in 1968 under the leadership of John R. Macnamara, who was then a Jesuit seminarian. In one neighborhood in Chicago it was found that 80 percent of the residents were buying under contract, and such buyers form the membership of the League. Although it encourages voluntary renegotiation of unfair contracts, the League has turned to legal action when necessary, charging that lending institutions practice racial discrimination in lending to white speculators but not to black homebuyers, who then are forced to accept extortionate contracts. One speculator counter-claimed that he *had* to charge high prices to black homebuyers because of FHA and lending-institution practices of racial discrimination in making their loans!

The League has won a majority of its court cases, and by 1971 was developing a computerized system of documents for use in future lawsuits, with some 4,000 suits pending. As of the beginning of 1971 it reported it had saved 106 contract buyers a total of almost $1.5 million through renegotiation, or nearly $14,000 per homebuying family, at an average of $60 saved for every dollar spent.[60] Perhaps most importantly, by taking the excessive profit out of real-estate speculation in "changing" neighborhoods, it will decrease the rewards for those who encourage racial segregation because of the money to be made from blockbusting and related activities. Not all states offer as little legal protection to contract buyers as Illinois, but the League's success is very likely to encourage similar activity in other places with weak statutes.

Tenants have generally had less success than buyers in using the law to improve their housing conditions. One means available to the tenant is the "rent strike." For greatest effectiveness the tenant should deposit the rent money with a neutral third party on the date it is normally due as a demonstration of his good faith. When the landlord institutes legal proceedings to evict the tenant for nonpayment of rent, the tenant replies that he will pay as soon as the unit is improved to meet the legal code requirements for housing and that the court should not force him to pay rent on a unit that is in violation of the law. In bringing the tenant to court the landlord brings his own violation to court as well.

Analyzing the Harlem rent strikes of 1963–1964 Lipsky judged, however, that they "did not succeed in obtaining fundamental goals. Most buildings in which tenants struck remained in disrepair, or deteriorated even further." [61] One difficulty is that rent strikes require mass action by all or most of the tenants in a building to be effective. The problems are increased by the powerlessness and relative ineffectiveness of slum residents. Mass action by powerless individuals requires strong leadership, and Lipsky concluded that problems of organization and leadership, plus the need for support by third parties, created problems that interfered with the attainment of goals.

The rent strike has been in a somewhat shaky legal position because courts have traditionally held that landlords are not required to make repairs unless they specifically promise to do so in a lease. In 1970, however, the U.S. Supreme Court agreed with a Washington D.C. Circuit Court ruling that landlords are responsible for furnishing adequate maintenance, heat, sanitary facilities, and so forth, and that a tenant has a right to withhold rent if these are not provided.[62] This decision could be of considerable significance in making rent withholding more effective by putting a protesting tenant in a stronger legal position, thereby reducing the amount of organization and mass action required.

---

1. Urban America, Inc., and The Urban Coalition, *One Year Later* (New York: Praeger Publishers, Inc., 1969), p. 115.
2. Allon Schoener, ed., *Harlem on My Mind* (New York: Random House, Inc., 1968), p. 22.
3. Chicago Commission on Race Relations, *The Negro in Chicago* (Chicago: University of Chicago Press, 1922; reprinted, Arno Press, Inc., New York, 1968), p. 645.
4. Gunnar Myrdal (with the assistance of Arnold Rose and Richard Sterner), *An American Dilemma* (New York: Harper & Row, Publishers, 1944), pp. 375–76.
5. Robert C. Weaver, *The Negro Ghetto* (New York: Harcourt Brace Jovanovich, Inc., 1948), p. 269.
6. *Report of the National Advisory Commission on Civil Disorders* (Washington, D.C.: Government Printing Office, 1968), p. 259.
7. Walter Firey, *Land Use in Central Boston* (Cambridge, Mass.: Harvard University Press, 1947), p. 222 (emphasis in the original).
8. Kenneth B. Clark, *Dark Ghetto* (New York: Harper & Row, Publishers, 1965), pp. 32–33.
9. U.S. Civil Rights Commission, *A Time to Listen . . . A Time to Act* (Washington, D.C.: Government Printing Office, 1967), pp. 9–10.
10. Lewis Mumford, *The Culture of Cities* (New York: Harcourt Brace Jovanovich, Inc., 1938), p. 179.
11. *City,* August 1969, p. 10.
12. *New York Times,* January 31, 1971.
13. Edith Abbott, *The Tenements of Chicago, 1908–1935* (Chicago: University of Chicago Press, 1936), p. 304.
14. Davis McEntire, *Residence and Race* (Berkeley and Los Angeles: University of California Press, 1960), p. 335.
15. "A Conversation with Herbert J. Gans and Robert W. Glasgow," *Psychology Today,* March 1970, pp. 58–82.
16. Francesco Cordasco, ed., *Jacob Riis Revisited* (Garden City, N.Y.: Doubleday & Company, 1968), p. 341.
17. Jane Addams, *Twenty Years at Hull-House* (New York: The Macmillan Company, 1910; reprinted, 1960), p. 100 (emphasis added).
18. Cordasco, *Jacob Riis Revisited,* p. 301.
19. Henry Pratt Fairchild, *Immigration* (New York: The Macmillan Company, 1913), pp. 234–35.
20. David R. Hunter, *The Slums: Challenge and Response* (New York: The Free Press, 1964), p. 3.

21. Miles L. Colean, *Renewing Our Cities* (New York: The Twentieth Century Fund, 1953), p. 41.

22. *City Chronicle,* November 1969, p. 3.

23. Glenn H. Beyer, *Housing and Society* (New York: The Macmillan Company, 1965), p. 450.

24. *Ibid.,* p. 507.

25. The National Commission on Urban Problems, Research Report No. 10, *Urban Housing Needs Through the 1980's: An Analysis and Projection* (Washington, D.C.: Government Printing Office, 1968).

26. *See* Urban America, Inc., *The Ill-Housed* (Washington, D.C., 1968), *esp.* pp. 32–33.

27. U.S. Department of Commerce/Bureau of the Census, *Housing Starts, January 1971,* Publication C20-71-1 (Washington, D.C.: Government Printing Office, March, 1971), Table 1.

28. Beyer, *Housing and Society,* p. 198.

29. *Ibid.,* pp. 344–45, 465.

30. *City,* August 1969, pp. 10–11.

31. *Time* magazine, March 16, 1970, p. 88.

32. Harrison E. Salisbury, *The Shook-up Generation* (New York: Harper & Row, Publishers, 1958), pp. 75–76.

33. Lee Rainwater, *Behind Ghetto Walls: Black Families in a Federal Slum* (Chicago: Aldine Publishing Company, 1970).

34. *Ibid.,* p. 8.

35. AP dispatch in Toledo *Blade,* February 7, 1971.

36. *City Chronicle,* September 1969, p. 1.

37. *Ibid.,* pp. 1–2.

38. Urban America, Inc., *The Ill-Housed,* pp. 29–30.

39. *Ibid.,* pp. 28–39.

40. *Ibid.,* p. 39.

41. *Ibid.,* p. 14. Whites are more likely to be homeowners than blacks and to benefit from tax policies favoring homeowners. *See* The National Commission on Urban Problems, Research Report No. 5, *The Federal Income Tax in Relation to Housing* (Washington, D.C.: Government Printing Office, 1968), pp. 27–28.

42. *Report of the National Advisory Commission on Civil Disorders,* p. 260.

43. Department of Housing and Urban Development, *Statistical Yearbook, 1968* (Washington, D.C.: Government Printing Office, 1970), p. 248.

44. President Richard M. Nixon, *Second Annual Report on National Housing Goals* (Washington, D.C.: Government Printing Office, 1970), Table 1, p. 12.

45. *Ibid.,* p. 3.

46. *Ibid.,* p. 2.

162 *Relieving Slum Problems*

47. According to Representative Wright Patman, Toledo *Blade,* February 2, 1970.

48. Richard M. Nixon, *National Housing Goals,* p. 1.

49. Miles L. Colean, *American Housing* (New York: The Twentieth Century Fund, 1944), *esp.* pp. 329 ff.

50. Urban America, Inc., *The Ill-Housed,* pp. 45–46.

51. Miles L. Colean, *Renewing Our Cities* (New York: The Twentieth Century Fund, 1953), pp. 28–29.

52. John C. Bollens and Henry J. Schmandt, *The Metropolis: Its People, Politics, and Economic Life* (2nd ed.) (New York: Harper & Row, Publishers, 1970), pp. 203–4.

53. Martin Anderson, *The Federal Bulldozer* (Cambridge, Mass.: The M.I.T. Press, 1964), pp. 91 ff.

54. Michael Aiken and Robert R. Alford, "Community Structure and Innovation: The Case of Urban Renewal," *American Sociological Review,* XXXV, No. 4 (August 1970), 651.

55. Bollens and Schmandt, *The Metropolis,* p. 207.

56. Herbert J. Gans, *The Urban Villagers* (New York: The Free Press, 1962), p. 304.

57. *Ibid.,* Chapter 14.

58. Herbert J. Gans, "The Failure of Urban Renewal," *Commentary* XXXIX (April 1965), pp. 29–37.

59. Article in the *Washington Post,* August 4, 1969.

60. *Ibid.; Chicago Sun-Times,* January 22, 1971; plus information supplied by the Contract Buyer's League, Chicago.

61. Michael Lipsky, "Rent Strikes: Poor Man's Weapon," *Trans-action,* February 1969, p. 11.

62. *Javins* v. *First National Realty Co.,* 428F 2d 1071 (D.C. Cir. 1970).

10 | Reducing Ghetto Segregation

Problems of the ghetto are those of involuntary racial residential segregation. Because whites have both initiated and maintained segregation, we should inquire into their reasons for rejecting a potential black neighbor. We thus come back to questions raised in the first chapter of this work regarding the relative importance to white attitudes of social class, racial prejudice, cultural differences, and the possible confusion of slum with ghetto. Material covered here has given at least some support to each of these possibilities, but we may now be in a better position to discuss them.

Banfield emphasizes the social-class differences between the slum dweller and the middle-class suburbanite and writes that the difference is mainly one of different life styles in terms of orientation toward the future: how far into the future one looks and how much influence a person believes he can have on the future.[1] He distinguishes four social-class levels and considers each to be a subculture, contending that much of what appears to be racial antagonism is instead that of social-class subcultures. While social class may frequently be relevant, the racial or ethnic factor appears to be of greater importance.

The earlier discussion of ghetto characteristics maintained that the native, white, middle-class person judges his neighbors according to whether or not they have traits characteristic of the ghetto. Certainly many of the characteristics of the slum-ghetto resident are simply those of the lower class and would result in his being rejected because of them. Social class will not explain, however, most cases of rejection of Jews, whom Banfield recognizes tend to be quite future-oriented and hence supposedly highly acceptable to other members of the middle class. Neither does simple social class seem to account for such phenomena as the Grosse Pointe (Michigan) point system (see pp. 91–92), with its concern for such matters as swarthiness of skin color and accented speech, nor for restrictive covenants that exclude Southern Europeans, and so forth. Middle-class, future-oriented whites in Deerfield, Illinois, fought off a private housing development that would have included 10 to 12 middle-class future-oriented black families among those in its 50 new homes (see pp. 93–94).

In instances such as these it seems that the native white has based his rejection more on the basis of the racial-ethnic cultural characteristics of a potential neighbor than on that of social class. In a recent article, Moynihan discusses ethnicity and social classes, noting that the two have frequently been closely associated, and concludes: "To be sure, there are class realities, but ethnic realities are there as well. Increasingly they are the *dominant* realities." Glazer and Moynihan judged that ethnicity and race dominated issues and problems in New York City far more by 1970 than seemed possible in 1963.[2] Krickus has a similar view, maintaining that new-immigration ethnic groups have not assimilated fully into American culture either in style of life or in patterns of social relationships, and that the neighborhoods which have been most successful in resisting black expansion have been the more homogeneous ethnic ones. He believes also that "the black revolution" has heightened ethnic-group awareness.[3]

A case in point is that of Warren, Michigan. This practically all-white working-class suburb of Detroit has already been mentioned as vigorously opposing black residence. Warren residents are described as of predominantly Polish background, and it is reported that "English is still a secondary language in some households."[4] Polish neighborhoods generally have been described as "particularly resistant to racial change."[5]

A recent study of a Near West Side slum area in Chicago indicates both that many ethnic-group cultural traits are still strong and that racial-ethnic cultural differences can cause hostilities and misunderstandings. The Italian way, for instance, is to deal with disagreements through private arrangements that avoid taking public positions. Italians consequently not only look down upon public-protest actions taken by blacks but feel resentful that they were not approached informally first. Blacks, in turn, believe that the Italians are being dishonest and should have anticipated their demands.[6]

Black-white cultural differences are not just social-class differences, then. To be black in 20th-century America is to have a history and set of experiences that are greatly different from those of whites. It is understandable that a black might want to live with neighbors who have shared the black experience, yet to do so frequently means living in or near a slum. "The middle- and upper-working-class Negro, then, if he is to be anywhere near his friends and relatives and in a community to which he feels he 'belongs,' must live among people whose style of life [because of social class] he finds repugnant." Moving to a white neighborhood involves "cutting himself off from relatives and friends, and risking insult and even injury from prejudiced neighbors. . . ."[7]

The white may say that blacks should live with people of "their own kind." But what is the middle-class black's "own kind?" In a society that emphasizes educational and economic accomplishment, one's own kind may well be considered those of similar social status, irrespective of race; but our society also has a long history of emphasizing race as determining one's own kind. Furthermore, there seems to be a greater tendency recently on the part of middle-class blacks themselves to feel a sense of identification with and responsibility for lower-class blacks.

It appears that a middle-class black's neighbors are likely to present difficulties for him regardless of the type of neighborhood he chooses. Given this, it is then more likely that his choice would be influenced by other factors—location with regard to place of employment, convenience to community facilities, quality of schools, suitability of type of housing, and so forth. Most individual housing decisions are probably based on such criteria anyway, rather than on selecting a cozy group of neighbors.

These considerations suggest that nonsegregation would probably produce a process similar to that characteristic of the immigrants. Many ghetto residents would want to remain in the black ghetto for social reasons, business or professional advantages, or because of familiarity with the area. With crowding reduced because of the elimination of back-pressure, many areas could "unslum" through a process of reducing density and improving the quality of housing, just as various immigrant areas have unslummed.[8] Also like immigrants, those who least identified with ghetto culture or who had the strongest motives for moving out of it would be the ones most likely to do so, and for these reasons they would be the ones tending to have the fewest ghetto characteristics. This would give them the greatest acceptability in nonghetto neighborhoods. Unslumming of the ghetto would give it a more attractive image and result in a higher status for its residents, which in turn would decrease the importance of ghetto characteristics. Just as some immigrant ghettos have remnants surviving more than 50 years after the end of mass immigration, so black ghetto communities are likely to exist in the 21st century, but because they would meet the needs of their residents and would be preferred by them, rather than because there was no alternative.

The goal in reducing residential segregation, then, is not necessarily integration—the even distribution of blacks about the city in a fashion that would produce a value of zero according to the Taeuber's segregation index (see page 40)—but rather nonsegregation, a condition in which a black would be able to locate wherever in the city he felt would best meet his needs.

Since at least the 1940s some black community and political leaders have favored continued segregation of the races because of advantages that result from territorial concentration.[9] Whereas black leaders would formerly admit this only privately, increased black militancy by the late 1960s saw them advocating this publicly.[10] Attempts by HUD to encourage the provision of housing for blacks outside ghetto areas have, according to one congressman, "produced angry charges from leaders of the black community of Pittsburgh that no attempt is being made by HUD to build in, and upgrade, their ghetto community." [11] One consequence of such black opposition was the stoppage of federal programs relating to housing in Pittsburgh, Washington, and a number of other cities.[12]

At the same time, federal programs to aid home ownership of low-income families through low-interest-rate mortgages have been criticized by various individuals and groups as aiding segregation, as most homes bought or rehabilitated by blacks under these programs have been in ghetto areas. It seems as though any federal program affecting ghetto housing is bound to be controversial. In any event, the crucial question is still whether or not blacks who do wish to move out of the ghetto will be able to do so, as did the immigrants and their children.

Involuntary racial residential segregation has proven to be an extremely important force that has affected black-white relationships and has caused much Negro discontent. Its elimination has been urged repeatedly—from the 1922 Chicago Commission on Race Relations recommendation opposing "forcible segregation or exclusion of Negroes" up to the 1968 National Advisory Commission on Civil Disorders conclusion that "fundamental is the elimination of the racial barrier in housing." [13] If American cities continue to have racial difficulties it will not be from a lack of knowledge of what is the cause, but rather from a failure to take action to deal with the cause.

COMBATTING INVOLUNTARY SEGREGATION

Consideration in detail of approaches and methods for dealing with involuntary segregation is beyond the scope of this book. Instead the reader is referred to works which concentrate on this topic.[14] Here we will attempt only to consider some general issues and recent developments.

Regarding action programs, one distinction is that between coercion and persuasion; just how much change can be brought about by forceful methods and with what consequences? [15] Sumner, an early sociologist, doubted the effectiveness of laws in changing behavior that was well-established in the folkways of a society.[16] Whites have frequently favored gradual programs that emphasize "goodwill" and "education," fearing, as in Chicago in the 1940s, that any substantial gains by blacks would "excite tension among white people." [17] Now the term "white backlash" is used to refer to the negative reaction (frequently only expected rather than actual) of whites to changes that take place "too fast" because they have resulted from the application of power, pressure, or legal authority.

Jack Greenberg has questioned the truth of the belief that "stateways cannot change folkways," however, and has cited a number of changes in race practices that have been brought about by legislative or judicial means.[18] The difficulty in the North, though, is that practices of racial discrimination have developed despite theoretical legal racial equality. Hence, there are no laws requiring racial discrimination that can be overturned in the North as there were in the South; there are instead a set of attitudes, beliefs, informal arrangements, and institutional practices that are all the more difficult to combat because they are so amorphous.

The first step taken on the national level toward eliminating housing segregation was Executive Order 11063, signed by President Kennedy in November 1962. This Order directed "all departments and agencies in the executive branch of the Federal Government" engaging in activities related to housing "to take all action necessary and appropriate to prevent discrimination because of race, color, creed, or national origin." The next major action was Title VI of the 1964 Civil Rights Act, which prohibited discrimination in federally assisted programs, chiefly public housing and urban renewal. Neither the Executive Order nor Title VI applied retroactively, one effect of this being that housing financed earlier by the FHA or the VA was not covered. Also, conventional (non-FHA or -VA) mortgages, which amounted to about three-fourths of all mortgages in the early 1960s, were not covered.[19]

Federal provisions were supplemented by fair-housing laws in 18 states and more than 40 cities by the beginning of 1968. Nevertheless, the Advisory Commission on Civil Disorders reported in that year that "the great bulk of housing produced by the private sector remains unaffected by anti-discrimination measures." [20]

In 1968 two major developments took place that made the federal ban on discrimination in housing complete. One was the passage of Title VIII of the 1968 Civil Rights Act, which provided for "fair housing throughout the United States." [21] Coverage under the act was extended in three phases so that it became fully effective by the beginning of 1970, when it included all housing except single-family housing sold or rented without the services of a real-estate broker and owner-occupied apartment buildings with no more than four dwelling units.

The other development was a landmark ruling by the U.S. Supreme Court upholding an 1866 law that reads: "All citizens of the United States shall have the same right, in every State and Territory, as is enjoyed by white citizens thereof to inherit, purchase, lease, sell, hold, and convey real and personal property." [22] Regarding this ruling, which was in the case of *Jones* v. *Mayer,* the U.S. Civil Rights Commission stated: "The *Jones* decision rendered all housing, with no exception, open without regard to race, at least as a matter of legal right." [23] The federal government thus changed from actively promoting segregation in the 1930s and 1940s, to a policy of neutrality in the 1950s, and finally to active opposition to segregation in the 1960s, beginning with Executive Order 11063 and culminating in the two-month period in 1968 that saw both the passage of the fair housing act and the *Jones* Supreme Court decision.

How much effect the federal fair-housing legislation will actually produce remains to be seen. State and local fair-housing acts were hardly revolutionary in their consequences. Regarding them, Eley wrote that real-estate brokers, who were among the strongest opponents of fair-housing legislation, tended to relax their opposition when they found that such laws did not "disrupt" the market. "In other words," he maintained, "the state and local laws have not yet brought any fundamental change in realtor practices or housing patterns." He suggested that the function of fair-housing legislation was "mainly symbolic and ritualistic," and pointed to the lack of a relationship between the degree of integration in a community or state and the presence or absence of fair-housing laws.[24] The effect of fair-housing laws would certainly be blunted when, as noted by Hecht, "the personnel of an enforcement agency" would try to discourage black families from going "where you aren't wanted." [25] In Buffalo, however, a citizens' group, HOME, was apparently able to secure substantial real-estate broker compliance with the New York state fair-housing law through particularly skillful leadership, which did not seek harsh penalties if compliance could be effected but stood ready to cooperate with the state in suspending the broker's license if other means failed.[26]

The existence of a national legal ban on racial discrimination in housing does not in itself guarantee that it will be enforced. Regarding the 1968 fair-housing act, the U.S. Civil Rights Commission notes that "while coverage is a strong point, enforcement is weak." [27] HUD "is charged with the principal responsibility for enforcement and administration" of the law, but is limited to "informal methods of conference, conciliation, and persuasion." [28] HUD can refer cases to states that have fair-housing laws and enforcement machinery and to the U.S. Attorney General for litigation, but this does not guarantee that action will be taken. The Justice Department did not follow up initially in the case mentioned earlier of Black Jack, Missouri; it was left for a private organization to institute proceedings. While the 1866 law cited in *Jones* v. *Mayer* is complete in coverage, it has no provision for enforcement except through private lawsuits by affected parties.

Weak enforcement provisions are undoubtedly at least one reason why an official of the National Association of Real Estate Boards was able to comment in 1970, after two years of federal fair-housing experience: "The act has caused very little ripple in the market. There's been much

less change than a lot of people thought there'd be." [29] Another reason
is that HUD, according to the U.S. Civil Rights Commission, "has not
made maximum use of the enforcement tools at its command nor has it
made the best disposition of the available resources." [30]

One factor that certainly tends to inhibit vigorous enforcement is that
there is hardly unanimous public demand for it. Earlier chapters have
provided a number of examples of the disfavor with which nonsegregation is viewed by many individuals and groups. When the Secretary of
HUD, George Romney, visited Warren, Michigan, during the 1970
election campaign he was hissed and booed by residents who resented
HUD efforts to reduce racial segregation there.[31] This is language any
public official can understand.

Furthermore, the Administration must obtain its funds from Congress, some of whose members favor a policy of "gradualism" and who
will not vote for substantial appropriations to enable vigorous enforcement. Ultimately, federal goals and policy are expressed by the President,
and in a news conference in December 1970 President Nixon said that
he would do no more than what was "required by the law," and that
he believed "that forced integration of the suburbs is not in the national
interest." The catch phrase *forced integration* is reminiscent of the term
forced-housing used by the National Association of Real Estate Boards
in opposing fair-housing legislation[32] and tends to direct attention away
from "forced segregation."

Even if enforcement of nondiscrimination in housing is limited to
what is required by law, the combination of the 1968 fair-housing law
and *Jones* v. *Mayer* is a formidable one indeed. Under the fair-housing
law, an individual who has been discriminated against can make a complaint to HUD through a regional or area office, which will investigate
the complaint and take action if the facts are found to support it. The
Civil Rights Commission, however, has called the complaint procedures
"cumbersome" and noted the limited sanctions and resources which
HUD can use.[33]

In approximately the first two years of the fair-housing law, 1,321
complaints were received by HUD.[34] During 1970, 51 percent of the
complaints made were settled satisfactorily through HUD conciliation
efforts. These settlements included cases where landlords or sellers paid
damages of from $250 to $3,500 to renters or buyers to compensate
them for extra costs, inconvenience, or embarrassment caused by the
discrimination.[35] That HUD, with its limited powers, could negotiate
such damage settlements may be due to the existence of an additional
weapon available to the person discriminated against (which he could
use either instead of a complaint to HUD or if a HUD settlement were
not satisfactory)—the private suit for damages, most likely under *Jones*
v. *Mayer*.[36]

While the private suit for damages may have some drawbacks in that it requires the individual to hire an attorney and proceed on his own, it has the advantage of not depending upon bureaucratic action. Furthermore, the damage award will ordinarily provide for the cost of taking the legal action. Whether resulting from administrative or private actions, the concept of awards for damages and suffering is a powerful one. In 1970 the New Jersey Superior Court ordered a landlord to pay $2,500 to two nonwhites who tried to rent a house of his. The award—for "humiliation, pain, and mental suffering"—was described as the first one ever granted for such reasons in New Jersey.[37] Court decisions in Massachusetts in 1970 and Oregon in 1971 have upheld the right of the administrator of state antidiscrimination laws to award damages for "mental suffering and humiliation" even if the state statutes did not specifically provide for payments.[38] Another recent ruling by a U.S. Court of Appeals held that a plaintiff is entitled to sue for damages resulting from refusal to rent even if the defendant subsequently rented an apartment to him.[39]

A 1970 Circuit Court decision in Illinois maintained that refusal to rent, even if only based *partially* on racial grounds, is prohibited by *Jones* v. *Mayer*.[40] Two 1971 court actions have the effect of prohibiting racial discrimination by a large real-estate rental firm using a practice of renting some of its buildings to whites and others to blacks. This constitutes a "pattern of discrimination," which is outlawed by the 1968 fair-housing act. Under the terms of a settlement in the U.S. District Court in Brooklyn one such firm has agreed to provide a month's free rent for up to 50 black families who had been refused admission by the firm to some of its buildings that it had reserved for whites. The firm agreed to accept blacks in any of its units and to process all apartment applications with a time clock to assure that a "first come-first served" policy is actually followed. As this firm controls more than 20,000 apartment units in New York City, the effects of this one agreement alone are considerable.[41]

As a body of court decisions and precedents builds up, the handling of discrimination matters could become a relatively routine matter. An individual who was turned down could inform the landlord or seller that he was ready to take legal action, if necessary, including seeking payments for damages. In some cities there are fair-housing organizations actively working to bring about open housing. One such group, the Leadership Council for Metropolitan Open Communities, has as its "ultimate objective . . . no less than the complete elimination, through legal tactics, of discrimination in the real estate industry throughout the Chicago metropolitan area." The organization aims to make discrimination "too expensive and too risky a proposition," and says: "When large real estate organizations are ordered by the U.S. District Court to pay large damage awards to minority homeseekers as a consequence of their racial prejudice, patterns of conduct on the part of those who control the sale and rental of housing will begin to change." [42] Hecht, drawing both from his experience in Buffalo and from other sources, discusses fair-housing groups in a recent book.[43]

Meanwhile, HUD is also working to see that real-estate advertising does not foster racial discrimination, that Negro real-estate brokers are not excluded from local multiple-listing services, and that blockbusting is stopped.[44] With individuals and private organizations adding their pressures to those of the federal and state governments, both the forces and the means to eliminate racial discrimination are immeasurably stronger than at any time in the past.

Enforcement need not come directly through lawsuits, but may be brought about through implementation of governmental policies. HUD, in particular, is in a position to require fair housing as a condition for a community's receiving federal funds through HUD housing and urban-renewal programs. The limit of enforcement through such means is determined by the readiness of the community to forego federal assistance in order to avoid nonsegregation provisions. It was mentioned earlier that the Toledo City Council was willing to take a chance on forfeiting $15 million in federal funds for various improvements around the city because of controversy over sites for public housing.

In 1970 the voters of Warren, Michigan, voted down an urban-renewal program already underway because its continuation would have made Warren subject to a HUD requirement of fair housing in the city (mentioned earlier as being practically lily-white). "In doing so, Warren became the first city in the country to forcibly eject a HUD program." [45] There is little question but that Warren desperately needed the urban-renewal funds as its "overburdened budget" had already led to a cutback in municipal services. Yet the Warren residents turned down $13 million of HUD money rather than open their city to blacks, even those who might be working in its own industries.

ETHNIC WORKING-CLASS WHITES

It seems evident that the Warren residents have strong feelings about racial matters. There are indications that they are not unique, however, but are typical of the residents of many working-class ethnic areas, whether suburbs such as Warren or simply neighborhoods in larger cities. It is important to inquire into the attitudes and feelings of such people, because, for some time in the future, most changes in racial residential patterns are likely to affect them more than those in high-status suburbs.[46] It seems an oversimplification to ascribe their reactions to racial attitudes alone. They are also likely to have antagonisms toward such white groups as student protesters, hippies, and peace demonstrators.

Although blacks may believe that whites, even at the working-class level, have so many advantages that it is ridiculous for them to feel on the defensive, this is not the picture given by a number of accounts of working-class whites; their accounts portray them with their backs against the wall and barely able to hold their own against the inroads made by the changing technology that threatens their jobs, the inflation that robs them of money, the taxes that make increasing demands on their income, and the threatening of their basic beliefs by the revolts against the traditional value system by middle-class young people.[47]

Given such a view, programs designed to improve housing for the poor and to implement a policy of nonsegregation seem to the working-class ethnic white to be an additional burden, to be borne primarily by him, for the benefit of the blacks, who are being given preferred treatment by the safely suburbanized middle-class whites. Psychiatrist Robert Coles quotes a Boston housewife of Irish descent:

> All you hear these days is news about them. You'd think Negroes were the only people in America that have a tough time. What about the rest of us? Who comes here asking us how we get by, or how we feel about what *we* had to go through?

A Boston lawyer voiced similar thoughts:

> This is a slum . . . but it's a white slum, so no one cares about it. There's no glamour in white slums, only Negro ones. The suburban housewives and the Ivy League students, they've gone poor-crazy, but only for the colored poor. . . . We have overcrowded schools. We have rotten buildings. . . . We have lousy parks. . . . We have our delinquents and our drop-outs—the works. Who cares, though? [48]

Coles considers that lower-status whites are going through a process opposite to that of the blacks. "At this time in history Negroes are being affirmed, while these white people feel increasingly deserted and alone. The Negro's excuse for his present condition is everywhere made known: it was not his fault, but ours. We carried him here by force and kept him in bondage for three centuries." [49] The poor white has no such excuse. If he is not successful, according to our society's conventional value system, he has to accept the blame as his own. It is not a pleasant pill to swallow. Resentment against black "intrusion," whether into jobs, neighborhood, or social life, thus seems to result from a complex of personal, social, political, and economic factors in which ethnic status provides a rallying point.

A constantly recurring theme that pervades the literature on race and housing and which this writer believes should be emphasized is that of the *fear* felt by whites. Again the black, whose Southern traditions include the fear of being powerless in the face of physical attack, including lynching, and at the mercy of Southern whites in all aspects of life, and whose experiences in the North generate frustrated rage because of white dominance,[50] may find it hard to believe that whites, who are both numerically and institutionally at such an advantage, could feel fear of blacks. Yet the literature dealing with black-white residential issues mentions white fear repeatedly. It seems appropriate to recognize and discuss it as an issue in its own right.

Weaver's 1948 book *The Negro Ghetto* has five subheadings under its index listing of "fear." (One such reference, interestingly enough, is to the fear of ignorant black Southern rural migrants felt by black Northern "old settlers" at the beginning of the Great Migration.) In Helper's discussion of whites' reasons for not wanting Negroes as neighbors, she uses fear words ("fear," "afraid," "scare," and so forth) 25 times in less than four pages.[51] Included are, for example, fear of being outnumbered racially, fear of personal danger, fear of neighborhood deterioration, fear of loss of social status, fear of decline in property values, fear of people simply because they are Negro ("Most colored people look dangerous; they scare you. . . ."), fear of what will happen to neighborhood schools, and of course the traditional fear of interracial sex and marriage. It does not seem an overgeneralization to say that practically any work dealing with residence and race will refer to white fears.

Whether the fears are justified on any realistic objective basis may be of very little importance in an actual situation. It is a sociological truism that what people believe to be true is more important in determining behavior than what is actually true. In earlier discussions we have seen how one common fear, loss of property values, does not seem to be justified by objective evidence and how in other situations fears can be made to come true through the operation of the self-fulfilling-prophecy mechanism. In many cases the most important factor is simply that the fear exists and influences behavior. It might be helpful, even in a therapeutic sense, for whites to admit their fears freely both to other whites and to blacks. Blacks have fears and resentments that they could admit, and, if nothing else, race relations could proceed on a more honest and realistic basis. Otherwise, the fear and other emotions remain in the background, influencing the course of events in various indirect ways because they are not admitted or acknowledged.

MODEL CITIES

The Model Cities program is not directed towards reducing segregation, but it has the potential for exerting an indirect influence by changing the image of the ghetto, with the consequent re-evaluation of ghetto characteristics. The Model Cities Act, passed by Congress in 1966, provides a program for deteriorated city areas that is concerned not just with housing but with a broad range of matters related to the quality of living within each area—including health and medical care, transportation, criminal justice, social welfare, education, recreation, employment, or whatever else is important in a particular city. By early 1968 some 75 cities had their initial proposals approved, and by early 1971 150 cities were participating in the program.[52]

An important feature of the program is that the residents of each Model Cities area are to be involved as fully as possible in determining the specific needs and plans for the area, working with public officials and drawing upon the resources of the city in devising a detailed proposal that will be the basis for the granting of federal funds. Because each local program is designed for the particular community, there can be considerable variation from city to city in goals, type of organization, and means chosen to attain goals. Another provision calls for regular evaluation of the success of the local program. Moyer, Kaplan, and Klein have suggested a design for evaluation that they developed in the course of working on the Toledo Model Cities program.[53]

Although the program is generally thought of as being for ghetto-slums, a local Model Cities area need not be either a slum or ghetto.[54] For ghetto-slums, though, the Model Cities program is important because it makes it possible to change both the self-concept of ghetto-slum dwellers and the image of the ghetto held by outsiders. Zorbaugh called attention to the "*set of attitudes* that . . . accommodates the family to the slum, and isolates it." [55] These attitudes of apathy and passivity, feelings of powerlessness, and a low self-image contribute to the perpetuation of the slum way of life. Clinard has written that successful slum-action programs lead to "newly created self-images . . . and recognition by others of new identities and roles." [56] By helping to plan and carry out successful improvement programs, residents of ghetto-slum areas gain increased self-respect, which tends to generate greater respect from others. If, as maintained here, ghetto characteristics are important in themselves in leading to rejection by others, changing the image of the ghetto can lead to increased acceptance of families moving from the ghetto.

Because of the time lag in planning and getting the local programs underway, most cities did not enter the action phase of their programs until 1969 or 1970. Given the multiple goals, the individualistic nature of each local program, and the newness of many of the approaches being tried, several years of experience will be needed to evaluate Model Cities adequately. Preliminary indications point to at least some degree of success in the planning and early action phases of local Model Cities programs.[57]

CONCLUDING REMARKS

Describing a new edition of *Beyond the Melting Pot,* by Glazer and himself, Moynihan wrote, "we conclude that, for racial and ethnic relations in the North, the decade [of the 1960s] was a near disaster." [58] There has not been much in these pages to support an effective rebuttal to that conclusion, as this writer has tried to avoid an unrealistic optimism. It seems, however, that there might be some consolation in the fact that the "near disaster" is more a matter of a failure of the situation to improve than a serious deterioration from earlier conditions. There has been abundant evidence in this work of a lack of change, of a continuation of the same kinds of condition for a half-century or more. It was this stagnancy that led Kenneth B. Clark to state to the National Advisory Commission on Civil Disorders:

> I read that report . . . of the 1919 riot in Chicago, and it is as if I were reading the report of the investigating committee on the Harlem riot of '35, the report of the investigating committee on the Harlem riot of '43, the report of the McCone Commission on the Watts riot.
> I must again in candor say to you members of this Commission—it is a kind of Alice in Wonderland—with the same moving picture reshown over and over again, the same analysis, the same recommendations, and the same inaction.[59]

That inaction also seemed to follow this Commission report was indicated by one study that inquired into changes made during the year following its release.[60]

Nevertheless, at the risk of being judged in the future as having been naively hopeful, this writer will suggest that there seem to be some indications of a change in both race relations in general and residential practices in particular.

On the race-relations scene as a whole there is evidence of a higher status for Negroes in both North and South. One need only compare the segregationist, race-baiting, campaign techniques of Southern politicians up through the early 1960s to the position currently taken by a number of southern public officials, recognizing that segregation is legally dead and that cooperation between the races is the goal in the 1970s.[61] In 1970 a Negro, Wilson Riles, was elected Superintendent of Public Instruction in California, a state in which Negroes made up less than 8 percent of the population. Northern cities in which whites were in the majority have elected black mayors. A number of black entertainers have TV shows whose popularity depends upon a mass audience that necessarily includes many whites. By the late 1960s black models were frequently being used in merchandising catalogs and advertisements aimed not just at blacks but at the mass market. Elementary-school readers now include black characters; some reading series have realistic inner-city illustrations rather than the traditional middle-class suburban settings.[62] There is evidence of genuine change.

There are also indications of change in ideas regarding race and residence. In studies of attitudes toward desegregation, Hyman and Sheatsley found that the percentage of Northern whites who expressed attitudes of support for residential integration increased from 42 percent in 1942 to 70 percent by the end of 1963.[63] Of course a person's behavior might be different when confronted by the actual prospect of a black neighbor, and cases documented here show that there is still much determined opposition. But the attitudinal climate does seem to be different.

The means for bringing about nonsegregation have become far more powerful than at any time in the past with the combination of the 1968 fair-housing law and the *Jones* v. *Mayer* decision. Given the countervailing forces in government and the nature of bureaucracies, it would be surprising if the fair-housing law were given maximum implementation; nevertheless, the penalties and the principle of payment for damages suffered by prospective buyers or tenants need not actually be implemented in every case to be effective. A landlord or seller who knows that he faces a possible damage suit would think twice before turning away a black person. His second thought might be not to do so. Each such instance would be another case of desegregation. There are certain to be enough blacks who are willing to use these resources to make discrimination much riskier than in the past.

It should be emphasized that desegregation in the 70s will not be taking place in the same ideological climate that existed in the past. In addition to their data regarding residential desegregation, Hyman and Sheatsley present evidence of a considerable change in racial views in the past few decades. Whereas in 1942 only 50 percent of Northern whites considered Negroes to be born with intelligence equal to that of whites, the figure had risen to 80 percent by 1964.

It has been stressed here that the basic practices of modern residential segregation were developed shortly before and during the early 1920s, a time during which racist beliefs maintained that behavioral characteristics or tendencies were inborn. It is now recognized that this is not so, and while the typical Northern white may resist desegregation simply because it is new, because of beliefs regarding property values, or because of cultural characteristics, he at least is not viewing the black as someone born with abilities inferior to his own, which could be a powerful factor even for someone with basically democratic values.

Given the decline in racist beliefs, it may turn out that the main support for residential segregation is residential segregation. In other words, even though there was a decrease in the factors that originally led to the development of involuntary segregation, the system developed its own dynamics—with a property-value mystique; real-estate beliefs and practices that were profitable to the real-estate broker, the blockbuster, the residential developer, and associated institutions; and self-sustaining patterns of interaction between whites and blacks that produced wrongs and hostilities on both sides. The role of involuntary segregation as a *cause* and stimulant of racial prejudice has been emphasized before. Although segregation may be a result of prejudice, at the present time the reverse may be more true.

Given the changed status of the black, the changed attitudes on the part of many whites, the outlawing finally of residential racial segregation (with means available for combatting segregation), it is difficult to believe that the 1970s will see a continuation of the same old ghetto pattern and the involuntary segregation that have been characteristic of the past half-century.

1. Edward C. Banfield, *The Unheavenly City: The Nature and Future of Our Urban Crisis* (Boston: Little, Brown and Company, 1970), chapters 3 and 4.

2. Daniel Patrick Moynihan, "Eliteland," *Psychology Today*, IV, No. 4 (September 1970), 70 (emphasis in original); Nathan Glazer and Daniel Patrick Moynihan, *Beyond the Melting Pot* (2nd ed.) (Cambridge, Mass.: The M.I.T. Press, 1970), p. ix; *see also* p. xxxv.

3. Richard J. Krickus, "White Ethnic Neighborhoods: Ripe for the Bulldozer," *Civil Rights Digest*, III, No. 3 (Summer 1970), 4.

4. *City*, January–February 1971, p. 77.

5. Dennis Clark, "Immigrant Enclaves in Our Cities," in C. E. Elias, Jr., James Gillies, and Svend Riemer, *Metropolis: Values in Conflict* (Belmont, Calif.: Wadsworth Publishing Co., Inc., 1964), p. 208.

6. Gerald D. Suttles, *The Social Order of the Slum: Ethnicity and Territoriality in the Inner City* (Chicago: University of Chicago Press, 1968).

7. Banfield, *The Unheavenly City*, p. 83.

178   *Reducing Ghetto Segregation*

8. *See* Jane Jacobs, *The Death and Life of Great American Cities* (New York: Random House, Inc., 1961), chapter 15.

9. St. Clair Drake and Horace R. Cayton, *Black Metropolis* (New York: Harper Torchbook, Harper & Row, Publishers, 1962), p. 201.

10. Urban America, Inc., and the Urban Coalition, *One Year Later* (New York: Praeger Publishers, Inc., 1969), p. 108.

11. *City,* June 1969, p. 18.

12. *Ibid.*

13. Chicago Commission on Race Relation, *The Negro in Chicago* (Chicago: University of Chicago Press, 1922; reprinted, Arno Press, Inc., New York, 1968) p. 645; *Report of the National Advisory Commission on Civil Disorders* (Washington, D.C.: Government Printing Office, 1968), p. 260.

14. George and Eunice Grier, *Equality and Beyond: Housing Segregation and the Goals of the Great Society* (Chicago: Quadrangle Books, Inc., 1966); James L. Hecht, *Because It Is Right* (Boston: Little, Brown and Company, 1970); *City,* January–February, 1970; U.S. Civil Rights Commission, *Federal Civil Rights Enforcement Effort* (Washington, D.C.: Government Printing Office, 1971).

15. Cf. John F. Cuber, William F. Kenkel, and Robert A. Harper, *Problems of American Society: Values in Conflict* (New York: Holt, Rinehart & Winston, Inc., 1964), pp. 54–56.

16. William Graham Sumner, *Folkways* (Boston: Ginn and Company, 1940).

17. Drake and Cayton, *Black Metropolis,* p. 95.

18. Jack Greenberg, *Race Relations and American Law* (New York: Columbia University Press, 1959), *esp.* chapter 1.

19. U.S. Civil Rights Commission, *Enforcement Effort,* pp. 138–40.

20. *Report of the National Advisory Commission on Civil Disorders,* p. 263.

21. Civil Rights Act of 1968, Title VIII, Sec. 801.

22. Quoted in U.S. Civil Rights Commission, *Enforcement Effort,* p. 142.

23. *Ibid.*

24. Lynn W. Eley, "Fair Housing Laws—Unfair Housing Practices," *Trans-action,* June 1969, pp. 59–60.

25. Hecht, *Because It Is Right,* p. 76.

26. *Ibid.,* chapter 4.

27. U.S. Civil Rights Commission, *Enforcement Effort,* p. 141.

28. *Ibid.,* p. 142.

29. James Batten, *Chicago Daily News* syndicated column, April 13, 1970.

30. U.S. Civil Rights Commission, *Enforcement Effort,* p. 176.

31. *Time* magazine, September 7, 1970, p. 51.

32. See Eley, "Fair Housing Laws," p. 59.

33. U.S. Civil Rights Commission, *Enforcement Effort,* pp. 144–47.

34. *Ibid.*, p. 146.

35. AP dispatch in Toledo *Blade*, February 11, 1971.

36. U.S. Civil Rights Commission, *Enforcement Effort*, p. 146.

37. AP dispatch in Toledo *Blade*, May 17, 1970.

38. Legal citations: *Massachusetts Commission Against Discrimination* v. *Franzanoli*, 38 L.W. 2476 (Sup. Jud. Ct. Mass. 1970); *Williams* v. *Joyce*, 39 L.W. 2616 (Ore. Ct. App. 1971).

39. Legal citation: *Cash* v. *Swifton Land Corp.*, 39 L.W. 2344 (6th Cir. 1970).

40. Legal citation: *Smith* v. *Sol D. Adler Realty Co.*, 39 L.W. 2307 (7th Cir. 1970).

41. AP dispatch in Toledo *Blade*, January 29, 1971, and *Time* magazine, February 22, 1971, p. 59; *U.S.* v. *West Peachtree Tenth Corp.*, 39 L.W. 2371 (5th Cir. 1971).

42. *City*, January–February 1971, p. 40.

43. Hecht, *Because It Is Right*.

44. U.S. Civil Rights Commission, *Enforcement Effort*, p. 141.

45. *City*, January–February 1971, p. 79.

46. Krickus, "White Ethnic Neighborhoods."

47. *See*, for example, Peter Schrag, "The Forgotten American," *Harper's Magazine*, August 1969, pp. 27–34; Haynes Johnson, "That White Revolt," *The Progressive*, December 1969, pp. 25–28; Jerome M. Rosow, *Memorandum for the Secretary*, Department of Labor, Washington, D.C., April, 1970 (mimeographed).

48. Robert Coles, "White Northerner: Pride and Prejudice," *Atlantic Monthly*, June 1966, pp. 54–55.

49. *Ibid.*, p. 56.

50. William H. Grier and Price M. Cobbs, *Black Rage* (New York: Basic Books, Inc., Publishers, 1968).

51. Rose Helper, *Racial Policies and Practices of Real Estate Brokers* (Minneapolis: University of Minnesota Press, 1969), pp. 78–82.

52. *A Comparative Analysis of The Planning Process in Eleven Cities*, Department of Housing and Urban Development (Washington, D.C.: Government Printing Office, 1970), p. 4.

53. L. Noel Moyer, Sidney J. Kaplan, and Thomas A. Klein, "Model Cities: A Design for Evaluation," *Social Science*, XLV, No. 2 (April 1970), 84–92.

54. *A History and Analysis of the Planning Process in Three Cities: Atlanta, Georgia; Seattle, Washington; Dayton, Ohio*, Department of Housing and Urban Development (Washington, D.C.: Government Printing Office, 1969), p. 42.

55. Harvey W. Zorbaugh, *The Gold Coast and the Slum* (Chicago: University of Chicago Press, 1929), p. 132 (emphasis in original).

56. Marshall B. Clinard, *Slums and Community Development* (New York: The Free Press, 1966), p. 318.

57. *A Comparative Analysis of The Planning Process in Eleven Cities,* Department of Housing and Urban Development (Washington, D.C.: Government Printing Office, 1970).

58. Moynihan, "Eliteland," pp. 35–36.

59. *Report of the National Advisory Commission on Civil Disorders,* p. 265.

60. Urban America, Inc., *One Year Later.*

61. One of the many examples of this change was a CBS documentary program, "New Voices in the South," broadcast March 9, 1971. See also *Time* magazine, May 31, 1971, pp. 12–20.

62. *See,* for example, The Skyline Series of readers, McGraw-Hill Book Company, New York; The Bank Street Readers, The Macmillan Company, New York.

63. Herbert H. Hyman and Paul B. Sheatsley, "Attitudes Towards Desegregation," *Scientific American,* CCXI, No. 1 (July 1964), 16–23.

Index